The **Rowman & Littlefield** Publishing Group

AltaMira Press

Bernan Press

Government Institutes

Hamilton Books

Jason Aronson

Lexington Books

Rowman & Littlefield Education

Rowman & Littlefield Publishers

The Scarecrow Press

Sheed & Ward

University Press of America

We are pleased to provide you with the enclosed book for review.

Upon publication, we would appreciate a copy of the review sent electronically or mailed to the address below.

Lisa McAllister and Emily Todd
4501 Forbes Blvd, Suite 200
Lanham, Maryland 20706
301-459-3366
www.rlpgbooks.com

Please e-mail all future requests to
reviews@rowman.com
Customer Service: 800-462-6420

Children's Literature and British Identity

Imagining a People and a Nation

Rebecca Knuth

THE SCARECROW PRESS, INC.
Lanham • Toronto • Plymouth, UK
2012

Published by Scarecrow Press, Inc.
A wholly owned subsidary of The Rowman & Littlefield Publishing Group, Inc.
4501 Forbes Boulevard, Suite 200, Lanham, Maryland 20706
www.rowman.com

10 Thornbury Road, Plymouth PL6 7PP, United Kingdom

British Library Cataloguing in Publication Information Available

Library of Congress Cataloging-in-Publication Data

Knuth, Rebecca, 1949–
Children's literature and British identity : imagining a people and a nation / Rebecca Knuth.
p. cm.
Includes bibliographical references and index.
ISBN 978-0-8108-8516-5 (cloth : alk. paper) — ISBN 978-0-8108-8517-2 (ebook)
1. Children's literature, English—History and criticism. 2. Children—Books and reading—Great
Britain. 3. Literature and society—Great Britain—History. I. Title.
PR990.K59 2012
820.9'9282—dc23
2012002337

Printed in the United States of America

Contents

Preface

There is something of inspiration in [writing], something of business, some-thing, at times, of agony, yet in the main, writing is just thrill; the thrill of exploring. The more difficult the country, the more untraversed by the writer, the greater (to me) the thrill. —A. A. Milne

My scholarly work owes much to Milneian thrill seeking and a prefer-ence for untraversed ground. Because I've been preoccupied with books, literacy, censorship, identity, and nationalism for many years, I wasn't surprised to find my preparations for a children's literature course side-tracked by a fascination with the messages that authors have passed on to children. I began, almost compulsively, exploring terra incognita—the role of children's stories in teaching worldviews and supporting iden-tity—and questions quickly arose. A long-standing interest in the politi-cal functions of books was coupled with a desire to understand why the relationship between children and books can be so threatening to some groups. That introduced the notion of probing the social effects of read-ing. An interest in nationalism and identity was parlayed into a fascina-tion with how children's books shape identity and character. Do they foster a common consciousness and national unity? How have a nation's geography, history, and cultural ideals influenced the development of a nation's children's stories? Also, what relationship exists between folk-lore and children's literature? As one question led to another, I found myself engaged in a full-scale exploration of the genre of children's litera-ture and the effect of that genre on national consciousness (character and identity).

Parameters were necessary, of course. I defined the materials encom-passed by the term *children's literature* as, loosely, books and materials written or illustrated for young people. These come in the form of poems, stories, novels, picture books, serials, and manuals, as well as nonfiction books. I defined "the child" as any young person up to the age of eight-een. This broad characterization of childhood as spanning many develop-mental stages acknowledges the contemporary trend toward splitting materials for young people into two categories: children's books for those aged five to about twelve and adolescent or "young adult" books for those approximately thirteen to eighteen. But collapsing the two catego-ries into one broad one—children's literature—more accurately reflects historic patterns where the demarcation of childhood was loose and, as well, twentieth-century notions in which children of younger and younger ages have been tasked with confronting frightening and disillusioning aspects of reality, forging identity, and finding a place in the world. Contemporary books for young people reflect increased precocity.

I began with a hunch that a common consciousness infuses (or is encouraged by) a nation's children's literature in so natural a way that it is virtually invisible. My challenge would be to bring this process into view. Cultural specificity emerged very quickly as a key element in the development of children's literature. It was useful to limit my inquiry geographically, to the effect that children's literature has had on a particular nation's consciousness (and vice versa) and how it has served as a form of intangible national heritage. That this study should focus on the United Kingdom of Great Britain and Northern Ireland (Britain) was probably overdetermined. There were personal reasons. When I read about the lives and goals of British children's authors, I was gripped by their passion for ideas, most evident in the work of J. R. R. Tolkien and C. S. Lewis. And I felt again the pull of England (both a geographical and an imaginative destination)—a recurrent force in my life. I am a raging Anglophile and believe that children's books have shaped the person I am—my values and ideals, what I think is funny, beautiful, and important—and a deep cultural wiring, an inner Englishness, that accompanies my birth identity as an American.

There were also, of course, compelling practical reasons, and these were the deciding factors. British children's literature has many iconic texts, and the country's books have been a dominant influence on children's literature for several centuries. There is evidence of a national ethos and ample raw materials that provide access to the ideas that propelled development of the genre in this nation. Preoccupied with childhood for over two centuries, the British have a literature for children that has undergone cycles and golden eras and has a well-documented history. Secondary materials were abundant. For context and perspective, I turned to literary criticism as well as historical and sociological studies of childhood, the role of women, the family, nationalism, and political and social thought in key periods. I gained access to the minds and hearts of British writers, readers, and thinkers through a seemingly inexhaustible supply of biographies and memoirs. Tapping into their extraordinary ruminations on a society in constant flux allowed me to explore the influence of social conditions and climates of thought on children's books, evolving notions of childhood, and what adults thought about their lives and society.

The emphasis is on national identity and values as a factor in children's literature. Notions of national consciousness (expressed in terms of "Britishness" and "Englishness" and concepts of national character) have had a presence since the eighteenth century, with interest cresting at the end of the nineteenth century and continuing through the twentieth. The debates over these concepts have roughly paralleled, in time, the development of the genre. My study explores children's literature in Britain over two and a half centuries: from the mid-eighteenth century, when a new notion of childhood led to the printing of books specifically for young people, to the 1990s and the phenomenon of the Harry Potter series. The development of British children's literature is discussed in periods and a roughly chronological fashion. There is no attempt at exhaustiveness, and readers may lament the exclusion of a favored text, especially one they consider to be "classic," but choices were based on the focus.

With the time, place, definitions, and theoretical perspectives set, I began to trace expressions of national consciousness. I found that children's books contribute to the development of character and, as well, to an ethos and national identity—in the case of Britain, the nebulous thing called *Englishness* and an overlapping identity that lacks its imaginative force, being British. Language immediately emerged as contested ground. The choice of the signifier "English" over "British" was an ongoing issue. "English" has never been a simple geographical, linguistic, or political reference. I use "English" when discussing periods in which it was the normative adjective. I use "Englishness" as it has been deployed, defined, and reconstructed over time, and I acknowledge the uses and abuses of the term.

An initial Romantic approach to Englishness was shaken by the contentious arguments over its existence in contemporary Britain. Currently, British intellectuals and social commentators shudder at the term for its connection with conservative mind-sets and the support of militant nationalism, war, and outmoded notions of class and race. While some wish to strip the concept of all credence (and British university students are often taught to shun the concept), it is too important a factor in English children's literature to be sidelined. I decided that my study, which was grounded in the broad terrain of national consciousness and identity, would address Englishness as a multivalenced and very real force in British thought: as a manipulated perspective within a convoluted history of national consciousness, as an emotional bond shared by many, and as an idealization that has haunted the nation's imagination for several centuries.

The audience I envision is one of intelligent, thoughtful readers, both academic and general. I used an interdisciplinary process that involved probing primary and secondary sources; studying the particularities of authors' lives and critiques of their works; and applying sociological, historical, and political perspectives. I chose a broad interdisciplinary and social approach, so this is not a narrow historical or literary study. I do not confine myself to the usual tools of literary analysis, bringing a particular critical perspective to bear (a favored disciplinary approach) or discussing a specific topic or deconstructive issue, such as whether the child in children's literature actually exists. I have purposefully kept disciplinary jargon to a minimum to keep the content and ideas accessible to a wider range of readers.

As I interacted with the materials, I wanted to capture the excitement I was feeling and convey it to my readers, as well as provide them with the opportunity to comprehend the dynamics of something previously unconsidered or viewed dimly. I sought jolts of insight for myself and my readers: a comprehensive understanding about the weblike effects of children's books. The frustration involved in working with such a complex topic was balanced by the ongoing interest of the material and the ultimate satisfaction of having the pieces fall into place. In the end, I offer a cosmography of the universe of British children's literature and a representation of its main features and effects as the genre has emerged over time. And I interweave a discussion of how children's works have influenced the development of character in general and national identity and consciousness in particular. To my knowledge, this is the first fully fleshed-out book on the subject. When similar studies of the development of children's literature in particular countries appear, it will be possible to compare patterns of development and the relative influence of a particular society's values on its children's literature. We can advance our knowledge about how the genre has developed globally and what effect reading has had on the identity formation of young people.

This project took five years and brought intellectual as well as emotional satisfaction. Constant reminders of the agendas of children's authors and society in general served as an anecdote to excessive sentimentality. However, I was left with a sense of the richness of the gift, children's literature, that each generation has given to the next for over two and half centuries—it is the gift of roots and wings. Children's authors have drawn on folk traditions but recast them to forge a new storytelling tradition. Their works serve an important cultural function by providing children with identity, ideals, a common consciousness, and the opportunity to share in an extended imaginative community, as well as thrive as individuals.

ACKNOWLEDGMENTS

No book is written without support. I wish to thank the University of Hawaii, the Library and Information Science Program, the University of Hawaii Study Abroad Program, and students who served as sounding boards. Thank you, Darcy Abe, Ryan Choy, Kelcie Awo, and Suzanne Winstedt from the first Roehampton University Group. And aloha to my LIS 693 HITS classes. I appreciate the encouragement of friends, such as Tony Olden, Sunyeen Pai, Debbie Nelson, Mara Miller, and Helen Nakano, who listened to tales of angst and pushed me forward with occasional tough love. Thank you to Charlene Gilmore who edited part of the book.

Aloha to Linda Fujukawa for her support and for sharing her grandchildren, Leah and Kai. Appreciation to Jeng-her (Alex) Chen, who modeled persistence and decency. Thanks always to Barbara Parker (my mother) and to Edwin and Tia Knuth (my son and daughter-in-law). This book is dedicated to Edith Wartburg, best friend and a lifelong friend to children. In Hawaii we have a word, *ohana*, which means "extended family and helping community." I am very lucky in my ohana.

ONE
Introduction

In order to have an identity, we need an orientation to the good, which means some sense of qualitative discrimination, of the incomparably higher.... This sense of the good has to be woven into my understanding of life as an unfolding story. —Charles Taylor

Children's literature in England began when childhood was acknowledged as a separate period of life and children were perceived to have special needs, including a literature of their own. The genre developed through the efforts of writers who sought to help young people decide who they were: with whom to identify, what to value, and what goals to aspire to. Stories were a means of fostering acceptable worldviews—mixtures of spiritual, philosophical, and social ideas that would sustain children through life and determine their choices. The worldview they were to acquire encouraged them to be "good" according to the way that their society defines a good person, and it was a legacy that each generation passed on to the next. To adults had fallen the charge of ensuring that children shared their values and were equipped to preserve—even improve—their world.

Over the past two and a half centuries, what philosopher Charles Taylor describes as a "sense of the good" has been explored and refined in stories for children. As a result, children have opportunity, through reading, to develop this sense—a skill of qualitative discrimination—that can aid them in understanding their lives as they unfold, in grasping their lives as a narrative and developing self-knowledge and direction as a result.[1] As children's authors have experimented with religion and reason as guiding principles on which to base education and character formation and, as well, with socialization and indoctrination techniques, there was, over time, a shift in understanding how we make meaning and

1

"learn" from stories. The imagination came to be valued as a powerful catalyst for stimulating growth and change.

The idea that stories have great impact and carry important values is a very old one. For centuries, tales (and values) were conveyed orally from person to person by storytellers who entertained while passing on strategies for survival and successful living. Traditions of oral folklore are still alive in modern children's stories, and it is widely accepted that a diet rich in folk and fairy tales as well as modern children's stories encourages personal growth in an organic way. A good story can penetrate to one's very core and, to paraphrase Joseph Campbell about myths, it's felt in the gut.[2] I remember the eerie impact of hearing as a child, for the very first time, the folk tale "The Boy Who Cried Wolf"—I never again sounded an alarm wantonly. *The Tale of Peter Rabbit* had the same effect: the story's lesson about the dangers of tempting fate hit home hard.

Folklore carries truth about what makes us human; it is distilled wisdom, rife with motifs and characters that have survived the crucible of time. In both of the quintessential English tales "Jack the Giant Killer" and "Jack and the Beanstalk," there is a plucky lad, an action-filled narrative, an exciting climax, and a compelling theme: that the weak may prevail against the strong. There is great satisfaction in the story's rendering of cause and effect. Folklore often speaks to deep psychological issues, such as loyalty, honor, and desire for power, through archetypal characters.[3] Ancient and contemporary myths and legends instruct as well as entertain: they offer guidance for daily challenges as well as for the large quests of a life. Embedded in the stories is content that allows one to see the effect of choices—and to make them, vicariously—and satisfy the need for heroism and justice. The fear and loss that we feel when Hansel and Gretel are abandoned is replaced by joy when they use their wits, triumph over the witch, and emerge as heroes.

From exposure to traditional lore, generations of people have learned basic survival skills (beware of witches; use your wits) and less basic skills, such as making sense out of chaos by assembling it into a narrative. We have experienced a full range of emotions vicariously and—often unconsciously—figured out what is beautiful, genuine, and good . . . also, what is evil and life denying. Traditional materials ring true at an elemental level, and children learn from such tales that certain virtues and choices can bring triumph over adversity. These stories have the power to bypass reason via the imagination and land right in the heart, where intuition and feelings grow and where, as a result, character forms.

When oral cultures gave way to the era of print, the process by which people experienced stories changed in many ways. Instead of telling and hearing stories, they began printing and reading them. Readers had access to complex renderings of the past through history books; through biographies, they were exposed to compelling role models and ideals as they played out in a specific life. Cognition changed when writers were able to pass on experience by means of elaborate plots and character development that stimulated perception and judgment. Readers could study situations and use advanced reasoning skills.[4] While oral cultures had been concerned with the present, written works allowed readers to examine the past and probe human motivation in a more complex way, over time. Adult readers turned to new story forms—romances and novels. As the parameters of imaginative journeys expanded, so did the range of behavioral models and choices that readers encountered through story.

It was the sheer entertainment value of folklore, fairy tales, legend, and myth that helped preserve them until they became a mainstay of English children's literature. With the development of the printing press, old tales found their way into print in cheap softcover publications called *chapbooks*. Though often ugly and poorly written, chapbooks preserved an ancient repository of lore that otherwise would have been forgotten. From 1700 to 1840, a pittance could buy access to Tom Thumb or Sinbad—to devil legends, Aesop's fables, riddles, nursery rhymes, and simple fairy tales, strange tales and bizarre images. As well, there were romances riddled with the lore of chivalry and magic and rags-to-riches tales, such as the story of Dick Whittington, the poor boy who became Lord Mayor of London. Dick—who "strolled about the country as ragged as a colt"[5] and came to the city searching for streets of gold—became forever associated with the notion that with hard work and a little luck, one's future was unbounded. The chapbooks made Dick the hero of a moral fable. For a penny, readers thrilled to the legend of Robin Hood and his commitment to justice. Robin Hood eventually acquired legendary status and became an integral part of English national consciousness. He was a hearty and just champion of freedom, quintessentially English. Readers absorbed hero and outlaw models and street-smart and subversive values as well as spiritual and mythological ones.

Through the introduction of children's books in the mid-eighteenth century and well into the nineteenth century, children thrived on chapbook marvels and, as well, on novels originally written for adults: *Pilgrim's Progress* (1671), *Robinson Crusoe* (1719), and *Gulliver's Travels* (1726). The legendary lands and exotic places that young people discovered through reading expanded their frames of reference and vicarious possibilities. Soon young imaginations were stocked with exotica, and play often modeled Indian massacres, pirate attacks, shipwrecks, and desert islands. The grip exerted by a book read in childhood is testified to by many adults. Author Rider Haggard recounted an incident when he was supposed to go to church and instead hid under the bed with *Robinson Crusoe*: when his older sister and a governess came to get him, there was a Homeric struggle: "The two ladies tugged as best they might, but I clung to *Crusoe* and the legs of the bed, and kicked till, perfectly exhausted, they took their departure in no very Christian frame of mind, leaving me panting indeed, but triumphant."[6] As a child, James Barrie absorbed the aforementioned three classics and as well reveled in the gruesome style and heroics of "penny dreadfuls" (the latest manifestation of chapbooks). Youthful reading inspired him to write his own stories. "From the day on which I first tasted blood in the garret my mind was made up; there could be no hum-dreadful-drum profession for me; literature was my game."[7] Barrie would go on to create his own deliberately unreal Never Never Land and a character (Peter Pan) that was a pastiche of well-known stories combined to such potent effect that Barrie's own son dubbed it the "terrible masterpiece."[8]

Children's authors to this day borrow freely from folk materials, often using the simple plots, clear language, and rhythmic patterns so common to popular tales. From Lewis Carroll on, authors have understood the imaginative appeal of traditional works. *Alice's Adventures in Wonderland* and *Through the Looking-Glass* have much the same anarchic, irreverent quality as nursery rhymes. C. S. Lewis delighted in filling Narnia with a medley of humans, animals, mythological beings, and unrelated figures from stories that had influenced him as a child. His friend J. R. R. Tolkien, a purist, thought the incongruity of elements in *The Lion, the Witch, and the Wardrobe* rendered it practically worthless. But Lewis argued that they existed happily in our minds in real life.[9] And so they do. Carroll, Lewis, and other writers mined and adapted folklore and brought new forms into being, such as fantasy. They ensured that traditional elements remained a dynamic factor in children's literature.

Some of the earliest authors of children's books, however, thought they were rejecting primitive and fanciful tales as they adapted emerging forms — including the cautionary tale and romance novel — to their purposes and to their audiences. Late-eighteenth- and early-nineteenth-century women, who had to enter the marketplace gingerly because of social norms that confined them to the home, justified writing by stressing their mandate, as women and mothers, to educate the next generation. Their notion of the character they sought to foster was either religious or steeped in rationality. Women pioneered the cautionary "moral tale" for use with children and the barely literate. Ironically, while they were rejecting old tales as too edgy and uncontrollable, they had to open the door to the imagination and use storytelling and narrative traditions as effective means of getting children to absorb their moral, educational, and behavioral templates.

Once the door to the imagination was open, moral tales gave way to novels, often romances, that targeted children. Like folklore, these were forms that adapted well to a young audience because of their entertaining qualities. Novels allowed for complexity, and one could follow the trajectory of a single life, as choices were made and fates sealed — they were ideal vehicles of socialization, the message well masked by interesting plot developments. Like the traditional tales, romances exaggerated human nature and displayed "a peculiar vagrancy of imagination."[10] Romance is characterized by passion and adventure of a scale that generally requires suspension of disbelief and rationalism, and it invites wholehearted involvement—a pleasure that is somehow childlike. Like folklore, romances are engaging, and they also have worthy heroes, interesting plots, a mingling of the unexpected and the everyday, and happy endings. They provide charismatic role models. Romances for children became a staple of the emerging genre of children's literature and often mirrored the basic concerns of folklore—how to fulfill one's desires and those of the community and how to be a good person and live successfully and well. Nineteenth-century domestic novels, such as those of Charlotte Yonge, charted an appropriate life for an Englishwoman, and late Victorian boys' books and serials nailed down a type—the manly, cleanliving, courageous Englishman.

Nineteenth-century English society was enthralled with traditional legends reworked into poems and novels as well as fairy tales that were literary in execution. As the century wore on, simple legends and tales, riddles, and nursery rhymes became the province of children. The thrilling and entertaining qualities of traditional material were retained, but there was an evolving expectation that folklore in service to children's literature was a vehicle for teaching children empathy and honor. Authors built on folkloric patterns of passing on cultural knowledge from generation to generation, but unlike traditional storytellers, they consciously geared themselves to a specific, developing audience of young people.

Children's authors used the power of story and language to entertain, mentor, and support children. Lewis Carroll wrote about survival amid chaos and the cleansing effect of nonsense. Maria Edgeworth produced works of morality that mapped a direct line between action and consequences, and Beatrix Potter wrote animal fables about human foibles. Henty created myths of adventure that supported imperialism and a code of manliness. Frances Hodgson Burnett wrote nostalgic stories about the power and goodness that are within each person. E. Nesbit wrote about the importance of family and comradeship and had magic serving as a counterpart to daily life. Kenneth Grahame and A. A. Milne produced rich explorations of humanness; Arthur Ransome celebrated the acquisition of skills and the solidarity of families; and J. R. R. Tolkien and J. K. Rowling provided heroes who waged mythic battles against the forces of evil. Like their storytelling predecessors, they enlisted the power of story to involve a child in the molding of his own character.

The character to be molded, of course, was British (or as it was most often referred to—English). The development of English children's literature can be seen, in retrospect, as part of the project of constructing a modern society and the identities that would support it. The genre's development occurred from the mid-eighteenth century onward, in tandem with the development of the nation as the focal point for identity. The processes of nationalization and genre development accelerated in nine-teenth-century England, when national ideals were embedded in stories that helped unify the population into a nation. A nation, according to Benedict Anderson, is an "imagined" community based on perceived companionship and consensus.[11] Children's literature had an important role in fostering common consciousness and helping the British to con-ceive of themselves as a unique people with a distinctive history and national character. The authors of English children's books were engaged in a semi-self-conscious exercise in creating useful citizens, imbuing them with common values, and making sure they would define themselves in terms of their country and culture: as Englishmen, as British.

During the eighteenth and early nineteenth centuries, the period in which children's literature really took off in Britain, the drive to discover cultural roots and use these as a basis for the development of national character was a feature of European scholarship. There were concerted efforts to gather and reconstruct traditional literature: Oral traditions were excavated for tales that could stimulate personal identification with the nation. In Germany the philosopher Johann Gottfried von Herder (1744–1803) pushed for the deliberate recording of folklore as a means of validating German culture and documenting the spirit and traditions of the German people. The Grimm brothers compiled a German mythology and a corpus of folk tales and legends first issued in 1812 as *Children's and Household Tales*. In Finland in the 1830s, Elias Lonnrot (1802–1884) re-worked ancient songs into a poem, the *Kalevala*, which is now the Finnish national epic. In Denmark, Nikolai Grundtvig (1783–1872) used saga, epic, and ballad literature to stimulate a sense of Danish national identity.

While European scholars were collecting and recycling folklore in the interests of national identity, English Romantics were promoting the no-tion that these traditional materials were nutritious fare for young and old. The Romantic movement was markedly concerned with folk culture and the past, and it had much to do with the substantial body of lore that was offered to children in England during the nineteenth century. As well, new stories for children were written to entertain and to inculcate values by invoking the imagination in the way of the old tales. The devel-oping genre of children's literature, influenced by Romanticism, spoke to age-old themes and preoccupations, including the very English notion of Arcadia and the fascination with human freedom, personal foibles and eccentricity, the small hero, and sympathy with the weak against the strong.[12] In late-nineteenth-century children's material, there was often a synthesis of Romanticism and nationalism. Ideas of "Englishness" emerged over time within this relatively new canon, and the term came to reflect a love of country and encapsulate a sum of qualities describing a basic character and its accompanying sentiments, beliefs, and practices.

To be English at this time was to be manly, courageous, chivalrous, and unabashedly patriotic.

Under the influence of romantic nationalism, stories and legends were repeatedly reworked to encourage the notion of timeless ideals and an illustrious history. A nation's legitimacy, after all, depends on its ability to affirm its antiquity and past glory and celebrate its heroes. In imagining England, authors had long drawn inspiration from Sir Thomas Malory's *Le Morte d'Arthur*, the substance for popular legends ever since its 1485 publication. A little over a century later, Edmund Spenser celebrated Queen Elizabeth I in his *Faerie Queen* by associating her dynasty, the Tudors, with Arthurian virtues (and was well rewarded as a result). In nineteenth-century England, the desire for national myths—whether real or imagined—resulted in even more reconstructed literature, such as Tennyson's *Idylls of the King*, which came out between 1856 and 1885 and retold the legend of King Arthur. In 1879, the *Encyclopedia Britannica* put forth the story of Arthur as "the epic of the English mind as the Iliad is the epic of the Greek mind." [13]

The Victorians made King Arthur a national hero and celebrated his virtues, seen as Christian in spirit and essentially English: he was merciful, brave, pure, humble, loyal, and true. Myths are coded messages from the culture as a whole to the individual member. [14] The Victorian Arthur embodied a new concept of masculinity and supported a code of ethics that posed British Empire builders as chivalric knights—Galahads and Percivals gallantly fighting to bring the benefits of civilization to inferior people. [15] In 1840 Sharpe's *London Journal* celebrated Arthur as "the beautiful incarnation of all the best characteristics of our nation"—someone willing to die for the country's glorious causes:

> I have not flinch'd from peril, nor counted pains;
> What adverse odds, what difficult steps to climb,
> What possible inconvenience or mishap,
> Troubled me never. I ask'd nought but this—
> May it serve thee? my Country! Welcome then. [16]

Over time Arthur's chivalrous spirit permeates the entire canon of English literature, including its children's literature.

Twentieth-century author J. R. R. Tolkien, a scholar of ancient English history and languages, eventually set forth with the same purpose as the Grimm brothers had in Germany the previous century. Disturbed by the lack of a substantive body of myth and legend that was truly English, Tolkien reconstructed the language through etymological clues and "recorded" the product of his imagination—a tradition that he thought of as "true," rooted in the soil of England and evoking its very air. [17] He ultimately created an entire cosmology for his country: it included myths and fairy tales and something he called the "heroic legend on the brink of fairy-tale and history." [18] His work gives breadth to the folkloric spectrum of children's literature by supplying original high myth. It is laced with rich and complex expressions of various kinds of Englishness, from relatively straightforward references to Anglo-Saxon history to beliefs about the nature of Englishmen in general—that they are peaceful and moderate unless stirred to action by duty.[19] Tolkien demonstrated conclusively that traditional oral folklore is still alive and operating—but in the form of children's literature and the practice of sharing stories with young people.

* * *

The imagination became paramount in children's literature as children themselves were recognized as having capabilities that opened them up to the experience of story, to being shaped by literary adventures. The adventures begin and end at home, in the little and big journeys "there and back." In Tolkien's blurb for the British edition of *The Hobbit*, the author specifically invites children on a fantastical adventure out of "the comfortable Western world, over the edge of the Wild, and home again." Bilbo, the story's hero, begins his journey when his imagination comes alive, sparked by the dwarves' songs and fierce love of their ancient home. He wants to see their great mountains, explore their caves, and wear a sword. Writers such as Tolkien or Grahame have frequently reminded readers that within any journey or adventure there is a yearning for home and hearth. Leaving home is perilous, and the peril built into adventures of all sizes can serve to transform experience into self-knowledge and confidence. Likewise, when we read, we travel to a new place and then return home to, as T. S. Eliot said, recognize it for the first time. There is a heightened perception of the goodness of home, and personal changes often rededicate us to our own culture and its core values.

Like Bilbo, children want adventure, but they usually can't embark on real adventures—that is one of the realities of childhood. They can, though, strike out with the heroes in stories. And when lost in a book, a child can experience everything from depression to euphoria—a range that may be far beyond the boundaries of the child's real life. The vicarious emotional journey allows insight: truth that comes suddenly in a stab of recognition or, more slowly, as the essence of an irresistible secondary world seeps into the child's being. As the child navigates the imaginary world through story, innocence falls away and new ideas take root. There is the possibility of bringing the experience back "home" and applying the lesson to real life, where real change—growth—can occur. And make no mistake: As J. R. R. Tolkien reminds us in his essay "On Fairy-Stories," while children journey hopefully in the land of make-believe, they must grow up and ultimately live in the real world.[20] Even behind James Barrie's entrancing world of Never Never Land, there is the real world to which one must return.

Stories have long helped generations of youth learn to discover themselves and respond to their own culture. C. S. Lewis was ravished as a child by his readings of northern myths and was moved by the authenticity of Potter's *Squirrel Nutkin*, and he in turn wrote works that sparked similar reactions for a new generation of children. Readers who broke into tears at the plight of Black Beauty thereafter retained a heartfelt empathy for mistreated animals. In 1914 soldiers who were little more than boys themselves were ready to die for an England they had learned to love through serials and historical novels. Tolkien's messages about the importance of fellowship and the corrupting influence of power gave the cultlike followers of his *The Lord of the Rings* trilogy a philosophy to live by. Young people seem particularly open to reading experiences that engender either acculturation or rebellion, responses involving emotional investment and choices. An inspiring story can produce a shift in consciousness that colors all subsequent experiences.[21]

For British youth, England is home—the arena for everyday adventures, the geographical start and end point for imaginative journeys, the mythological backdrop for small heroes venturing far from home. Authors have often woven the texture of everyday English life into their works. It is a tone, a portrait of familiar rituals (such as tea drinking and country walks) and environments (such as the nursery or kitchen). Some authors convey passionate attachment to the country by incorporating place names, historical snippets, and images of snug cottages, country estates, and London scenes. Like other wayfarers, Bilbo and Frodo experienced their destinations as exotic, in direct proportion to the lack of Englishness about the new place and along the way. Cultural strangeness is tied up with quest and danger; cognitive disturbance is part of the experience. Home, in contrast, is a place where one can relax and feel secure and comfortable in one's own identity. It's a place of right thinking and living. Surviving; testing and forming values; and fighting for empire, home, and a familiar lifestyle gives purpose to an imaginary journey: returning home is a goal in itself and allows for closure.

Often, the ideals written in British children's stories have been agrarian and nostalgic. Tolkien's Shire, for example, is a bucolic, timeless portrait of rural England. The countryside plays a profound role in shaping character in children's stories (as seen in *Tom Brown's Schooldays*), but a decidedly English lifestyle, often with Victorian and Edwardian undertones, is apparent in both rural and urban settings. The appeal of *The Wind in the Willows*, replete with the attractions of life along an English river, and the Mary Poppins stories, set in London, has much to do with their historical anachronisms and the Edwardian sensibilities they celebrated. Not coincidentally, these stories had yin and yang. Grahame's tranquil river world was bordered by the Wild Wood, with the wood representing freedom and recklessness. Travers used magic to provide an exotic dimension (and spice) to daily life at Number 17 Cherry Tree Lane.

The authority figure in Travers's *Mary Poppins* (1934) switches back and forth from nanny to playmate and matter-of-factly ushers her charges, the Banks children, between realms of magical adventures and prudent domesticity. Travers wrote, "We cannot have the extraordinary without the ordinary. Just as the supernatural is hidden in the natural. In order to fly, you need something solid to take off from. It's not the sky that interests me but the ground."[22] Expressing the changing sensibilities of childhood, Travers combines an ironic, biting tone with a safe setting, and though unsentimental, she provides comforting moments. Her magic is firmly grounded. The context that underpins most English children's stories is a culturally consonant environment of stability, substance, and creature comforts, warmed by the existence or possibility of loving relationships. This provides the platform for imaginary journeys, large and small.

Child readers often respond to the England they encounter in their books as an imaginary country with great numinousness, experienced in the same way that child readers experience Narnia and "Ringers" experience "Middle-earth." There is recognition and joy as well as deep cultural attachment even in those who are not English. American Anna Quindlen had been to London so frequently in the pages of books that setting foot there for the first time "felt less like an introduction and more like a homecoming."[23] Many readers associate England with wonderful stories and timeless values. The favorite book of another American writer, Phyllis McGinley, was *A Little Princess*. In introducing a new edition, she commented,

> The England of Mrs. Burnett—even my imaginary England—has changed. There are still the elms, the rooks, the fogs, the skylarks. But little beggar girls don't have to sit starving in doorways any longer. . . . Still, courage doesn't change. Mysterious good deeds do not change. There are still wicked people and good people and brave unhappy little princesses left in the world. And as long as those things endure. . . . This book is just about the most interesting, funny, sad, exciting, wonderful story anybody ever told.[24]

The destination of the literary journey that McGinley took when reading this book was England; the ideals that she absorbed along the way moved her deeply. Images and basic values associated with this country, first assimilated by childhood reading, were retained by McGinley for life.

* * *

From the mid-eighteenth century onward, English writers and readers engaged in an inquiry into youth and its distinction from adulthood that had a revolutionary impact on Britain and the world. From this effort emerged the notion that childhood is a separate state of being, with the child limited in experience but capable of a full range of human emotion, from hilarity or hatred to transcendence. In the twentieth century, children's literature had reached a point where books written for young audiences captured and transmitted conventional and experimental truths about character and goodness, social obligation, and what it meant to be human. They ultimately reminded their adult audience of the limitless potential of youth and the importance of choices made during this time. Of course, because writing for children was such a powerful tool of socialization and indoctrination, some choices were foreclosed.

Adults have been the producers and consumers of children's books in all eras, and the tone and content of children's materials have been set by their ideas about childhood and their own childhood experiences. Children's books involve the deepest values and interests of those who concern themselves with them. In their writing, children's authors respond to the crosscurrents of thought and competing forces at play in their particular time and place, and, in turn, authors influence their societies. Writers, parents, and critics often set their sights on more than entertainment. They've sought to help children to grow up, to become "good" people who will believe and behave in ways that they as adults think best serve society. Children's books model aspirations and worldviews (which can be religious, secular, or some combination of the two), and because these differ within geographical and cultural boundaries and over time, there has been disagreement throughout the genre's history over what a good person is and how goodness is to be inculcated — in other words, what kind of an adult is desirable and what kind of society is the goal.

The development of English children's literature can be seen as an experiment in defining and instilling a productive goodness that supports contemporary notions of a strong and healthy society and nation. Early authors favored piety, morality, and a consequences-based approach to life. Children were schooled in responsibility and duty. Morality was a major factor in children's stories for years, but it became more and more matter of fact. In the later part of the nineteenth century — the midpoint of the development of the genre — we can see a clear turn toward assumptions of national character, as parents (and authors and publishers) decided that what they really wanted was for their children to grow into strong English men and women. The values and cultural rituals portrayed to children in books served ideological purposes: girls were schooled in domesticity and charged with maintaining the home, while boys were socialized to be clean-living Britons and to defend the nation and empire. In story after story (in adventure novels, historical fiction, and serials), nationalism and imperialism were romanticized. Ideological Englishness enshrined obedience, racial pride, and heroism for its own sake. Duty to country and empire was a sacred obligation.

This changed in the aftermath of World War I, but what persisted was a generalized notion of Britain as a place where right thinking was prevalent and supported conservative notions of the correctness of existing social hierarchies. When individualism took center place, it was an individualism rooted in collective identity, a common cultural consciousness, and a pride in the innate decency of the British people. Mid- and late-twentieth-century writers have taken on the task of writing more inclusive stories that support diversity, multiculturalism, and social equality.

Children's writers express notions about what it means for a child to be a good person—in temperament, morality, and ethics. In an effort to work through their own issues, doubts about existing institutions, and hopes for an improved society, they have projected their yearnings on children and made offerings to them—and, in the process, shaped a new genre. Their exploration of childhood and ideas about children has set in motion the evolution of a diverse, often contradictory, body of literature that carries important messages and values. Children's books have played a key role in the evolving notions of British national character or, as it is more often referred to now, national identity. They conveyed perspectives that unified the British into an imagined community, a sense of being a people linked by virtue of a common culture.

Like the storytellers who came before them, children's authors have offered role models and archetypes, values to live by, celebrations of humanness, and a means of being in touch with the divine. Like folklore, their works carry a powerful ethos. The great cumulative value and worth of the genre, including its cultural role, suggests that children's literature has become a tradition in itself—drawing on folk traditions as rich and fully developed as traditional lore but also replacing them. In effect, English children's authors have forged a new storytelling tradition, a nouveau folklore of an evolving people that has fostered cultural consensus and a common and constantly morphing national consciousness and identity. This book tells the fascinating story of how this came about.

NOTES

1. Taylor, *Sources of the Self*, 47.
2. Campbell, "Mythic Reflections," 52.
3. Carpenter, *Secret Gardens*, 168.
4. Ong, *Orality and Literacy*, 54–55.
5. Parrinder, *Nation and Novel*, 220.
6. Cohen, *Rider Haggard*, 23.
7. Barrie, *"My Lady Nicotine" and "Margaret Ogilvy,"* 255.
8. Carpenter, *Secret Gardens*, 170.
9. Sayer, *Jack*, 312–13.
10. Beer, *The Romance*, 4.
11. Anderson, *Imagined Communities*, 7.

12. Summerfield, *Fantasy and Reason*, 32.
13. Barczewski, *Myth and National Identity*, 114.
14. Green, *Dreams of Adventure*, 5.
15. Barczewski, *Myth and National Identity*, 220.
16. Barczewski, *Myth and National Identity*, 13.
17. Day, *The World of Tolkien*, 13–14.
18. Dickerson and O'Hara, *From Homer to Harry Potter*, 25.
19. Hopkins, "Tolkien and Englishness," 278–79.
20. Tolkien, "On Fairy-Stories," 44–45.
21. Smiley, *Charles Dickens*, 56.
22. Lawson, *Mary Poppins*, 161.
23. Quindlen, *Imagined London*, 9.
24. McGinley, "Foreword," 5–6.

TWO

Creating "Good" Children

Why should the mind be filled with fantastic visions. . . . Why should we vitiate their taste, and spoil their appetite, by suffering them to feed upon sweetmeats? —Maria Edgeworth, *The Parent's Assistant*

In the eighteenth century, reading became associated with "improvement" and the cultivation of virtues acceptable to both God and Mammon—major influences on British character, Puritanism and mercantilism.[1] Adults wanted lessons in thrift, godliness, and conduct for themselves and their offspring. Early publishers and authors of books believed that an educational function justified a specific literature for children. Their goal was to foster goodness in children and ultimately affect their whole life. They sought to instill mind-sets and social codes that would support an honorable society and national culture. The rub came in defining "goodness" and "honor," and an early preoccupation with ideals and their practical expression became a dominant factor in the development of English children's literature throughout its history.

In the beginning, when England's economy was vital and social life energetic, the vision of a desirable English child was a jolly one. John Newbery (1713–1767), the first major figure in English children's literature, was a kindly fatherly figure, a family man, and a savvy publisher who spotted a prospective market among middle-class parents of mid-eighteenth-century England. A self-made man, Newbery associated learning with success and believed in the possibility of worldly advancement. His nation was one in which internal peace, rising incomes, and a decrease in infant mortality had resulted in childhood being taken seriously but not somberly. Medieval notions of children as imperfect adults were abating. Newbery capitalized on emerging notions of childhood as a separate state and on Enlightenment views of the child as a reasoning being and of childhood as a time for education.[2] Developing high-func-

15

tioning children was an important venture because "the nation's moral health and economic prosperity resulted from the collective character and effort" of all Britons.[3] Newbery saw the purpose of publishing books that spoke directly to children and offered them practical advice, laced with good cheer and optimism.

With prosperity and the heady scent of progress in the air, Newbery made common cause with parents seeking upward mobility for their children: the goal was to help children acquire the habits and values that would propel them toward financial and social success. Newbery authored and published tolerant little stories that encouraged mercantile values of honesty, shrewdness, and hard work, as well as optimism. *The History of Little Goody Two-Shoes* (1765), his most popular work, was dedicated to poor children aspiring to the good life: wealth, fame, and the ability to "gallop in a Coach and Six." The story told of an orphaned girl, Margery (Goody) Meanwell, forced into homelessness by an avaricious squire. A good child, then a virtuous and resourceful young woman, she educates and helps herself and her neighbors and eventually reaps her reward by being loved and attracting a rich husband. Message and story combine to memorable effect in this book, and like Newbery's others, it was fondly remembered for its happy ending.

Newbery had zest for life and an appreciation for children that jumps off the pages of the tiny books that bear his imprint. He introduced the possibility of playfulness in children's stories, filling *A Little Pretty Pocket-Book* (1744) with riddles and selling the book with the option of acquiring a ball or pin cushion. *Mother Goose's Melody* (1791) featured English rhymes. He used humor as an incentive to learning, as in the following poem:

> To Master John the ENGLISH Maid
> A Horn-book gives of Ginger-bread:
> And that the Child may learn the better,
> As He can name, He eats the letter:
> Proceeding thus with vast Delight,
> He spells, and gnaws, from Left to Right.[4]

Children were portrayed as anxious to learn in titles such as *The Entertaining History of Tommy Gingerbread: A Little Boy Who Lived upon Learning.* Science was fun when acquired by reading Newbery's books about Tom Telescope.

But his moderate approach and humorous tone were far too relaxed for the educators, theorists, and writers to come, however. From 1780 to 1840, there was radical political and social upheaval as the nation underwent a revolution in agriculture and processes of industrialization and urbanization that triggered class conflict. In rural England, the Luddites destroyed factory equipment; in the cities, protesters rioted over food and social and political issues. In the Gordon Riots of 1780, London endured three days of uncontrollable mob violence. The larger picture was of a country at war: the Revolutionary War in America persisted from 1775 to 1783, and England was then embroiled in wars with France from 1789 to 1815. The vital economy of the eighteenth century was faltering and basic security eroding in the face of external threats and social unrest, and lightheartedness in children's stories was out of place. In the face of economic depression and mass unemployment, it was unrealistic to teach children to expect upward mobility; in addition, the notion of social ambition resonated with radical ideals filtering in from France. Republican ideas about equality threatened the monarchy and class system, and the middle-class establishment felt that English children needed to be schooled in contentment and compliance—as did the poor, who were grouped with the young because of their common powerlessness and ignorance. Religious piety and the cultivation of reason were prudent responses to social chaos.

So the next generation of writers, concerned with the influence that reading might have on children, rejected what Newbery had offered to the fledging genre. With the new century approaching, these writers felt that the country was in dire need of moral stiffening, starting in the arena of education. A healthy social order would require well-schooled children who would grow into disciplined adults. These writers saw children's books as instructional tools, a view that left little room for amusing stories. After all, as educator Maria Edgeworth asked parents in 1797 in *The Parent's Assistant; or, Stories for Children*: "Why should we vitiate their taste, and spoil their appetite, by suffering them to feed upon sweetmeats?"[5] Filling children's minds with useful knowledge and morality rather than ambition seemed only practical. Edgeworth became famous for feeding children "English pills of instruction in coatings of anecdote."[6] Newbery's example of offering the medicine with a dose of sweetener (entertaining narrative) was not entirely forgotten, but the acceptable amount of sweetener was significantly reduced. There was a new chilling vision of the teacher as austere and humorless.

It is important to remember that the recognition of childhood as a separate stage of life is a relatively new concept. With its acceptance came a literature written specifically for children and addressing their needs (as determined, of course, by adults). It took a long time for notions that we now take for granted to develop: that emotional and intellectual stimulation should be tailored to a child's developmental level and that children should be encouraged to read for pure enjoyment. In the second half of the eighteenth century and early years of the nineteenth century, reading was a serious business, for parenting had become more fraught with general social anxiety than in the robust, casual era that had preceded this time. Parents knew that it was important to educate their children and instruct them in morality, and these parents were looking for assistance from books.

Soon the works of certain writers were in high demand—authors assumed an in loco parentis role. Their stories, which came to be known as moral or cautionary tales, spelled out the consequences of error and reflected the authors' own deep-seated fears about the security of the social order (and their position in it). They wrote out of a sense of concern for children and fervently tried to reassure parents that children could be raised in such a way as to ensure that they could function as responsible adults. Their vision of society was one in which all behavior was controlled, through either religion or rationality. The authors were not out to empower children (a modern vision) but to tutor them in correct behavior and align their thinking to fit with society's. The storyline followed a simple formula: bad deeds are punished, and good children make the right choices. The desired response from child readers was acceptance of these truths and the making of good choices.

Two movements influenced the content and tone of cautionary tales. One was the Edgeworth school, which held that the upbringing of the child should instill rationality—an awareness of cause and effect. The other group, the Evangelicals, employed religious dogma as the backbone of education. The Evangelicals labored exhaustively to control children's literature from 1780 onward, and their efforts exerted a powerful influence on the genre well into the nineteenth century. The literature they produced was part of a faith-based initiative to restructure society in its entirety, and the Evangelicals' energy and sincerity profoundly influenced Victorian values. Both movements served to shift the relatively complacent culture of the mid-eighteenth century into the earnest moralism of the nineteenth.

Evangelicalism was the neo-Puritanism of the industrial age.[7] Its disciples revisited attitudes that had gained foothold in the seventeenth century. Disgusted by what they perceived as the ignorance, extravagance, and vice of their times, they ambitiously set their sights on the top-to-bottom reform of English society. Their stories explicitly championed discipline and social stability. Books that advanced their religious agenda were promoted; others were publicly attacked. They waged relentless campaigns against folk and fairy tales, which they considered perverse and unfit for children—probably for the wildness that gave them their appeal but just as likely for their themes of justice and empowerment. The Evangelicals' efforts to dominate the children's book market came to a head in the late 1780s and 1790s with attempts to control publishers and ensure the exclusive publication of pious literature.[8]

Under Evangelical influence, the tone of children's literature became authoritarian and stern. Parents were instructed to break the child's will, instill guilt, and stifle sexuality, imagination, and individuality. Self-denial was fundamental to the desired goal of habitual restraint. A child's life was vigilantly controlled, for obedience and duty were paramount parenting goals. In their child-rearing philosophies, the Evangelicals adamantly rejected lightheartedness and imagination. Children were often isolated, kept from playing with other children or talking to servants for fear of worldly contamination. In the interests of sobriety and austerity, nurseries were spartan. To the Evangelical mind, children were conceived in sin and fundamentally corrupt. With moral danger all around, a child's innate depravity had to be stamped out—and time was short; death lurked just around the corner.

Haunting many a child raised in the late eighteenth and early nineteenth centuries were images of pain and violence associated with—by today's standards—the mildest of behavioral infractions. One children's poem opined: "Satan is glad when I am bad / And hopes that I with him shall lie / In fire and chains and dreadful pains."[9] The precedent for this kind of material can be clearly seen in *A Token for Children* (1671–1672) by Puritan author James Janeway. He warned children to be good or they would go to a hell—"a terrible place, worse than a thousand whippings." The tiniest infraction, such as losing one's temper or disobeying authority, was sternly punished, for every action was to serve the divine order and the family. Stories often contained examples of "tough love" that, to modern readers, border on cruelty. Characters and readers alike were assured that punishment was an expression of a parent's love and desire to save children from the eternal consequences of depravity.

By making sure that religion dominated emerging notions of childhood and the developing genre of children's literature, Evangelical writers were claiming a role in the sweeping reforms that were transforming English society from approximately 1780 to 1840. Many of the writers were women. With urbanization and the rise of a middle class, women were confined to the home, their realm of influence restricted to housekeeping, private charity, and child rearing. For ambitious and literate Evangelical women, childhood was one of the few domains in which their men would cede them. Claiming that because of their gender, they were natural experts in child raising, these women justified advances into the public arena and commerce that were otherwise forbidden to women. Stressing the great potential (for good and for bad) that existed in the childhood years, they gave themselves unprecedented importance as parental advisors and, in addition, offered mothers a new sense of purpose as educators of young children. The authority that women authors found through their writings gave them the potential to save children—and, by extension, the entire social order.

This sense of mission was particularly compelling for Hannah More (1745–1833). She reacted to a perceived climate of immorality, fed in part by access to cheap chapbooks that contained hair-raising tales of crime and fantastical beasts, as well as thrilling accounts of chivalry and magic. Evangelicals feared any texts that overexcited the sensibilities of the young and deranged their minds: reading Shakespeare could lead to a "dangerous elevation of fancy" in which the reader imagines himself to be a king, a warrior, a lover—and thereby loses touch with sober reality—"a terrible calamity at the stage of life when the mind should be achieving a permanent insight into things as they are."[10] One can imagine their revulsion against appalling and ungodly chapbooks that were perceived as promoting passion and vice to children and the poor. In 1795, More spearheaded a counteroffensive against the influence of these lurid tales by writing and distributing a flood of easy-to-read materials that functioned as alternatives to the chapbooks. Cheap repository texts (as these stories were called) engaged the reader through interesting story lines, but they were written with an eye to instructing in basic morality and Evangelical values. More, who wrote many of them, summarized the publications as tales of "striking Conversions, Holy Lives, Happy Deaths, Providential Deliverances, Judgments on the Breakers of Commandments, Stories of Good and Wicked Apprentices, Hardened Sinners, Pious Servants & etc."[11] The distribution network was already in place: the vendors of secular chapbooks were paid to distribute moral tracts instead.

More and other Evangelicals were responding to the threat of Jacobinism, radical ideas filtering in from France. As More's biographer Anne Stott has pointed out, in the 1790s the vague term *Jacobinism* worked in the way that *Bolshevism* did in the early twentieth century. It was emotive "shorthand for a comprehensive revolutionary ideology" that, like a plague, had the potential to undermine the status quo: England's constitution, the church, and morality of public and private spheres.[12] To counteract this threat, More and others set up an extensive network of Sunday schools that offered poor children religious instruction and taught them simple reading skills. By 1820 there were over five thousand such schools in England, many providing the only education available to poor children.[13] In these schools, children were taught to read (to access the Bible) but not to write. Describing her plan for instructing the poor as "limited and strict," More specified, "They learn of weekdays such coarse work as may fit them for servants. I allow of no writing. My object [is] . . . to form the lower class to habits of industry and virtue."[14] Reading was for the purposes of accessing the Bible, the catechism, and approved works such as the cheap repository tracts. According to Richard Altick's *The English Common Reader: A Social History of the Mass Reading Public 1800–1900*, Evangelicals believed that if reading led to thinking, the poor might become conscious of their misery and question their place in the social order—this would invite chaos.[15] So the tracts with their "sugar-coating of religious and moral counsel" concealed "a massive dose of social sedation."[16] The poor were taught to be dutiful and obedient to their superiors. Poverty and a low position in the social hierarchy were presented as circumstances to be accepted as God's will, with resignation and grace. It is clear in the third verse of the immensely popular Anglican hymn "All Things Bright and Beautiful" that Victorian society as a whole subsequently internalized this notion:

> The rich man in his castle,
> The poor man at his gate,
> God made them, high or lowly
> And ordered their estate.

More made a significant contribution to keeping the poor man happily at his gate in her popular story *The Shepherd of Salisbury Plain*, a Romantic depiction of an impoverished rural family. In this story, More portrays a poor and virtuous shepherd with eight children who lives in a spotless cottage and counts his blessings daily. A charitable gentleman comes along and provides a job for the husband and aids the wife in opening a school. His kindly effort eases their poverty and makes them, as he says, more "useful." In the story, More argues that the poor are poor because it is God's will—without any hint of the brutal mechanisms behind systemic poverty—and that virtue lies in the pious acceptance of one's lot in life and gratitude toward benefactors. According to More, "beautiful is the order of Society when each, according to his place—pays willing honor to his superiors—when the servants are prompt to obey their masters, and masters deal kindly with servants; when high, low, rich, and poor . . . sit down satisfied with his own place." [17]

The Evangelicals provided role models for children of all classes. In their stories, the poor learned what was expected of them. Middle-class girls were shown women exercising their special duty to make themselves useful through charity and worthwhile works. Good women visited the poor and gave them food baskets and hand-me-downs. Indeed, More's popular novel for adults, *Coelebs*, promoted charity as a calling. The subtext that charity work was sexy, a demonstration of qualities guaranteed to attract young men, was not lost on young middle-class women of the times. [18] Pious women were heroines in the eyes of many but despised as hypocrites by a few. Elizabeth Barrett Browning had an Evangelical aunt in mind when she took aim with her pen in 1856 in *Aurora Leigh*. Browning abhorred Englishwomen's penchant for trivial, small-minded "missionariness," combined with the fact that they were expected to "keep quiet by the fire / And never say 'no.'" It was a sort of "cage-bird life."

More's portraits of appropriate behaviors for little girls (and their mothers) to aspire to were the product of a passionate, conflicted woman. She struggled with issues of identity and a compulsion to please male authority figures. [19] Under the patronage of playwright David Garrick, she wrote an acclaimed play, *Percy*, in 1777. Judging from the trajectory that her life took, being a blue-stocking celebrity may not have been enough for her; or, perhaps fame conflicted with her notions of what was appropriate for a woman. But soon after, More experienced a religious conversion, and it was through Evangelicalism that she made her lasting mark and secured her place in middle-class society.

More and the Evangelical leadership worked hard at using their influence to preserve the class system in England, which they used as the scaffolding for reforms aimed at creating a religious-based society. Other children's writers of the time seconded More's defense of the existing social hierarchy. In Sarah Trimmer's stories, the wealthy and wellborn are consistently portrayed as generous and scrupulous, and the subservient position of children and servants is assumed to be natural. In her insightful study of children's literature titled *Engines of Instruction, Mischief, and Magic,* author Mary V. Jackson notes Trimmer's scornful handling of Newberyesque books such as *Primrose Prettyface,* in which a maid marries above her station. And Jackson quotes More as also lamenting the state of a world in which one could be a waiting maid in the morning and a Duchess at night.[20] Even the classics were viewed with suspicion: Trimmer thought that *Robinson Crusoe,* for example, might engender an early taste for a rambling life that was at odds with one's duty to remain in the place and station assigned by God.[21] In an expurgated edition of *The History of Little Goody Two-Shoes,* published after Newbery's death, the squire's unjust policies—which orphaned and impoverished the book's heroine—were modified to not encourage children to turn against their social superiors. Readers were *not* asked to ponder what a terrible situation the poor must be in when at the mercy of greedy authority figures.[22] Authority was unquestionable. The relative power of children and subordinated groups in general is a recurrent thread in children's literature.

One of the chief proponents of the sanctity of paternal authority was the wife of a military officer, Mrs. Sherwood, who returned from years in India a fervent Evangelical. Her conversion was brought on by the agonizing death of her second child, Henry, and she became highly vested in the notion of human depravity and the need to prepare for eternity. Sherwood set up schools in India and England and, driven in part by financial need, wrote over three hundred popular and well-crafted stories between 1802 and 1851. Known for her deathbed scenes and pious presentations of family life, Sherwood supported a God-ordained hierarchy in which the father was supreme, the mother and servants were below the father-master, and the children were below their mother. Just as everyone was to obey God, children were "under heavenly command" to obey their parents—no matter how neglectful, harsh, or cruel a parent might be.[23]

We know that Mrs. Sherwood's own mother subjected her daughter to a regime of self-denial: she was fed mostly dried bread and milk, the former severely rationed. She never sat in a chair in her mother's presence; she studied while standing in stocks with an iron collar pressing into her neck; and every morning she had to translate fifty lines from

Virgil.[24] Yet Sherwood insisted throughout her life that she was happy as a child. Sherwood and other authors of moral tales seemed to have had an important stake in promoting the parental norms they were raised under. They had been raised not to question authoritarian child-rearing schemes and often ended up staunchly reinforcing them. The characters in their stories were expected to conform; parental love, after all, was rightly contingent on compliance to adult will. Authors of the era repeatedly warned children about disappointing their parents. A poem by Jane and Ann Taylor, written in the early nineteenth century, gives a taste of these attitudes.

> And when you're good and do not cry,
> Nor into angry passions fly
> You can't think how Papa and I
> Love Baby.
> And when you see me pale and thin
> By grieving for my baby's sin
> I think you'd wish that you had been
> A better Baby.[25]

The moral imperative of obedience was reinforced by the knowledge that failing to comply to parents' expectations meant wounding parents. Fear of forfeiting parental love became a constraining influence in the lives of many Victorians.

In children's literature, the purposes of imagination were subject to contemporary influences. In the early nineteenth century, the imagination, when deployed at all, was evoked to drive home lessons. In Sherwood's best-known work, *History of the Fairchild Family*, siblings who fight over a doll have their hands soundly whipped, but this isn't enough. Their concerned father further drives home the message by waiting until dark and then taking them to view a gibbet and the putrid corpse of a man who murdered his brother. In another episode, the children are taken to pray over the decomposing corpse of an old man: their father points out that the corruption of the man's body is a result of the "exceeding sinfulness of sin." He bids them to pray to God that their spirits should be saved from such corruption. Ironically, while children raised by Evangelicals were protected from exposure to fairy tales (and the passionate responses that they were thought to evoke), many children were traumatized by horrific images like this and lurid tales that recounted in grotesque detail the fearful wages of sin. For example, Robert Louis Stevenson apparently suffered mentally and physically because of night terrors and insomnia engendered by the good intentions of a devout nurse who told him gruesome cautionary tales.[26]

Sarah Trimmer emerged as chief censor of the Evangelical period. The mother of eleven children, she appointed herself a champion of children for all of England, and she assiduously reviewed children's books in the

Family Magazine (1778–1789) and the *Guardian of Education* (1802–1806), hardly missing a title—nor any trace of insubordination and immorality. Any work that summoned passion or emotion other than godly piety and filial love was criticized for competing with religious pursuits and encouraging sinful frivolity. In her reviews, Trimmer warned parents of a vast conspiracy against Christianity and the social order that was attempting to infect the minds of children through children's books. She urged them to be vigilant and to counter these threats by impressing upon the child, from birth, the principles of Christianity.[27]

In spite of her influence, Trimmer did not escape her own critics, and they were as unflinching as she. In an 1806 *Edinburgh Review* essay, she was described as an "uncandid and feeble lady [who] seems to suppose, because she has dedicated her mind to the subject, that her opinion must necessarily be valuable upon it; forgetting it to be barely possible, that her application may have made her more wrong, instead of more right." She was, according to the essay's author, Sydney Smith, "a lady of respectable opinions, and very ordinary talents; defending what is right without judgment, and believing what is holy without charity."[28] Smith was not alone in finding Trimmer's reviews offensive. In *The Gates of Paradise* (1793), William Blake rejected the dogmas of good and evil, virtue and vice, that were drummed into tender minds by Trimmer and other "monitorial handmaidens" of tyranny. He lamented lives like hers, spent "in Curbing and Governing other people's passions by the various arts of poverty and cruelty." Blake, a prominent figure of the Romantic movement, had an optimistic vision of life and viewed children (as Dickens and others would later) as holy innocents and the imagination as conducive to healthful growth and joy.

Trimmer dismissed the criticism because she perceived her efforts as loving and—because they were Christian in orientation—beyond human reproach. Like Trimmer, Hannah More saw herself as a soldier in a war again sin and radicalism and armed by moral certainty. And they had the endorsement of each other and other powerful women writers, such as Mrs. Sherwood. These writers helped give birth to the repressive, sanctimonious tones of Victorian society. On children's literature, their mark is evident in several qualities and notions that persist to this day. From the Evangelicals, we have the notion that children can learn to be good through reading and that stories written for them should have moral purpose; we also have the idea that children's stories can be instruments of social influence—preserving the status quo, promoting social reform, and sometimes both simultaneously.

* * *

While economic depression and social turbulence encouraged dependence on religion and a passion for purification among Evangelicals, another group turned instead to the cognitive faculty of reason. This group built on Enlightenment notions that education was an important tool for creating healthy societies, and they adhered to Jean-Jacques Rousseau's belief that a more perfect adult could be engineered by controlling the influence of society on the child. Rousseau and his followers believed that the child was pure upon entry into the world and thereafter corrupted by exposure to a corrupt society. He advocated raising children in natural settings, keeping them from interacting with other people, and isolating them from such sullying forces as formal lessons and books.

Well-known English educationalist Richard Lovell Edgeworth (1744–1817) took Rousseau's ideas a step further by arguing that children's books could play a part in social progress. Edgeworth started his movement by experimenting with his own son's education. The result was, as Edgeworth later acknowledged, an ignorant and unsocialized individual, who was subsequently banished from the family. Edgeworth revised his ideas somewhat and, with the help of spinster daughter Maria (the second of his twenty-two children), created an educational plan that was published in 1798 as *Practical Education*. The book presented morality as the rational process of making good choices, rather than a strict adherence to religious principles. The Edgeworths promoted utilitarianism, teaching the children facts and emphasizing the child's learning from experience and reasoning. Middle-class parents eagerly adopted their ideals and the rigorously monitored environment they favored.

While Rousseau had believed that children were unable to reason, the Edgeworths turned to John Locke's notions that the child, a tabula rasa (blank tablet), could be taught to be moral and that even very young children could learn to exercise judgment. Also, Lockean was the idea that children could learn to govern themselves through the wise instruction of adults. While Rousseau thought that reading was the curse of childhood and that only one book — *Robinson Crusoe* — was acceptable for a child's education, the Edgeworths embraced the power of books and incorporated literature into their program, though with discrimination. It's interesting that Rousseau wanted his protégée to be "infatuated" with Crusoe[29] and to identify with him absolutely; the Edgeworths were much more rigid: reading was a means of absorbing specific lessons rather than a personality type.

Maria Edgeworth, who was a talented writer and storyteller, set out to compose rational children's stories that could serve as active agents for good. She believed that one could regulate human behavior by cultivating the human heart and inducing useful and agreeable habits: this would constitute a new and more effective method of policing.[30] Her books spelled out consequences and taught lessons. In her stories, Edgeworth rewarded virtue and punished vice in a way that may have seemed eminently fair to young readers. She gave charisma to the virtues of working hard and being honest, thrifty, and morally courageous. We can see the role that her tales were designed to fulfill, as aids for parents, in the title of her collection of stories, *The Parent's Assistant*. Her stories were educational tools. In contrast, she recommended that texts that did not support her prescribed goals be banished from the carefully engineered environment; at best, they were distractions and at worst, a pernicious influence.

The lens of reason is a powerfully clarifying one, if only because it can give the viewer the certainty of being correct. Followers of the Edgeworths envisioned the child as a chrysalis from which a fully rational (i.e., morally responsible) adult could emerge—with education. If ignorance was to blame for wickedness, then education was key to redemption. The education the Edgeworths envisioned consisted of controlling exposure to undesirable influences and filling the empty vessel of the child with scientific facts and other practical knowledge. The child's world, under the Edgeworths' program, became a laboratory for absorbing facts and, as well, skills of rational choice making. It was a highly manipulated environment in which parents provided structured experiences and in which books provided lessons and illustrations of good behavior contrasted with bad. The useful knowledge and rational goodness they fostered would become dear to the hearts of Victorians. The Edgeworths' self-conscious morality, as taught in children's books, was a good fit with the seriousness and dedication to duty that was a legacy of Evangelicalism.

Of course, there were those (most notably, the Romantics) who protested the narrow emphasis of the Edgeworth and Evangelical movements. In *The Prelude*, William Wordsworth (1770–1850) pined for the unselfconscious effect of free reading:

> Oh! Give us once again the Wishing-Cap
> Of Fortunatus, and the invisible Coat
> Of Jack the Giant-killer, Robin Hood,
> And Sabra in the Forest with St. George!
> The Child, whose love is here, at least, doth reap
> One precious gain, that he forgets himself.

The critic Charles Lamb, who would try (rather unsuccessfully) to write his own children's stories, complained to Samuel Taylor Coleridge in 1802 about authors who would attempt to stuff the child with insignificant and vapid knowledge. Like Wordsworth, he felt it bred self-consciousness and intellectual hubris. Lamb invited his friend to imagine what he would have been like if he had been raised in this era when science had supplanted poetry: "Think what you would have been now, if instead of being fed with Tales and old wives' fables in childhood, you had been crammed with geography and natural history?"[31] In a public lecture a few years later, Coleridge protested that the Edgeworth approach led not to virtue but vanity and that it taught not goodness but "goodyness."[32]

The Romantic movement's emphasis on feeling and freedom was in stark opposition to the Edgeworths' focus on reason and regulation, the Evangelical inclination toward piety, and, later, Victorian conformism. In *The Water-Babies* (1863), Charles Kingsley introduced readers to a fictional, overtutored child who turned into a turnip because "the more he listened, the more he forgot, and the more the water ran out of him. Tom thought he was crying: but it was only his poor brains running away, from being worked so hard." The child dies, and his parents put an inscription over his tomb about his wonderful talents and unparalleled precocity. Kingsley raises the question, "But perhaps the way of beating, and hurrying, and frightening, and questioning, was not the way that the child should go; for it is not even the way in which a colt should go, if you want to break it in, and make it a quiet serviceable horse."

Edgeworthian-influenced programs produced some remarkable infant prodigies, such as John Stuart Mill (1806–1873), who learned Greek at three years of age and went on, as an adult, to write the brilliant essay "On Liberty." But these same programs bred their fair share of hothouse plants that wilted when exposed to the world outside the nursery walls and were plagued with self-doubt, emotional coldness, and depression. Mill, for example, had a nervous breakdown at age twenty and restored himself to wellness by reading large doses of Wordsworth. What made Wordsworth's poems a medicine for his state of mind was that they expressed "states of feeling, and of thought colored by feeling, under the excitement of beauty. They seemed to be the very culture of the feelings, which I was in quest of. . . . I seemed to draw from a source of inward joy, of sympathetic and imaginative pleasure, which could be shared in by all human beings."[33] It is tempting to believe that he read the Wordsworth stanza later quoted in *The Water-Babies*: "Enough of science and of art: / Close up these barren leaves; / Come forth, and bring with you a heart / That watches and receives."

Nevertheless, many parents sought fulfillment by transforming their blank infant into a highly educated and behaviorally sound child. The behavioral component of the Edgeworths' program was very important, and right conduct was taught as systematically as facts. Parents (usually mothers) sought to monitor their child's every action and thought. Requiring absolute obedience and compliance, parents designed immediate consequences to bad behavior. The logical extension of the child was the future of English society, so there was no room for error in parenting. The preface of the Edgeworths' *Practical Education* explains to parents that "we should associate pleasure with whatever we wish our pupils should pursue, and pain with whatever we wish they should avoid." Affection was a parent's most persuasive tool, and it was provided or withheld according to the child's obedience and purposefulness. The psychological manipulation of a child's affections through fear and guilt was often more effective than corporal punishment, as many biographies from the nineteenth century attest.

In the Edgeworth and Evangelical schools, reading was key to eradicating irrationality and inappropriate aspirations. Thus, while the moral tales from both schools were somewhat sweetened by story, an independent imaginative life was forbidden to children. In *The Parent's Assistant*, Maria Edgeworth warned parents against books capable of inflaming the imagination and exciting a restless spirit of adventure, for, she explained, they painted false views of life and created hopes that, in the ordinary course of things, could not be realized. In her tales and those she influenced, there was no ambitious hankering after a dashing coach and galloping horses and very little fun for fun's sake. Instead, there were tales of dutiful sons looking after their widowed mothers, a twelve-year-old girl who acts as mother to her orphaned siblings, and an orphan boy who becomes an honest and trustworthy servant.

Unlike the Evangelical stories that were based on the assumption that children were born sinful and had to be saved, most of the children in Edgeworth's stories were portrayed as rational actors who ultimately chose to be good. Their goodness was shown as attracting rewards while shiftless behavior brought retribution. Edgeworth's characters undergo trials, but in the end, their rectitude is acclaimed, and they are rewarded by affection and gifts. Jackson describes the children in Edgeworth's stories as being tested to see whether the lessons had "taken," like a vaccine against a childhood disease. In "The Purple Jar," Rosamond purchases an alluring jar filled with what turns out to be colored water rather than the shoes she actually needs. She must then live with the pain of old shoes that pinch her feet. Rosamond makes the connection, and her final comment is that she hopes she will be wiser another time. The lesson of the story, of course, is the folly of choosing beauty over practical necessities, and Maria Edgeworth's tough-minded priorities in stories like these helped shape the content of children's literature for half a century.[34]

Edgeworth's characters were honest, thrifty, hardworking, and dedicated to serving and pleasing their parents and adults in general. The reward was often simple acknowledgment of the child's goodness, particularly precious when it came from parents. In a poem by Edgeworthian acolyte Mary Sewell, we meet George the Gentleman:

> George was the prince of boys! morn, noon, or night,
> Whate'er he had to do, 'twas always right;
> No murmur, nor excuses, nor debate
> That 'twas too early, or it was too late;
> For when by George his mother's will was known,
> In little time, his mother's will was done.[35]

It is striking the degree to which child characters in the literature of this era are fixated on adult approval and validation. The behavioral expectations of children were extraordinarily high, and for modern readers, humor and irony are conspicuously lacking. Child rearing, not entertainment or pleasure, was the raison d'etre of early children's stories. It was a serious calling.

Evangelical and utilitarian/rationalist authors were characterized by deep seriousness: neither group had time for frivolity or self-indulgence. Both groups believed that life must be lived methodically and that one read for a fixed end, which wasn't amusement.[36] One must take responsibility, be industrious, uphold authority, and live a moral life. These ideals, conveyed to children through stories, supported the Victorian social, moral, and educational codes that would dominate the century.

NOTES

1. Altick, *The English Common Reader*, 24.
2. Heywood, *A History of Childhood*, 24–25.
3. Jackson, *Engines of Instruction, Mischief, and Magic*, 84.
4. Jackson, *Engines of Instruction, Mischief, and Magic*, 33.
5. Wullschläger, *Inventing Wonderland*, 98.
6. Royde-Smith, *The State of Mind of Mrs. Sherwood*, 57.
7. Altick, *The English Common Reader*, 27.
8. Jackson, *Engines of Instruction, Mischief, and Magic*.
9. Adrian, "Dickens's Crusade for Children," 51.
10. Altick, *The English Common Reader*, 112.
11. Stott, *Hannah More*, 178–79.
12. Stott, *Hannah More*, 230.
13. Bradley, *The Call to Seriousness*, 44.
14. Kinnell, "Discretion, Sobriety and Wisdom," 180.
15. Altick, *The English Common Reader*, 32.
16. Altick, *The English Common Reader*, 105.
17. Altick, *The English Common Reader*, 105.
18. Stott, *Hannah More*, 277.
19. Kowaleski-Wallace, *Their Fathers' Daughters*, 11–12.
20. Jackson, *Engines of Instruction, Mischief, and Magic*, 175.
21. Summerfield, *Fantasy and Reason*, 196.
22. Jackson, *Engines of Instruction, Mischief, and Magic*, 181.
23. Cutt, *Mrs. Sherwood and Her Books for Children*, 41.
24. Royde-Smith, *The State of Mind of Mrs. Sherwood*, 27–28.
25. Brown, *The Captured World*, 40.
26. Harman, *Myself and the Other Fellow*, 21.
27. Summerfield, *Fantasy and Reason*, 193.
28. Darton, *Children's Books in England*, 160.
29. Green, *Dreams of Adventure*, 93.
30. Armstrong, *Desire and Domestic Fiction*, 15.
31. Talfourd, *The Letters of Charles Lamb*, 118.
32. Summerfield, *Fantasy and Reason*, 266.
33. Mill, *Autobiography*, 89.
34. Jackson, *Engines of Instruction, Mischief, and Magic*, 163.
35. Sewell, *The Children of Summerbrook*, 62.

36. Altick, *The English Common Reader*, 132.

THREE

Socialization: Loyalty, Duty, and Self-Sacrifice

If he'll only turn out a brave, helpful, truth-telling Englishman, and a gentle-man, and a Christian, that's all I want. —Father in *Tom Brown's Schooldays*

Authors spent the early decades of children's literature sorting out the relative roles that instruction and amusement would play in children's books. The initial hopefulness regarding children that ensured a light touch gave way to negativity and intense earnestness—children's stories became cautionary and dark. As we have seen, deteriorating social conditions in the late eighteenth and early nineteenth centuries led to a plethora of formulaic tales that offered bracing advice and religious and behavioral templates. Parents sought books that affirmed the existing social order as a way of assuaging their own fears about social chaos. Writers, under the influence of Evangelicalism or fervid rationalism, conveyed little optimism about children or their world and ultimately faulted children for their own circumstances—for childishness and childhood itself, denying them zest and possibilities.

Charles Dickens (1812–1870) had a role in restoring people to the innocence of children and the joys of narrative. His books, first appearing in the 1830s, exerted a tremendous influence on the way children were perceived within English culture—and ultimately on the evolution of children's stories from conscripted tools for indoctrination to more imaginative forms of storytelling and from moral smugness to social criticism. Dickens is not generally claimed as a pioneer of the genre of children's literature. He was, however, a pioneer in a certain portrayal and conception (in literature, at least) of children as rightfully innocent and of poverty and misfortune as not their fault but society's. Dickens was a towering figure in England's literary quest to find out what it means to be modern, fully human, and English.

With Dickens, the novel became respectable. For four decades in the mid-nineteenth century, Dickens wrote stories that Victorian England consumed eagerly in serial publications and then soon after in book form. He wrote to entertain, and he wrote for money. But he also leavened his stories with satire to needle the conscience of a society he saw as cold, even cruel, especially to children. Decency and love were recurring themes throughout his work. His stories captured people's attention with riveting plots, vivid characters, and mawkish sentimentality—but with his social criticism and irony, he gradually changed minds and hearts. While never claiming childhood as his arena, Dickens's tales of innocent child victims drew attention to the vulnerability of children, and his works prompted society to take greater responsibility for their care. When the child Oliver Twist, "desperate with hunger, and reckless with misery," rose from the table and uttered those fateful words, "Please, sir, I want some more," he confronted not only the inhumanity of his master but the apathy of England's reading public as well.

Dickens came by his unfortunate child heroes honestly, for he had been such a child himself. The precocious, aspiring child of a feckless civil servant father and a self-absorbed mother, he was fortunate only in that he escaped the stringent monitoring that most of his peers would have endured in Evangelical or Edgeworthian homes. He was permitted to read whatever he wished—*Tom Jones*, *Robinson Crusoe*, and thrilling tales of all kinds. But his parents' inability to manage money sent the family into a downward spiral. Reading became a major consolation when his bankrupt father was jailed for indebtedness when Dickens was thirteen. While his mother and siblings joined his father in prison, young Charles was put to work in a factory, and he lived, humiliated and alone, in a London slum. When his father was released from jail by a small legacy, Dickens was able to go back to school (against his mother's wishes, as she wanted to keep his income). Ultimately, of course, Dickens achieved middle-class respectability and then celebrity as an author. But his experience as a child laborer left him with a jaundiced attitude toward the society that would allow such a thing. Echoes of the disillusionment and loneliness he experienced reverberate in his stories. He had seen how church and state treated the poor, and for the rest of his life he would vehemently reject the hypocrisy and self-conscious goodness that enabled this negligence.

Pitiful child characters inhabit some of Dickens's most famous works, and he used them to evoke empathy. *Oliver Twist* (1838) was one of the first novels in English literary history with a view of life through the eyes of a child. Passive Oliver was alternately victimized by the self-interest of some adults and blessed by the goodwill of others. His pathos and vulnerability are duplicated in Little Nell in *The Old Curiosity Shop*

(1840–1841) and in Tiny Tim, the waifs, and the young Scrooge in *A Christmas Carol* (1853). Little Nell epitomizes innocence: Dickens describes her as fresh, spiritual, slight, and fairy-like—alone, unwatched, and uncared for (save by angels). When frail Nell suddenly has to help her wastrel grandfather flee London, her story takes readers on a hair-raising journey through the polluted countryside. When the scene depicting Nell's death was published (the book first appeared in serial form), readers across the country were devastated and bound together by grief. It has been suggested that her character aptly expressed the vulnerability and loss of innocence people were feeling at the hands of industrialization.[1]

In *A Christmas Carol*, the personification of Ignorance and Want as pathetic, mistreated waifs brings Scrooge to the realization that, in an effort to heal childhood wounds, he has mistakenly chosen money over love and defeated his deepest desires in the process.[2] Dickens's recognition of the importance of connection and love as a deep human need and not something to be turned on or off, apportioned in response to good or bad behavior, was absent in the moral tales of the preceding era.

Dickens's compelling child characters were created out of an earnest desire to counter the emotional apathy that plagued Victorian England. He was quietly rebelling against the stifling effect of Evangelical piety and rationalism. Dickens was aiming his message at the heart, not the mind. He paved the way for others, who took up the cause of social reform with books about saving innocent child victims and philanthropic themes. The brutal life of the chimney sweep, which Oliver Twist escaped, was later brought to literary life by Charles Kingsley in a book titled *The Water-Babies* (1863). This strange work graphically exposed the exploitation and cruelty of using children as chimney sweeps: to force them up the narrow flues, it was commonplace for homeowners to build a fire beneath them, sometimes causing horrible burns and even asphyxiation. The public was so horrified by Kingsley's story that within a year of its publication, the Chimney Sweepers Regulation Act was enacted, prohibiting children from being forced to work as sweeps.[3] Both Dickens and Kingsley used the imagination to clear the social fog of complacency and target the adult conscience.

Dickens never left his readers in doubt about the moral of a story: as one literary critic has written, the "angles of his absolute opinion stood up out of the confusion of his general kindness."[4] His agenda was to make visible the plight of England's poor and expose the hypocrisy of his times. But he was not exactly a revolutionary, either. A stable social order was important to Dickens; after all, it was the backdrop for his own spectacular success. To maintain his respectable image, Dickens kept secret his factory past and the companionship he found in later years with a young actress. In addition, he seems to have valued freedom of thought too much to fight social injustice with radical solutions; perhaps he realized that revolution can lead to a new and even more stifling orthodoxy. Nevertheless, he clearly held hope that the heartless injustices of the existing system could be alleviated.

In probing essential questions about how we respond to the needs of others, as individuals and as a society, Dickens formulated an idea about the purpose of the childhood years that was new to English society. This notion is most apparent in the semiautobiographical *David Copperfield*. Through telling of the ups and downs of David, an orphan child trying to find a place in society, Dickens models how a child learns how to be a good person.[5] The goodness to which Dickens aspires for David is not of religious piety, unquestioning allegiance to authority, or behavioral perfection; rather, it consists solely in common decency.

Dickens portrays the innocence of children as inspirational, suggesting that adults would do well to revisit their own childhoods and to learn from the children around them. This approach to childhood was in stark contrast to religious and rational models that had dominated the development of children's literature from its inception midway through the eighteenth century and well into the formative years of Dickens's writing career. Primarily a storyteller rather than a moralist or didact, he trusted his imagination—his creative skills—to deliver message through story. Because that message did not have to be boiled down, mashed, and spoon-fed, Dickens evaded what in other writers amounted to a strident and dogmatic tone. Dickens, who wrote in partial reaction to the Evangelical and Edgeworthian generation of authors and their influence on society, exploded their notions and profoundly influenced consciousness about children. Dickens saw children as actors and, though too often victimized, nevertheless admirable and even inspirational. He suggested a way to view children with compassion and empathy. He indicted society for cruelty and encouraged other authors (even those reared according to the harshest schemas) to use their pens to question social norms and stand up for decency. Earnest and didactic children's authors had opened the door for emotional engagement through stories, and Dickens (no less earnest) pushed it further ajar. The stage was set for the next wave of children's stories: novels written with determined social agendas but agendas heavily camouflaged by entertaining plots and endearing characters. Girls and boys would learn their roles through reading and from fictional role models.

* * *

The novel became the new darling of socialization. Its structure and emphasis on the everyday made it an ideal medium for inculcating life habits and acceptable worldviews. The English novel was already serving as a kind of biography or history: a form for delineating consistent human behavior and tracking the manner in which a character responds to successive circumstances.[6] As in biographies, a fictional subject is caught in what Hukacs called "the process of becoming," and the reader can absorb the subject's experiences and understandings in a way that engenders coping skills and a satisfying "philosophy" of life.[7] Novels provide basic moral instruction and, as well, carry what Craig Saper calls "artificial mythologies," the myths that replace existing ideas and rewrite the sociocultural rules.[8] Authors stage cultural interventions, drive home new cognitive maps, and influence personality development. By giving an inside view of society, they express and help define a particular nationality.[9]

Late-eighteenth- and early-nineteenth-century children's authors had been leery of the subversive potential of fiction. Their cautionary tales were a tentative experiment with social engineering, the making of good children. Their tales were basically religious and educational tools augmented with a modicum of plot and appealing elements. Authors drove with one foot on the brake, the imperatives of teaching and preaching offset by the necessity of engaging the reader. Nevertheless, they opened the door to the imagination. As attitudes toward imaginative literature relaxed and the novel became respectable,[10] children's literature benefited from trends in which romance—with its notions of beauty, hope, and social progress—became tamed in the novel, which taught knowledge of the world as rooted in reality.[11] From Dickens's time onward, his model of social earnestness carried by compelling narratives rose to dominance in books for children. Children's authors built on the primitive "cautionary tales of the bad endings awaiting those who step out of line through pride or ambition" and provided reservoirs of normative experiences that young people could draw on.[12]

Writers with their focus on domesticity provided social codes that would dominate English life for many generations. They thought they were advancing religion by providing templates of pious living. But in shifting the emotional focus from church to the home and family, they gave secular worldviews a boost and provided social maps that were useful for the purposes of the practical middle class and emergent capitalism.[13] Puritanism remained an influence, most notably though a terrifying stress on personal responsibility and a habit of self-consciousness and relentless scrutiny of one's inner life.[14] But Evangelicalism could not keep the next generation within its fold. Responding to social forces, authors sought to build a consensual moral climate through literature. Both men's and women's lives were reoriented to focus on the domestic sphere. Their roles had to be sorted out.

The home became absolutely central. "Home" conjured up magic, "bright memories of happy hours spent with loved ones, endeared by ties of consanguinity and affections, hours of sweet and holy communion in this blest retirement from a cold and calculating world."[15] There was the whole modern meaning of retreat and return. The home functioned as a symbol promoting the unity of the family in the same way that homeland promoted the unity of the nation.[16] In *Family Fortunes: Men and Women of the English Middle Class, 1780–1850*, Davidoff and Hall point to the influence of notions of home promoted by two influential late-eighteenth-century writers: the poet William Cowper (1731–1800) and the Evangelical author Hannah More. Cowper wooed the public with images of peaceful rural life and the comfort of tea and family: "intimate delights / Fireside enjoyments, homeborn happiness."[17] His vision of manliness was of living modestly, in retreat and reflection, and looking to God to "Improve the remnant of his wasted span, / And, having lived a trifler, die a man."[18] The Evangelicalist Hannah More targeted middle-class men and women with *Coelebs in Search of a Wife: Comprehending Observations on Domestic Habits and Manners, Religion and Morals* (1809). More's hero was a serious Christian, an "exempla of true manliness" who made it acceptable to enjoy domestic life and educating children.[19] More also emphasized a separate sphere for women and gave them roles in the hierarchy of home life.

As nineteenth-century children's authors shifted from tales to novels, they did their part in grounding the home, the family, and the nation in moral purity. They portrayed households in which experiences contrary to the development of faith were excluded.[20] The fulcrum of domestic happiness was the home, a "nursery of virtue."[21] Their characters modeled domestic virtues such as devotion, duty, mercy, and loving kindness, and young men and women had lofty moral aspirations. Both men and women could find gratification within the framework of the home. But while men were expected to value their domestic life, they were judged by their public and economic presence. Women's significance was linked exclusively to their performance in the domestic sphere.[22] Purity of the home was viewed as a matter of national security. Women who failed to vest their homes in peace and harmony were a threat to prosperity, society, and the nation.[23] They had moral authority over family relations, and their meaning in life was tied to their relationships with others. However, women's claims of moral superiority created a tension in the face of their social subordination. While women had little agency — things happened to them — their responses were critical; in contrast, agency and action were coded as masculine behavior. Feminine moral authority was tied to modesty, inconspicuousness, and adherence to rigorous codes of female deportment. Women policed themselves and domestic relations in general. To depart from accepted stereotypes was to risk social ostracism and the loss of their persuasive power and moral force.[24] Retaining moral superiority was paramount.

* * *

If More, Trimmer, Sherwood, and Edgeworth can be considered the midwives of Victorianism, Charlotte Yonge might be aptly called the understudy who became the era's governess. In the second half of the nineteenth century, she almost single-handedly provided a second wave of earnestness in children's literature that took up where her predecessors had left off. Her sights were on the older child and the process by which they became adults. Yonge began writing at sixteen and dedicated her life to helping young people, especially young women, learn to live according to church principles.

The template for her ideas about an appropriate developmental path for girls was her own life. Born in 1823, Yonge was raised in isolation by principled and devout parents who had studied the Edgeworths' *Practical Education*. Her mother taught her until age seven, when her only brother was born. Her father educated her until she was twenty, and though he yelled at her when she made errors, he engendered an intense emotional attachment.[25] For the rest of his life, his daughter would do anything to please him. The shy, awkward, and solitary young girl was kept on a short rein, fed only plain food, and discouraged from frivolity. She was drilled in truthfulness and the importance of the Fifth Commandment: *Honor thy parents*.

Yonge never questioned her upbringing, her parents' values, or the need for filial obedience. In her books, any child that disobeyed an adult came to a bad end.[26] She also never questioned religious tenets that held women to be innately inferior; her female characters knew or learned the value of being submissive and molding themselves to the wishes of husbands, fathers, and brothers. Their character benefited from male guidance and the natural superiority of males' reasoning abilities.

Yonge's entire life (1823–1901)—by all accounts a tranquil, upper-middle-class existence—was spent in the self-contained village of Otterbourne. This part of Hampshire was the center of the Oxford movement, which emerged in the 1830s and sought to reverse liberal reforms within the Anglican church. John Keble, the leader of this reaction against secularism, lived nearby and tutored young Charlotte in religious matters. Keble and her father were the key influences in her life; she thought them responsible for the whole cast of her mind. Keble fleshed out Tractarian principles in his book *The Christian Life*, and this Victorian best-seller may have shown Yonge the value of literature in bringing religious truths to the popular imagination.[27] Her characters learned to live according to Keble's lines:

> The trivial round, the common task,
> Will furnish all we ought to ask;
> Room to deny ourselves—a road
> To bring us daily nearer God.

It was Keble, after all, who had had much to do with her belief that self-denial was the key to making one's life into a spiritual journey.[28]

The primary impulse behind her writings was, of necessity, always religious. When she began writing in the late 1830s, her family had to approve first: writing was acceptable only if she wrote as a Christian, for the glory of God, and did not neglect her domestic responsibilities.[29] Fortunately for Yonge, her irresistible passion for writing could be posed as "her God-given duty," and her qualms about earning money were assuaged through philanthropy.[30] Charlotte's first book coincided with a turning point in British social history, the night in 1837 when eighteen-year-old Princess Victoria awoke to find herself queen. Over the course of her sixty-four-year reign, the queen's values dominated England. The rules that governed the princess's childhood were similar to those imposed on young Charlotte. The princess was overprotected by her pious mother, who shared her bedroom every night until she became queen and tried (though unsuccessfully) to cultivate dependency in her daughter. One technique was subjecting to her an elaborate set of rules and isolating her: she was not allowed to interact with other children, and she lived an austere life. Victoria later described her childhood as rather "melancholy." Because her mother was scandalized by the king's mistresses and bastard children, Victoria was drilled in the avoidance of impropriety, and sexual repression was a hallmark of her era. She married a conscientious and rigid German prince, Albert, and the royal parents were determined to school their children in the virtues of self-denial and duty. They found fault easily and went to great lengths to stamp out pride, considered to be vulgar and un-Christian.[31] Unlike that of the Georgian kings who preceded her, Victoria's lifestyle was governed by propriety and mirrored middle-class family values.

Parents in the Victorian era, who like the Queen had been subjected to rigorous educational and religious programs, were increasingly preoccupied with the moral development of the next generation. At the time, Dickens was bringing child characters to center stage: *Oliver Twist* appeared in 1838 and *The Old Curiosity Shop* in 1840–1841. *David Copperfield*, his semiautobiographical *Bildungsroman* (novel of personal development), appeared in nineteen monthly installments from 1849 to 1850. Writers continued to use stories as a tool for moral instruction, in the tradition of moral tales authors. But audiences, young and old, now turned to novels rather than story collections as a means for exploring and shaping the developing psyches of children.

Like other women authors of the Victorian era, Yonge used education as a tool for promoting her ideals. Through her writings, she taught females how to carve out a meaningful existence within the established hierarchy. She showed them that their daily activities and social contributions were important. Yonge put spinsters to work in an era when, according to population statistics of 1851, thirty out of every one hundred women were unmarried—and redundant.[32] Spinsters were entrusted with the care of aging parents and invalids, stepped in when the mothers of large families died young, kept house for bachelor brothers, and provided charity. Yonge's overarching vision of life as a spiritual journey gave girls' and women's lives purpose and significance.

The agenda for children's books during this period became long-term acculturation and socialization rather than drilling in the consequences of actions, the formula that had defined the didacticism of the moral tales. Yonge popularized the portrayal of moral development as a process (a series of choices) rather than as a stimulus-response reflex. She targeted older children and young adults with exciting narratives that reined in overt preaching and made "being good" interesting and ideals alluring. Indeed, her romanticized blueprint for development was so compelling that few readers questioned her underlying assumption that fitting into and serving society is worth any price. Yonge set the standard for a century of children's books in which the collective (family, society, nation, empire) was paramount and characters were judged on the basis of their contributions to the greater good. Reading was a means through which girls and boys learned sharply differentiated roles and types of goodness.

Charlotte Yonge had unparalleled influence, and like Queen Victoria, she cast a large shadow. Her first work appeared in 1838 and the last in 1900, shortly before her death and that of Queen Victoria. Her oeuvre was diverse and geared toward educating through examples. Yonge produced popular school texts (including *A Book of Worthies* and *A Book of Golden Deeds*) and historical fiction that celebrated battle and disciplined courage. To fill the need for school texts, she wrote cottage stories and tales about working-class children and the rural poor. A Tory conservative, Yonge posed honesty, diligence, and humility as the best policy for the lower classes; like the Evangelicals who preceded her, she believed in personal, hands-on philanthropy by the upper classes and a proper show of gratitude by the poor. She shared the Tractarian obsession with bringing religion to all through building churches and parish schools, but secular education and liberal emphasis on equality and individualism appalled her.

Yonge abhorred the overt dogmatism and scriptural references in children's fiction. And she knew how children read, having done so herself when reading Evangelical stories: children were proficient in what Yonge called the "noble art of skip"—"diligently extracting the small sandwiches of story, and carefully avoiding the improving substance."[33] Her religious ideals stressed emotional control, and the Christianity she inscribed into her narratives was implicit and lived, minute by minute, rather than declaimed or preached. The world of faith was portrayed as exciting: the stained-glass environments and church-related events (missionary meetings, retreats, bazaars, and fetes) functioned as balls or battles do in other writers' fiction—they elicited "enthusiasm or boredom, aesthetic rapture or distaste, high resolve or frivolity from her characters."[34]

Yonge's popularity as a novelist was cemented by masterfully crafted family chronicles, portraits of domestic realism that corresponded with contemporary visions of an ideal life.[35] She was fascinated by large families—life as experienced during visits to her cousins' homes; she may also have been responding to the contemporary reality of large families, their numbers in this era swelled by a survival rate among children of 90 percent. It wasn't unusual to have families with as many as ten or more children. Queen Victoria had nine. Lewis Carroll was one of eleven siblings, and accounts of his childhood (and life) are uncannily similar to one of Yonge's novels. Yonge's chronicles traced the fate—sometimes intertwined—of young members of upper-middle-class Victorian families, most notably the Underwoods and Mays, with thirteen and eleven children, respectively. Shifting from character to character, Yonge chronicled the siblings' development—their growing pains, religious and ethical crises, education, devotion to parents, love interests, and marriages. She showed the consequences of their choices, and religious, social, and domestic usefulness was shown as infinitely preferable to fame or fortune.[36]

Yonge focused on how young people formed their characters and responded to challenges. By modern standards, her books contain an extraordinary amount of self-doubt and soul-searching as characters scrutinize their every sin, internalize norms of self-sacrifice and self-control, and avoid the cardinal sins of "willfulness." In learning to submit to higher authority, young people were subjected to frustration and pain—both considered essential in transforming religion into a source of strength. Yonge's characters were perceived at the time as heroic, and she made duty seem romantically desirable. Her characters were so engaging that readers worried about their futures and snapped up sequels that addressed their fates.

Yonge was obsessively concerned with femininity: Her books spelled out clearly what behavior, concerns, and aspirations were appropriate for women and what were not. She popularized the notion of the "angel in the house," and the home as the natural sphere of influence for girls and women. Her twenty-plus domestic novels and ruminations on the role of women in the *Monthly Packet*, a girls' magazine that she edited for fifty years, profoundly influenced the aspirations and choices of upper-middle-class girls and women. Yonge's avowed aim was to help girls from fifteen to twenty-five become "steadfast and dutiful" daughters of the Church of England.[37] She initiated young girls into womanhood through illustration: her characters modeled the process of learning how to master themselves and absorb the codes of conduct and self-sacrifice expected of Victorian women. Her prefaces and subtitles often drew attention to the themes and principles that she was trying to illustrate in each book, as witnessed by such titles as *Henrietta's Wish: Domineering* and *The Daisy Chain, or Aspiration: A Family Chronicle*. In the latter, aspiration is framed, of course, in spiritual terms. Her domestic novels had an autobiographical character, and she wrote the story of her own socialization into womanhood over and over again.

Yonge was concerned about women who were poorly educated—taught senseless facts and parlor skills, such as drawing and French. If allowed to be frivolous, she believed, their thoughts would turn to worldly things; if intelligent, they might become desperate for meaningful work and step out of their proper sphere. Public life, after all, was harmful to true femininity.[38] *The Clever Woman of the Family* (1865) explores the frustrations of an intelligent woman, Rachel, unable to respond to the wretchedness and crime around her because of social convention and her mother's expectations. Rachel finds outlet eventually, not in self-directed action, but in church-sanctioned good works and surrender to the guidance of her husband: Yonge believed firmly that women had to be molded by the masculine intellect, which in one form or another becomes the master of her soul.

In her essay *Womankind*, she affirms "the absolute need of the feminine nature for discipline and obedience." There could be no true success or happiness for a woman who has not learned to efface herself. Some Victorian women, of course, effaced themselves into a permanent state of invalidism. It was a way out of onerous responsibilities and a role that carried with it entitlement, usually the assurance of receiving female care and attention. Many an unmarried daughter, Yonge among them, danced attendance on an invalid mother whom she dreaded disappointing.

Yonge was also worried that women would acquire a taste for learning that might lead them to neglect their domestic responsibilities. For women (as well as men), intellectual hubris was a sin.[39] Yonge returned repeatedly to the theme of the unfortunate consequences of giving girls a substantive education, especially in the classics. In *The Daisy Chain*, we have the intellectual Ethel, who is not allowed to have glasses, because it is considered unladylike. She is warned by her brother to stop studying or she would become "good for nothing." Persistence in learning Greek was already interfering with her duty as a Christian—taking care of her father, invalid sister, and younger siblings. When Ethel complies and assumes her proper role, she is awarded esteem as a moral center for the family. The life of Ethel most clearly sums up the Tractarian ideals that guided every aspect of Yonge's life and work: a woman must serve the church and her family in noncompetitive ways that don't threaten conventional notions of gender. In her books, Miss Yonge teaches the lessons of her own life—that subordinating her intelligence and autonomy in this way brings private rewards of surpassing value. The ideal Victorian girl and Yonge heroine loves goodness above all and leads an exemplary life of prayer, submission to authority, good works, and useful domestic service.

* * *

Middle-class boys, however, were to be groomed for leadership. After all, England and the British Empire would soon be theirs to govern and guide. Domestic masculinity had to be stiffened and duty channeled outward. From the mid-nineteenth century onward, it became common for boys as young as seven to be removed from the influence of their mothers and sent away to live as boarders in monastic "public schools" (private boarding schools) where they were toughened up and taught responsibility. Public school education meant moral education above all.[40] Traditional public school rituals stripped them of their previous identity, and they were taught the correct way to play games and fit into a hierarchy based on age, prestige, skill, and something called "character." Each public school had its own traditions and atmosphere, but in all, loyalty to the school was inculcated through rules, rituals, school songs, school magazines, and competitive games. Poet laureate Cecil Day-Lewis wrote of his school days, "We were children practicing to be men, as in a sense all savages are: and like any primitive community, we created by a sort of communal imagination the myths needed for our development."[41]

A new subgenre of children's literature emerged to address the needs of public school boys, for which W. F. Farrar's *Eric; or, Little by Little* (1858) and Thomas Hughes's *Tom Brown's Schooldays* (1857) were prototypes. The "school story," which flourished for the next century, typically traced the development and life of a boy from his entry into public school at approximately seven years of age until exit, at eighteen. Both Farrar and Hughes saw their books as instructional texts, but they took a page from Dickens by embedding their lessons in riveting plots and fleshing out their stories into the form of a novel. The view that these authors provided into the public school experience was fascinating for readers of all ages, and the expectations and aspirations that the books engendered had a great influence on the notions of boyhood and nationalistic ideals that came to define the Victorian era. Boys were expected to serve God, Queen, and country—at home and in the empire.

The Evangelical influence, well entrenched in Victorian society, influenced the school story in its early stages. Farrar, a former headmaster and preacher who served as chaplain to Queen Victoria, was a well-connected, energetic, and devout Evangelical. His *Eric* (1858) is little more than a cautionary tale adapted and extended into a novel by a male author for an all-boy audience. The public school that Eric attends is a testing ground and school life a perpetual exercise in self-examination, moral failure, and religious flagellation. Farrar's goal for boys was early acceptance of self-conscious piety and rigid adherence to the path of earnestness.

Eric and his brother enter school as children: "The small, shining flower-like faces, with their fair hair—the trusting loving arms folded round each brother's neck—the closed lids and parted lips—made an exquisite picture." But by his teen years, Eric has moved from innocence to corruption, and Farrar's portrait poses him as perennially on the brink of destruction. Despite recurrent crises of conscience, Eric keeps sinning—disobeying, smoking, swearing, and, worst of all, an unnamed sin, likely masturbation or sodomy. The book contains many exhortations, such as this one against swearing:

> Now, Eric, now or never! Life and death, ruin and salvation, corruption and purity, are perhaps in the balance together, and the scale of your destiny may hang on a single word of yours. Speak out, boy! Tell these fellows that unseemly words wound your conscience; tell them that they are ruinous, sinful, damnable; speak out and save yourself and the rest. . . . The knowledge of evil is ruin, and the continuance of it is moral death.

While Eric continually vows to be a better boy, dying young emerges fairly quickly as his only path to redemption. Farrar's book is a pessimistic study of a boy slipping into depravity, written by a man wishing to save other boys from this fate.

The book had a steady readership because it made school life and boyhood choices highly dramatic; the book—like Victorian society in general—took childhood seriously. Parents (often mothers) remained enamored with the book for decades and bought it as an exemplar for their sons. Mothers named their sons after Farrar's character: George Orwell's real name was Eric Arthur Blair. *Eric*'s influence peaked with boys in the 1860s and 1870s; it did not wear well as time passed. In the school story *Stalky and Co.* (1899), Rudyard Kipling has a group of boys mockingly read one another passages from *Eric*.

It was Thomas Hughes who successfully created a role model for English boys that would stand the test of time. Hughes was a respectable moralist with a "Christian tint," who like many Victorians rejected an intense spiritual orientation while remaining within a generally Christian framework.[42] In *Tom Brown's Schooldays*, published a year before *Eric*, Hughes tells the story of a high-spirited squire's son, following his life from his early years at home through his experiences at public school and, finally, into manhood. The model of learning that Hughes and subsequent school story authors promoted was socialization through total immersion in public school life. *Toms Brown's Schooldays* is set in a real school—Rugby—in an imaginary landscape of high drama and small pleasures: school matches, cheating scandals, and crushes; sausages cooked in the fireplace, cozy studies, jokes, and pranks. The boys are the center of action, and everything that happens to them matters. The book's credibility hinged on its portrayal of a real boy with the usual schoolboy's preoccupation with food, fun, and mischief. Tom was a breath of fresh air, the type of boy that children wanted to read about. He develops into the kind of man that Victorian society, saturated with Evangelical notions but restive, now wanted to cultivate. Rugby succeeds in that Tom is made into a good English boy, a good future citizen, to paraphrase Hughes.

Hughes himself was a bighearted, sports-loving man, described in his obituary as "typically English—English of the best."[43] He attended Rugby when it was undergoing reforms by its renowned headmaster, Dr. Thomas Arnold. There, he absorbed Arnold's belief in godliness, good learning, and character development as the basis of school life. Hughes went on to attend Oxford and became a liberal member of Parliament, a prime mover in a movement called Muscular Christianity (in which religion is the basis for action), and a fond father of nine. *Tom Brown's Schooldays* (1857) is semiautobiographical and expresses Hughes's goal for his son and other schoolboys: a down-to-earth robustness rather than the fire-and-brimstone piety of Evangelicals and the self-consciousness goodyness encouraged by moral tales. For him, Christianity was foundational rather than encompassing. His vision is evident through the musings of Squire Brown on his son Tom's departure for school: "If he'll only turn out a brave, helpful, truth-telling Englishman, and a gentleman, and a Christian, that's all I want."

In *Tom Brown's Schooldays* Hughes presents the process through which boys like Tom are socialized and inculcated with morality through life at school. The public school, Rugby, is an intense environment that allows boys to work out their character through competition, friendships, and the shouldering of ever-increasing responsibilities. They learn about spite, jealousy, and vanity, as well as love, loyalty, honesty, and cooperation. Character is developed through interaction and choices. For example, Tom must share quarters with a sickly boy; when he chooses to make friends with him, he learns a lot about empathy and quiet courage.

Public school boys taught themselves how society works through a quasi-formulaic process, designed and imposed by teachers and other boys. They were held responsible for the behavior and well-being of all students in their house (organizational and living unit). Ultimately, older boys in the public schools were given tremendous power over the younger boys. The justification was that it would teach them to be able administrators and leaders and they would leave school equipped for effective participation in society.

The book begins with Tom's upbringing in the country. He is a sturdy little rascal who plays with local boys, fishes and wrestles, and gets into mischief. This part of the book is a tribute to the healthy rightness of rural living. The country folk among whom Tom grows up are the backbone of England: Hughes links them to the heroes of British wars. Tom comes from an old Saxon fighting family, and fighting and loyalty become major themes in Tom's coming of age. The Muscular Christianity movement (to which Hughes ascribed) placed high value on those who embrace life as a struggle and fight for just causes: subduing the earth (imperialism) and protecting the weak. Hughes maintained that belief in God was a central attribute of a good man, but he shied away from the self-conscious piety of the Evangelicals.

Tom Brown's Schooldays was used by Hughes as a vehicle for the expression of ideas in a day when novels figured importantly in intellectual and moral debate[44] and religion was a source of both inspiration and confusion. Hughes's book is avowedly didactic—in fact, Hughes later said that his sole object was to preach. But it is also upbeat and unsanctimonious. At Rugby, Bible stories serve as discussion points as the boys ponder the implications of certain kinds of behavior, and religion (acquired through mandatory chapel attendance and the example of the headmaster) becomes an essential habit that fosters a hearty kind of goodness. Hughes presented religion as a wholesome foundation for character rather than as an obsessive preoccupation. Hughes was conveying and disseminating through story a new ethos, Englishness, which amalgamated Saxon manhood and matter-of-fact Christianity. School was a microcosm of the larger playing fields of the nation and world.

Hughes's philosophy of Muscular Christianity linked physical fitness with moral worth. Games were seen as building character. Tom and his peers loved games and also understood the importance of games in developing unity and team spirit:

> "It's more than a game. It's an institution," said Tom.
> "Yes, said Arthur, "the birthright of British boys old and young, as habeas corpus and trial by jury are of British men."
> "The discipline and reliance on one another which it teaches is so valuable, I think . . . it merges the individual in the eleven; he doesn't play that he may win but that his side may."

The love of games and the sense of their validity portrayed in this book and school stories in general played their part in fostering an obsession with sports that came to a head in the public schools of late-nineteenth-century England. In Hughes's words, a rugby match became "worth living for; the whole sum of schoolboy existence gathered up into one straining, struggling half-hour, a half-hour worth a year of common life." The schools' sports heroes—those who embodied the virtues of the playing field—were worshipped and given great privileges. Developing the intellect was considered a poor substitute to developing physical prowess and the capacity to shine on the playing field.

"Playing the game" became a central metaphor (for life) within the cult of the public school. It had to do with being true to the ideals of a superior race.[45] It is summed up in the flourishes of Henry Newbolt's poem "Vitai Lampada" (They pass on the torch of life):

> There's a breathless hush in the Close tonight—
> Ten to make and the match to win—
> A bumping pitch and a blinding light,
> An hour to play and the last man in.
> And its not for the sake of a ribboned coat
> Or the selfish hope of a season's fame,
> But his Captain's hand on his shoulder smote—
> "Play up! Play up! and play the game!"

"Playing the game" had evolved into an ideal, "an all-embracing principle of conduct applicable to every circumstance in which an individual might find himself."[46] The second stanza of Newbolt's poem links the playing field to the battlefield:

> The sand of the desert is sodden red,—
> Red with the wreck of a square that broke;—
> The Gatling's jammed and the Colonel dead,
> And the regiment blind with dust and smoke.
> The river of death has brimmed his banks,
> And England's far, and Honour a name,
> But the voice of a schoolboy rallies the ranks:
> "Play up! play up! and play the game!"

"Playing the game" became shorthand for adhering to ideals and a code of behavior that was paramount.

This code was strongly influenced by the invocation of the virtues of an idealized medieval King Arthur and his Round Table—purity, chivalry, loyalty, self-sacrificing courage, and unselfish duty. Arthur, a warrior king, was a compelling hero for the ruling class. Public schools encouraged boys to identify with Galahad and Percival, who were held up as exemplars of modern Christian knights, willing to sacrifice all for the empire. As inspiration, a copy of G. F. Watt's painting of Sir Galahad was hung in Eton College in the 1890s.[47] According to Stephanie Barczewski, the chivalric ethos of the public school boy formed a new code of colonial conduct that distinguished the British from the barbaric people they ruled over.[48] Schoolboys turned administrators were to bring firm government and the benefits of British civilization to native populations. The Arthurian ethos began a constant factor in British consciousness of masculinity and gentlemanliness.

It was on the playing fields and in the halls that England's elite absorbed notions of themselves as supremely important icons of Englishness. But it was through *serialized* school stories that young working-class and lower-middle-class boys were exposed to middle- and upper-class codes of behavior that involved doing the right thing and exhibiting pluck and an aura of command as well as "traditional British phlegm, reserve, understatement, unflappability, the stiff upper lip, a result of the inculcation of modesty in victory and defeat, the all-male society in which emotion was sissy, the encouragement of restraint in the exercise of power."[49] As the school story became part of popular culture, boys who could never aspire to attending a public school could nevertheless experience the almost fantastical life of the public school with its special attitudes, jargon, clothes, and ceremonial trappings. They absorbed something of its ethos through story. According to one working-class boy, it was through serialized school stories that he and his friends "learnt that boys of the higher class boarding-schools were courageous, honorable and chivalrous, and steeped in traditions of the school and loyalty to the country. We tried to mould our lives to this formula."[50]

For the century following its publication, *Tom Brown's Schooldays* fostered nostalgia for the world of the public school, even for those who had never attended one. The new genre that Hughes introduced would make its mark in terms of literary forms (through memoirs and novels) and popular culture (serials and, later, films). It met different needs for children and adults. Young boys read stories because it gave them an idea of what to expect at school and then something against which to measure their own experience. Adults who had attended public schools could relive their youth and the intensity of experience that often made subsequent life an anticlimax. The school story encouraged a sense of common identity focused around fair play, responsibility, and loyalty. Through actual experience, novels, and the pages of serials, the rituals and myths of public school life became part of what George Orwell called an "imaginative background" that English youth then carried through life.[51] As adults, they had a common well of images and experiences, shared as siblings share family memories.

NOTES

1. Ackroyd, *The Life and Times*, 64.
2. Stone, "Fairy-Tale Form," 80.
3. Chitty, *The Beast and the Monk*, 221.
4. Chesterton, "Harsh Truth in *Hard Times*," 134.
5. Smiley, *Charles Dickens*, 85.
6. Parrinder, *Nation and Novel*, 86.
7. Backscheider, *Reflections on Biography*, 17.
8. Saper, *Artificial Mythologies*, xii.
9. Parrinder, *Nation and Novel*, 1.
10. Altick, *Lives and Letters*, 89.
11. Parrinder, *Nation and Novel*, 13.
12. Porter, "Introduction," 6.
13. Armstrong, *Desire and Domestic Fiction*, 37.
14. Cockshut, *Truth to Life*, 66.
15. Gillis, *A World of Their Own Making*, 112.
16. Gillis, *A World of Their Own Making*, 113.

17. Davidoff and Hall, *Family Fortunes*, 165.
18. Davidoff and Hall, *Family Fortunes*, 164.
19. Davidoff and Hall, *Family Fortunes*, 169.
20. Conway, *When Memory Speaks*, 41.
21. Davidoff and Hall, *Family Fortunes*, 149.
22. Herrera, "Introduction," 2.
23. Barczewski, *Myth and National Identity*, 171.
24. Conway, *When Memory Speaks*, 16.
25. Coleridge, *Charlotte Mary Yonge*.
26. Brownell, "The Two Worlds of Charlotte Yonge," 172.
27. Dennis, *Charlotte Yonge (1823–1901)*, 45.
28. Sturrock, *"Heaven and Home,"* 107.
29. Sturrock, *"Heaven and Home,"* 20.
30. Hayter, *Charlotte Yonge*, 16.
31. Hibbert, *Queen Victoria*, 184.
32. Roberts, "Marriage, Redundancy or Sin," 57.
33. Hayter, *Charlotte Yonge*, 14.
34. Hayter, *Charlotte Yonge*, 19.
35. Sandbach-Dahlstrom, *Be Good Sweet Maid*, 60.
36. Sturrock, *"Heaven and Home,"* 30.
37. Mare and Percival, *Victorian Best-Seller*, 140.
38. Sturrock, *"Heaven and Home,"* 93.
39. Sandbach-Dahlstrom, *Be Good Sweet Maid*, 81.
40. Ashley, *George Alfred Henty*, 23.
41. Day-Lewis, *The Buried Day*, 115.
42. Davidoff and Hall, *Family Fortunes*, 184.
43. Quigly, *The Heirs of Tom Brown*, 59.
44. Richards, *Happiest Days*, 26.
45. Ashley, *George Alfred Henty*, 55.
46. Rosenthal, *The Character Factory*, 97.
47. Barczewski, *Myth and National Identity*, 221.
48. Barczewski, *Myth and National Identity*, 220.
49. Richards, *Happiest Days*, 13.
50. Richards, *Happiest Days*, 20.
51. Orwell, "Boys' Weeklies," 482.

FOUR

Creating Manliness and the Boy Hero

When all the world is young, lad,
And all the trees are green;
And every goose a swan, lad,
And every lass a queen;
Then hey for boot and horse, lad,
And round the world away;
Your blood must have its course, lad,
And every dog his day.
—Charles Kingsley

Victorians worshipped heroes. Rather than looking to the church and saints for inspiration, they turned to historical or contemporary figures as exemplars of virtuous living. Worshipping great *English* men was a form of self-help. A person was improved by pilgrimages to sites associated with famous men, such as Shakespeare's birthplace, or by worshipping at "secular shrines," such as the National Portrait Gallery, which opened in 1856.[1] Lord Stanhope, who proposed the gallery collection, believed that it would incite honorable exertion and great deeds.[2] Visitors—it was open to everyone—were to make the link between great men and great actions and see themselves as part of a race of heroes. But paintings and busts paled in contrast to the effect of reading, and writers gave the cult of hero worship great imaginative force. Thomas Carlyle, for example, fervently believed that "all that mankind has done, thought, gained or been: it is lying as in magic preservation in the pages of books." His *On Heroes and Hero Worship and the Heroic in History* (1841) touted great men's actions as a useful and reinforcing source of moral guidance; if heroes could master brute circumstance,[3] so could others: their triumphs were shared. Carlyle touted the English as new Romans, tasked with the heroic mission of civilizing the world by spreading their civilization, religion, and freedoms.[4]

Biographies displaced the Bible, as late Victorians turned to secular sources for moral inspiration. With heroism the basis for all possible good,[5] the lives of the great were treated as legends. They were personal stories with cultural interpretations built in.[6] By following the trajectory of a single life, readers gained access to the inner myth of famous people, the moral impulses that had made them exceptional. Biographies were useful; through them, readers were taught how to act for their own good and that of the world.[7] In addition, heroes were dynamic figures, and biographies provided an infusion of life force that contrasted sharply with the impotency that many experienced on a daily basis. Constrained and oppressed by social pressures, Victorians found bracing inspiration in strong characters who exercised free will and chose noble courses of action.[8] There was a preference for a man of action over the intellectual.[9] Biographers presented pictures of worthiness that resonated with English culture. It was "virtue embodied in a particular character and outlet"[10] — in effect, national character.

The greatest legendary hero was King Arthur, and for much of the nineteenth century, historians mobilized his legend as a rallying point for the development of national identity, social unity, and imperialism. It was part of the manipulation and fabrication necessary to construct a new history that focused on English accomplishments and exceptionalism.[11] Arthur was an ancestral hero whose charismatic fusion of chivalric virtue and fighting prowess continually served as a source of inspiration:

> Arthur's glorious name shall live;
> Warm'd like him, with worth sublime,
> Patriots rise from time to time;
> Through later ages, Britons be
> Ever happy, ever free.[12]

By the end of the century, Lady Magnus confidently wrote in *First Makers of England* (1901), "The seeds of our national character are to be sought in the lives of the heroes of early England, from whom we trace the beginnings of our best habits and institutions." Arthur was invoked to reinforce the continuity of English institutions and culture and serve as a basis for current aspirations, most notably imperialism.

Victorians adored Arthur, often naming their sons for him. Writers adapted his legend to support various interpretations of virtue. King Arthur provided a concept of masculinity that formulated the image of the gentleman as "an idealized medieval knight embodying the virtues of bravery, loyalty, courtesy, generosity, modesty, purity, and compassion."[13] In Yonge's *The Heir of Redclyffe* (1853), Sir Guy Morville reads *Morte d'Arthur* and admires Sir Galahad. Yonge uses Morville to demonstrate the potential of a domestic outlet for Arthurian values. But Arthur was also a source of inspiration for imperialists, who were interested in transforming public school boys into self-sacrificing propagators of empire. In 1849, a journalist described King Arthur as the "beautiful incarnation of all the best characteristics of our nation."[14] Arthur was a man who never held back from danger and was willing to die for his country. His self-sacrificing nature, and that of his knights, was much invoked by propagandists who wrote boys' adventure stories. For example, in *Percival: A Story of Past and Present*, a young colonial administrator named Percival dies on an expedition and is compared to the knight who risked all in his pursuit of the Holy Grail. Knighthood was constantly in flower in Victorian books for boys.

The greatest contemporary hero of the century was, of course, another Arthur—the Duke of Wellington, victor of Waterloo. He saved England when prospects were bleak and was soon idolized as the epitome of English virtues. Wellington carefully cultivated this image, editing his dispatches to emphasize his own discipline and steadiness. His biographers stressed Wellington's self-denial (he slept on a horsehair couch) and his sense of duty, reputation as a man of honor, and overall superiority. The honors heaped on Wellington and a peaceful death in his own armchair demonstrated the rewards and honor of staying within the system rather than trying to change it (as his nemesis Napoleon had).[15] Pure, vigorous, manly, courageous, and successful, Wellington was a gentleman, a satisfactory conveyer of mercantile and aristomilitary caste-based values. The nation and its place in history were embodied in him.[16] He was the essence of how the English liked to see themselves, and they admired themselves in him and basked in his reflected glory.[17]

Victorians wanted to improve themselves, morally and financially. Because meritocracy counted as well as birth, heroism and its rewards were accessible to middle-class Englishmen. Self-help books, flooding from the presses, instilled the necessary mercantile values. Biographers profiled professional men, lawyers, merchants, engineers, those who were at the top of their profession. Boy readers were told, "Read that; there is a man—such a man as you ought to be, read it, meditate on it; see what he was, and how he made himself what he was, and try and be yourself like him."[18] Normal men were transformed into heroic exemplars who could take the place of kings and knights and Christian martyrs in public consciousness.[19]

Midcentury heroes were often domestic professionals. For example, Samuel Smiles's *The Life of George Stephenson, Railway Engineer* (1858) portrays the railway pioneer as a "hero of peace," whose rags-to-riches story was the best sort of adventure.[20] Stephenson was put forth as a manly man: an athlete who worked hard, abstained from drink, and detested frippery. His entrepreneurial efforts vitalized England's economy. Smiles achieved his greatest fame with *Self Help, Illustrations of Character and Conduct* (1859), which gave Britons portraits of men whose continuous effort, persistent valor, daring ingenuity, and ever-active intellect had gained worldly rewards and respect.[21] Smiles's heroes modeled manly virtue; their successes provided hope for young boys with a life to make.

Writers who provided Victorian children with books about worthies (and unworthies) had a hidden agenda. The values embodied in fictional characters were to direct young lives in such a way that the status quo was reinforced and a plentiful supply of youths would serve England and stand ready to defend the empire. Authors emphasized Christian and Arthurian values. Charlotte Yonge was self-consciously pious. Thomas Hughes favored an action-based Christianity and used the public school story as a tool for instilling social codes. Morality and expediency trumped piety as fictional boys left school, cast off their fetters, and became autonomous. The new myth of adventure demonstrated that myth involves what people are really excited about and that the "one worshipped respectably on Sunday may not be the one that was really working in your heart."[22] With an eye toward the empire, boys' authors fostered grit and enterprise, as opposed to obedience and conformity.[23] While duty and selflessness remained important, duty was now to be bolstered by ingenuity and initiative.

In the second half of the nineteenth century, adventure stories became the medium for capturing the imagination of young boys, eleven to fourteen years old, and for convincing them that schoolboys turned adventurers had a key role to play in the high-stake games of imperial domination. The public school codes were expanded on as readers identified with fictional characters, who were usually fifteen when the action began and around twenty-five at the end. These boy heroes supplied manly role models for those who had their way to make and the empire to run. Beginning where the school story ended, adventure stories scattered boy heroes far and wide and tasked them with making it on their own. Their virtue reaped the rewards of prosperity, and journey's end was a return to the good life in England and rural domesticity.

Embedded in bloodthirsty accounts of fighting pirates, savages, and England's rivals was a simple but effective model of how to behave and rise in life, a serious preoccupation of Victorian parents. Surviving, being recognized, and making a fortune in exotic places was shown to be dependent on one's character. The new boy characters embodied all the masculine values that the Victorians admired most: clean living, honesty, bravery, and perseverance. Historical fiction and adventure stories for boys made dash, pluck, and self-reliance a part of the consciousness of new generations and fueled their aspirations.

These adventure books owed a lot to *Robinson Crusoe* (1719). Like Crusoe, boys leave home for remote places and display virtues that ensure success and survival. In the previous century, Daniel Defoe had introduced the notion of castaways, tropical islands, cannibals, and survival dependent on coolheaded resourcefulness. Crusoe is an archetypal Englishman and a quintessential British Imperialist. According to Leslie

Stephen, editor of the *Dictionary of National Biography*, "Drop him in a desert island, and he is just as sturdy and self-composed as if he were in Cheapside. . . . [He] calmly sets about building a house. . . . Cannibals come to make a meal of him, and he calmly stamps them out with the means provided by civilization. Long years of solitude produce no sort of effect upon him morally or mentally. He comes home as he went out, a solid keen tradesman, having, somehow or other, plenty of money in his pockets."[24] *Robinson Crusoe* is a tale of character, "a story of individual enterprise, Protestant piety, hard work, and self-help."[25]

Defoe's influence on children and children's literature has been immeasurable. Readers have testified as to how *Robinson Crusoe* fired up their imaginations for life. For pious authors in Western countries, it became a model for inculcating values in the young. In *Swiss Family Robinson* (1812), Swiss pastor Johann David Wyss wrote about a family marooned on an island in the East Indies. It was a vehicle for educating his four sons in Christian values, such as self-reliance. Nineteenth-century English authors became masters of using the Robinsonade as a medium for promoting English virtues in a boy hero. In Captain Marryat's *Masterman Ready; or, the Wreck of the Pacific* (1841), the Seagrave family is shipwrecked; the eldest son performs well and is encouraged by the value-laden talks of a God-fearing seaman. In a telling anecdote, the seaman recounts how the Dutch treated captured English boys badly. The plucky boys seized some weapons and told their captor that they would shoot him if he hit them one more time: "'Yes,' cried I, 'we are only boys, but you've got an Englishman to deal with!'" Self-sufficiency, pluck, resourcefulness, and racial superiority became dominant themes. Soon there would be a plethora of works that reinforced a racial message. In Henty's *In the Heart of the Rockies*, a boy survives Indians and avalanches, secure in the knowledge that "he had in his blood a large share of the restless spirit of enterprise that has been the main factor in making the Anglo-Saxons the dominant race of the world."

Author Robert Ballantyne (1825–1894) capitalized on Crusoe mechanisms as well and wrote stimulating tales of survival based on his own experiences. In 1841, at sixteen, he had sailed off to Canada in a three-masted sailing ship and spent five years in the wilderness working for the Hudson Bay Company. Frontier living changed him profoundly. After returning home, he dipped quill in ink and wrote 80 books and 150 stories, beginning with *The Young Fur Traders*. Boys identified most intensely with his second book, *Coral Island* (1857). It's a Robinsonade of six boys who fend for themselves after being marooned on an island. They improvise with rudimentary resources, as Crusoe did, and fight off cannibals and sharks. Ballantyne wrote in an easygoing and accessible style, and his bloodthirsty stories riveted boys, leaving many with a lifelong passion for the romance of shipwrecks and tropical islands. James Barrie, in his preface to the 1913 edition of *Coral Island*, described Ballantyne as "my man" and likened waiting for his next title to appear, "as if for the pit door to open." Fifteen-year-old Robert Louis Stevenson thought Ballantyne was a genius, waylaid him outside of church, and invited him to dinner.[26] *Coral Island* is believed to have laid the foundations for *Treasure Island*, and Stevenson honored his idol in the introduction:

If sailor tales to sailor tunes,
Storm and adventure, heat and cold,
If schooners, islands, and maroons,
And buccaneers, and buried gold,
And all the old romance, retold
Exactly in the ancient way,
Can please, as me they pleased of old,
The wiser youngsters of today:
So be it, and fall on! If not,
If studious youth no longer crave,
His ancient appetites forgot,
Kingston, or Ballantyne the brave,
Or Cooper of the wood and wave:
So be it, also! And may I
And all my pirates share the grave
Where these and their creations lie!

Like Wellington, Ballantyne managed his image. He portrayed himself as a Romantic hero. A handsome, strapping man, he gave performances decked out in trapper's clothing and standing before a table strewn with Indian headdresses, snowshoes, and animal skins. The bearded Ballantyne had a gun under his arm, sang canoeing songs, and, as a finale, fired a gun at a stuffed eagle that, with a jerk of a string, came tumbling down.[27] In his personal life, he hunted and fished avidly. His books took for granted the pleasures of slaughtering wild animals. This is dialogue among the three boys in *The Gorilla Hunters* (1861):

"It seems to me, [said Jack] not withstanding the short time we stayed in the gorilla country, we have been pretty successful. Haven't we bagged thirty-three altogether?"

"Thirty-six, if you count the babies in arms," responded Peterkin.

"Of course we are entitled to count those."

"I think you are both out in your reckoning," said I, drawing out my notebook; "the last baby that I shot was out thirty-seventh."

"What!" cried Peterkin, "the one with the desperately black face and the horrible squint, that nearly tore all the hair out of Jack's head before he managed to strangle it? That wasn't a baby; it was a big boy, and I have no doubt a big rascal besides."

"That may be so," I rejoined; "but whatever he was, I have him down as number thirty-seven in my list."

"Pity we didn't make up forty," observed Jack.

The boy heroes in Ballantyne's and others' nineteenth-century adventure books were enthralled with killing wild animals, such as sharks, hyenas, gorillas, and lions. They found it "capital." It seemed to have been equal parts sport, empowerment over fears, and youthful bloodlust.

Ballantyne fostered an image of himself as a rugged frontiersman, a man's man. He consciously prepared boys for a kind of manhood based on a blend of the moral solidity of Crusoe and the chivalry of King Arthur—an amalgamation of mercantile and caste-based values. By incurring risks and grappling with danger in vicarious adventures, they would learn cool self-possession and be prepared for any eventuality. Boys loved Ballantyne because he was a great storyteller and one of the first authors to wrest them, imaginatively, from their homes and schools and drop them in dangerous, exotic locales where they had to sink or swim. His characters gave heft to youthful dreams and fantasies of survival and triumphing over pirates, Indians, and grizzly bears. Boys relived his tales "shipwrecked in suburban gardens; marooned on muddy backyard islands; or while they retreated before overwhelming odds—badly wounded, but still fighting bravely—up the attic stairs."[28] He gave boys a place in the empire and enveloped them in an aura of British superiority.

He also gave them useful knowledge and facts. Like other Victorian boys' authors, Ballantyne had a passion for accuracy and was meticulous in his details, though he spun his yarns in a rattling, breezy style. Boy readers absorbed a lot of geography and information about how things worked. The author's own experiences gave his work authenticity. For Ballantyne, unlike later authors Rudyard Kipling and G. A. Henty, living adventurously was a lifelong pattern rather than an affair of youth. Throughout his writing career, he traveled off the beaten path to collect technical data, immerse himself in a lifestyle, and prove his courage. For example, for *The Iron Horse; or, Life on the Line* he served as a fireman, shoveled coal, and operated the controls on the Edinburgh-to-London express. This book has been described as four hundred pages of dramatic stories about thieves, compensation claims, rescues, and railway accidents, all woven into a factual account of the British Railway system.[29] Ballantyne wrote from his experiences with fighting crime and fires, being a miner, fishing on a trawler, posing as an Arab in Algiers, and living rough in exotic places.[30]

Ballantyne's passion for stirring consciences led him to support initiatives such as building lighthouses along the Scottish coast. He gave a human face to his causes. His tragic account of ships going down in *The Lifeboat* inspired people to support lifesaving initiatives. The book recounts the story of young Guy, who barely survives the crack-up of his greedy uncle's poorly equipped ship. He subsequently inherits the business and puts lifesaving equipment on all of his ships. Guy prospers and lives a happy, virtuous life ever after. Virtue always pays in Ballantyne's books.

A strict Presbyterian, Ballantyne made sure that his boys were also good and God fearing. The author couldn't resist sermonizing. He gave boys clear and stern messages about moral purity and godliness. Smoking, drinking, and swearing were unacceptable. In 1859, in a letter to his sister-in-law, he mused that he had come to see writing for juveniles as part of an evangelical call: he saw young people as his "mission"—they liked what he wrote, and he had a hold over them.[31] Ballantyne's narrative was pitched somewhere between the Evangelical fire-and-brimstone of Farrar and the Muscular Christianity of Hughes. Love of God was paramount, although the narrative had force of its own. Like all subsequent boys' adventure books, sexuality was unmentionable. Ballantyne played forward the "legacy of prudery that millstoned Victorian juvenile fiction and castrated the teenage heroes of adventure tales."[32]

In 1855, British youth were given a charismatic new symbol in Charles Kingsley's Elizabethan-era character, Amyas Leigh. In *Westward Ho!* Amyas volunteers to become a cabin boy and ships out to fight the Spaniards: "As he stands there with beating heart and kindling eye, the cold breeze whistling through his long curls, he is a symbol, though he knows it not, of brave young England longing to wing its way out of its island prison, to discover and to traffic, to colonise and to civilise until no wind can sweep the earth which does not bear the echoes of an English voice." Kingsley blatantly offered up adventure cloaked in the ideology of imperialism. Amyas and the men of Devon were chivalrous and loyal to Queen Elizabeth; they overcame Spanish jealousy and "won their markets at the sword's point, and then bought and sold honestly and peacefully therein."[33] They were heroes "in the right causes."[34] Kingsley reinforced notions of British superiority, a civilizing mission, and the concept of service to the empire—it was "a fighting sermon to quicken nationalism."[35] In his dedication, Kingsley expresses his admiration for the "English virtue" of the Elizabethans that he modeled Amyas after: they were "at once manly and godly, practical and enthusiastic, prudent and self-sacrificing." With *Westward Ho!* Kingsley hit the mark by amalgamating heroism, adventure, and history as a force for energizing Britain's youth.

Kingsley attributed the past glories of England to her men of action.[36] He also aligned with those who believed that English literature expressed the aspirations of the national culture at its best and most characteristic and conveyed the cultural soul or essence of the English nation.[37] The idea that history could be explained by "character"—the character of individuals, a nation, or an age—was commonplace in the nineteenth century.[38] "Self" came to be seen as a social construct, and the new history (and biography and novels) gave accounts of how a character acts under successive circumstances.[39] As history evolved into a popular medium with imaginative punch, real events, such as the Black Hole of Calcutta, became folklore.[40] Teachers of history were very concerned with interpreting the national character and ideals and stimulating patriotism and right thinking and feeling. The new history resonated strongly with beliefs about English superiority and imperial aspirations.

So many nineteenth-century authors wedded political history and literary narrative that sometimes half the fiction for children published in the nineteenth century was historical.[41] Though Kingsley, like Ballantyne, still laced his narratives with sermons and was a bit florid, the great era of secularized adventure stories was at hand. Historical fiction became the preferred genre for offering up adventure tales that appealed to children's love of story and heroes. And the king of historical fiction for boys was G. A. Henty. His one hundred volumes sold an estimated twenty-five million copies between 1868 and 1902. He was a propagandist for British imperialism and specialized in writing about military campaigns and skirmishes within the empire. He encouraged patriotism and celebrated Britain's missionary nationalism and quest to civilize the world. When reading Henty's *With Clive in India; or, the Beginnings of an Empire* or *With Roberts to Pretoria: A Tale of the South African War*, boys felt themselves a part of history and contemporary military campaigns. They learned the importance of fearlessness and discipline. The exemplary British virtue of valiant battle, always tempered by the principles of fair play, is celebrated in every single story and became deeply embedded in the consciousness of English children.[42]

Henty personalized history and made it palatable by inserting a boy hero into historical events. The boys were endowed with qualities that had made the British Empire great. That the greatness came in the form of the average English boy enhanced reader identification. As one author puts it, Henty was just the man to "translate the national imaginary into everyday reality," and stimulate aspirations.[43] Henty made boys want to be heroic and enlist in serving the empire, and parents repeatedly thanked him for preparing their sons for the civil service.[44] He made military life exciting to boys, touting its emphasis on duty and obedience as good for making men of them.[45]

Henty made the code of manliness and service to the empire stand for something with boys. Certainly, as testified in memoirs and autobiographies, such as those of C. S. Forrester and P. G. Wodehouse, Henty's stories charged the imagination of future writers. He also profoundly affected foreign policy. One measure of Henty's influence on the inner circle of British policy makers, most from public schools, was a study of the circulation records (1902–1903) of the libraries in four great public schools: Henty's books were checked out most often.[46] The books inspired generations of Englishmen to selflessly serve the empire or be a certain kind of man. In *George Alfred Henty and the Victorian Mind*, Leonard Ashley gives boys' books a role in Anglo-American espionage. He quotes spy Robin Winks: "One could always count on people like me being familiar if not with the Henty books then with the principles they advocated. If you knew Henty's works, you knew who you were—or

wanted to be. You could count on us to be not only prepared but principled—with Henty's principles."[47] Henty encouraged men to crave adventure: Richard Meinertzhagen, who developed the British secret service, once declared, "I loved the raw naked life, bereft of all trappings
and tomfoolery of modern civilization. Wide horizons in thought and
vision, freedom and always more freedom, fresh air and exercise and a
contempt for Death."[48] Henty got inside his readers' heads and hearts to
such an extent that in 1963, the bishop of London confessed in the House
of Lords that after fifty years, he had still not got G. A. Henty out of his
system.[49]

In Henty's books, readers interacted vicariously with real men, such
as Clive of India, credited with securing India for the British Crown.
Henty's mental construct was Victorian: he believed that history could be
explained as the biography of the great and their deeds and that charismatic male personages could inspire boys to greatness.[50] Real military
and political figures became mentors for his characters and, in a process
of transference, for his readers. Henty also became a surrogate father
figure or perhaps kindly uncle, a role he reveled in. We see this most
clearly in the paternal tone of his prefaces, always addressed to "my dear
lads."

Henty's empathy for his readers may have stemmed from being sickly
as a child. While bedridden, he read voraciously and experienced what
reading could mean to children. As a young adult, he led a life of adventure and daring in far-flung places. Skills, such as wrestling and boxing,
and public school values acquired at Westminster School were useful
when he served as a volunteer in the Crimean War and as a war correspondent. Henty witnessed every European war of his time and, as well,
English campaigns in the Crimea, Abyssinia, and Ashanti. At thirty-six,
Henty turned to what would be his life work and set out to write historical fiction for boys, notably accounts of all of Britain's wars since the
revolution. His own experiences and yarn-telling oral style gave his
works authenticity and dash. He shared enough details of his own life to
cue his readers that he was the real deal. In *Union Jack*, the penny journal
that he edited for three years, Henty told of having men beside him killed
in the act of speaking to him, of leaning against a horse that was then
disemboweled by a shell; he was shot at so many times that he couldn't
say when he had been in the greatest danger. In a line guaranteed to
titillate his readers, Henty allowed that he had never felt more uncomfortable than he did when he was once sentenced to be hung as a spy.[51]

A stickler for accuracy, Henty packed his books with historically accurate background material: maps, battle plans, the names of regiments and
officers, and detailed descriptions of local customs and geography. In
With Kitchener in the Sudan (1902), the reader becomes privy to a mind-
boggling amount of information about military life (eating, packing,
marching, fighting), held together by the exploits of a plucky young hero,

Gregory Hilliard. Gregory finds it "glorious" to be one of a band on its way "to meet the hordes of the Khalifa, to rescue the Soudan from the tyranny under which it had groaned, to avenge Gordon and Hicks and the gallant men who died with them!" Gregory survives captivity and wounds and has great success. In the end, it turns out that he is the long-lost Marquis of Langdale, and he goes to England to claim his inheritance.

Henty taught boys the value of "rising." He knew his audience: young middle-class boys, often younger sons, with some education and the need to make their way in a competitive world. Henty gave them possibilities, role models of boys abruptly separated from home and plunged into adventures in far-flung stretches of the empire; they surmount fearful odds (battles, shipwreck, capture, deprivation, and other tribulations) and make their fortune. Henty made sure that they are never permanently scarred or traumatized. In *For Name and Fame; or, Through Afghan Passes*, my personal favorite, a baby boy is stolen by gypsies, grows up in a workhouse, and is shipwrecked several times. Will saves a ship from pirates and then joins the British army in Afghanistan, where he is recognized for valor and rises to the rank of captain in three years (although he isn't even twenty). He is captured and wounded several times and seems to have nine lives. Will finally meets up with his real father, a British colonel. In all cases, he acts "right and straight and honorable" and constantly seeks to improve himself. His gentlemanliness, coolness under fire, enterprise, and dash bring him recognition and rewards and an ultimate safe haven on the family estate in England. Henty's heroes are white Anglo-Saxon Protestants, Victorians through and through. Success on the testing ground of empire meant acquiring money and status and retiring home to England and a blameless domestic life.

Henty held conservative views, and position, class, and loyalty are always suitably established in his books.[52] Selfless and loyal followers often saved their masters' lives in battle or by hiding and nursing them. If English, they were often installed on the hero's estate to live their own version of happily ever after. This dialogue in the *The Cornet of Horse* conveys Henty's orientation very well: returning from war, Rupert and his loyal retainer and comrade in arms, Hugh, renegotiate their relationship:

> "Not a lackey, perhaps, but a sort of confidential retainer. That will be best, Master Rupert, in every way."
>
> Rupert was silent for a moment.
>
> "Well, Hugh, perhaps that would be best; but you must remember that whatever we are before others we are always friends when we are alone."
>
> "Very well," Hugh said, "that is understood; but you know that alone or before others, I shall always be your faithful servant."

The good life for returning heroes involved public service and charity, maintenance of the status quo, and overt respectability. The ultimate fate of the dashing boy hero was to become a pillar of the community with a proper sense of his own consequence.

Henty boys always had something special about them; though, invariably, they were all the same type, gentlemanly and possessed of a public school morality that emphasized reliability and responsibility. In late Victorian children's literature, the assumption was that Christian behavior was congruent with gentlemanly behavior, "behavior becoming to an Englishman."[53] While boy heroes were desirous of doing right in the name of God, their unsanctimonious goodness was driven not by doctrine but by a masculine code that emphasized clean living, honesty, courage, and initiative. They had a horror of being milksops, timid "muffs" that displayed emotion. To be a gentleman was to make "a fine art, almost a religion, of Stoicism."[54] They had average brain power, but that was okay because they were well connected. The vicar in *One of the 28th: A Tale of Waterloo* praised the young hero for his manliness: "I don't mean to say that he has any exceptional amount of brain, is likely to set the Thames on fire; but if he comes into the Penfold property that will not be of much importance."

The boys often saved themselves and others by ingenuity and strategic thinking. They got close to famous people who would acknowledge their good deeds and reward them. In *Jack Archer: A Tale of the Crimea* (1884), Jack tells his friend, "We did a good night's work. We saved sixteen lives, we got no end of credit, and the chief says he shall send a report in to the Admiral; so we will be mentioned in dispatches, and it will help us for promotion." Henty's scripts for transforming virtue into success involved an eye for the main chance and never putting a foot wrong.[55] His characters always found prominent men willing to push them forward. Yorke mused, "I am the luckiest fellow going. . . . I get a commission in the army. . . . I obtain Mr. Rhodes's goodwill and now Mr. Chambers, one of the richest men in Johannesburg, is going to take me up, and all from a series of accidents." Henty made his position explicit in the prefaces to his books. In *Sturdy and Strong; or, How George Andrews Made His Way*, he tells his boy readers, "We are all living on a hill-side, and we must go either up or down. . . . To be successful one must not only be steadfast, earnest and true, but to have the faculty of turning every opportunity to the best advantage." What the empire offered, particularly to educated younger sons with their way to make, was a plethora of opportunities.

By modern standards, Ballantyne's heroes were righteous prigs. While less pious, Henty's boys can still be criticized for their absolute qualities—they have all the manly virtues and none of the common vices.[56] In his study of Henty, Guy Arnold finds the boys to be innately mature. Never showing weakness or deviating from a mold of heroic capability,[57] they are straight, and their moral fiber is such that they never backslide. They tended to be "sober, farsighted, earnest and wise before their time" and possessed with little sense of humor.[58] The idealization of virtue was typically late Victorian, when the Puritan character or "temper" retained its vitality by virtue of its separation from dogma.[59] Of course, his boys professed religion (as did all Victorians), but Henty offered readers a broad-based masculine moral and behavioral code, being an Englishman, in which morality was lived. His was an alternate gospel of manly independence, tenacity, and bravery, and there were standards to live up in this new "secular religion of self-sufficiency."[60] Piety was of less interest than decency and powerfulness.[61] Ashley theorizes that the code favored by Henty may have served as a new conscience; in any case, Henty taught more about Christian virtues than the church did. He showed what was right and wrong (and that was a matter of black and white) and provided a sound moral background that could be effortlessly absorbed.[62]

It was "sound" for its day, as racism had yet to become problematic. Ballantyne, Henty, and Victorian children's authors in general wrote in the heyday of national character, when an Englishman was defined in contrast to anyone of a different nationality. Manly Englishmen operated in contrast to stock stereotypes, which served to encapsulate each nation; these, along with histories and biographies, "illuminated, reinforced, and in some measure created differences in national character."[63] "The British were terribly British—and worth ten of any foreigner alive, by Jingo," and "the British straight left was more than a match for any half-dozen skulking foreigners, though the blackguards were armed to the teeth."[64]

The cult of adventure supported an ideology, imperialism, which was rationalized by open and completely unselfconscious racism. The typical native was childlike, undeveloped, and backward in the rationality that had allowed the West to gain and maintain power.[65] The "savages" needed the white man to bring them civilization and help them evolve, and who better than the most superior race in the world? Henty was a propagandist for the British Empire and his novels, the African ones in particular, highlight his attitudes toward empire and the general concept of white and British superiority.[66] In *By Sheer Pluck: A Tale of the Ashanti War*, a naturalist on an expedition to the Gold Coast explains to young Frank why they won't hire negroes from Sierra Leone:

> "They are just like children," Mr. Goodenough said. "They are always either laughing or quarreling. They are good natured and passionate, indolent, but will work hard for a time; clever up to a certain point, densely stupid beyond. The intelligence of an average negro is about equal to that of a European child of ten years old. A few, a very few, go beyond this, but these are exceptions, just as Shakespeare was an exception to the ordinary intellect of an Englishman. They are fluent talkers, but their ideas are borrowed. They are absolutely without original-

ity, absolutely without inventive power. Living among white men,
their imitative faculties enable them to attain a considerable amount of
civilization. Left alone to their own devices they retrograde into a state
little above their native savagery."

His patronizing attitudes and contempt for those he often referred to as
"niggers" also crop up in books on Haiti and the American South, such as
With Lee in Virginia: A Story of the American Civil War (1890). Henty was an
apologist for slavery, arguing that blacks were happier and better cared
for under that system, despite a few bad masters.[67]

Henty's stereotypes were representative of general British opinion of
the day.[68] For almost forty years, Victorian racial attitudes were inculcated in children through their books, serials, and history texts.[69] The effect
of such prejudice on national consciousness and attitudes toward
foreigners has lingered and become a factor in the contemporary rejection
of traditional Englishness, perceived by some as exclusivist and an inappropriate evocation for a multicultural Britain.

* * *

"Culture" has many definitions. Those relevant to children's literature
often have to do with the notion of culture as developing intellectual and
moral faculties and as patterns of human knowledge, belief, and behavior
that must be transmitted and learned. Clifford Geertz characterized the
culture concept as denoting "an historically transmitted pattern of meanings embodied in symbols, a system of inherited conception expressed in
symbolic forms by means of which men communicate, perpetuate, and
develop their knowledge about attitudes toward life."[70] As books became
a significant vehicle for the transmission of culture—values and models
of behavior—Victorian and Edwardian authors set up the boy hero as a
cultural icon. They inspired generations of middle-class boys to do their
duty, serve the empire, and live up to national cultural ideals. The package that Henty delivered was played forward by others.

Henry Rider Haggard (1856–1925) lived an early life that could have
been scripted by Henty. He was a younger son who was shipped off to be
an administrator in Southern Africa. He thrived on living rough in the
hinterlands and was recognized and promoted. Haggard married well,
returned to England, and became the foremost writer of the imperial
romance genre. Haggard's famous *King Solomon's Mines* (1885) is supposed to have been written in six weeks, to show his brother that he
could better Stevenson's *Treasure Island*. It introduces Allan Quatermain
and is a raw and bold account of a band of adventurers who penetrate
deepest Africa and return with pockets full of diamonds. Haggard has
been credited with inventing the "lost world" genre. In his books, Haggard pitched Henty's code at the level of heroic hypermasculinity, as

displayed in the physical prowess and heroic actions of his characters.[71] Haggard did not have young characters; however, he expected that boys would read his novels, and he dedicated *Allan Quatermain* (1887) to his son in the hopes that he and other boys might be inspired by his hero's actions, to reach to "the highest rank whereto we can attain—the state and dignity of English gentlemen."

Danger, adventure, heroism, biography and history were bundled into other exciting works for youthful readers. A list of popular titles published in 1891–1893 includes *Stories of History, Stories of Peril and Adventure, Stories of Brave Lads and Gallant Heroes, Adventures of Two Brave Boys, Stirring Adventures Afloat and Ashore, Stories of Adventure and Heroism, Fact, Fiction, History and Adventure,* and *Brave Tales of Daring Deeds and Adventures.*[72] They all carried the same message and promoted the same virtues.

But many boys did not have access to these books. British education, literacy levels in general, and access to books through libraries and purchase were held back by powerful conservatives who didn't want the lower classes to read and by publishers who fought to keep the price of books high.[73] The upper class feared that reading would radicalize the poor and lead to revolution. The new middle class thought that their hard-won economic and social security depended on maintaining the status quo.[74] Victorian books for boys were geared for those whose families could afford to educate them and support their reading habit. Ultimately, High Victorians took on the task of using printed material to stimulate responsibility and patriotism in a wider range of boys, those who would remain in England and be counted on to defend it in a crisis. Getting possession of lower-middle-class boys became a type of social experiment. Popular culture, particularly serials, could shape their characters and foster identification with England and a common national consciousness.

To clear the way for respectable publications, the grip of trashy, thrill-oriented publications had to loosened. An abundance of cheap paper and the invention of rotary steam printing presses led to the proliferation, between 1830 and 1850, of inexpensive eight-page "penny bloods." The melodrama and terror of these publications thrilled those with a penchant for the macabre. The legends of Robin Hood and tales of highwaymen such as Dick Turpin gave the urban poor and boys a taste for outlaw behavior and gore. Here, born in a penny magazine (the *Tell Tale*), was the story of the evil barber of Paris, who turned his clients into meat pies (its recently resurfaced in musical and movie form as *Sweeney Todd: The Demon Barber of Fleet Street*). In a similar vein, *The Monster of Scotland* chilled readers with the story of the cave-dwelling Sawney Beane family, who waylaid and cannibalized innocent travelers. When caught, the family was publicly executed: the men bled to death after their hands and

feet and private parts were severed; their bodies were then cast into large
bonfires along with the women and children of the family.[75]

In the 1850s, 1860s, and 1870s, there was a dramatic surge in cheap
publications called "penny dreadfuls." With titles such as *The Boy Brigand*
and *The Boy King of the Outlaws*, these were simple narratives with boy
heroes and melodrama. Serials such as *The Bad Boy's Paper* and *Wild Boys
of London* (the latter suppressed by the police in the 1890s) delivered
hard-core titillation that made them a favorite of working-class boys. For
conservatives leery of mass literacy, the penny dreadfuls sent up all sorts
of red flags about unfettered stimulation of the imagination: they felt that
these stories of prostitutes, rogues, and cutthroat criminals were encouraging crime and corrupting the millions of children who relished them.[76]

To counteract this influence, critics created the respectable boys'
weekly—adventure at a higher literary level and with sound content. In
1879 the Religious Tract Society, a Christian publishing house, moved
away from its traditional didacticism and sponsored the sixteen-page
Boy's Own Paper. Gratuitous violence was avoided, but violence that was
for a good cause or represented historical fact was a permissible sop to an
appetite for gore. The society's religious narratives and earnest accounts
of missionary work were transmuted into tales of heroic adventure that
celebrated imperialism and fostered identification with the nation and
the monarchy. Nationalistic fervor was encouraged by publishing the
lyrics of the songs such as "Old England's Heroes":

> Come, boys, let us tell of the heroes
> Who have fought and dar'd to die,
> For St. George and merry England,
> In the brave days gone by . . .
>
> Tell how England won her glory,
> Tell how England won her fame,
> We'll sing aloud for we are proud
> Proud of our English name.[77]

Other respectable magazines aimed at boys soon appeared after the *Boy's
Own Paper*, notably *Boys of England: A Young Gentleman's Journal of Sport,
Travel, Fun and Instruction*. This magazine stressed self-help, a work ethic,
and the moral robustness of Muscular Christianity. From it came a new
hero in 1871, Jack Harkaway—a resourceful, brash, full-blooded, and
cocky practical joker, consciously British and proud of it. He was a good
English boy who valued honor. In *The Road to Adventure*, Jack is introduced as a boy who is on the run, escaping from school to go to sea.
When reminded that a sailor's life is a hard one, he replies, his face
flushing with pleasure at the prospect, "I am strong, and young, and
hardy. Beside, it is a life of adventure, and what can be more delightful?"
Several generations of readers would follow Jack (and his son and grand-

son) in adventures to exotic places where he was pitted against criminals and assorted dangers. The Harkaway stories made *Boys of England* so popular that newsagents fought one another in the street outside the publisher's offices to get their copies of the latest edition.[78]

In 1890 Alfred Harmsworth (later Viscount Northcliffe) of Amalgamated Press sought to corner the market on healthy stories by ensuring that his stories were not *too* pure. To combat the corrupting effect of the penny dreadful, Harmsworth came up with the *Half-Penny Marvel*, the *Union Jack*, and *Pluck*, all priced at one half-penny. The high moral plane they began on soon deteriorated, and as A. A. Milne quipped, "Harmsworth killed the penny dreadful by the simple process of producing the ha-penny dreadfuller."[79]

Boys' serials aimed to excite but not incite boy readers, so it featured mainstream adventure rather than outlaw tales; the magazine's pages also contained school stories and articles about the hobbies and games that filled boys' leisure time. The publishers' real agenda, according to Joseph Bristow's *Empire Boys: Adventures in a Man's World,* was to encourage boys to size up and control their world. Bristow notes that the *Boy's Own Paper*'s pages were filled with a "jungle book" of predatory and domestic animals: beasts that were fierce and friendly, exciting and sentimental at once, in a domain based on emotional extremes of protecting and fighting.[80] A useful Englishman, especially one stationed in the far reaches of empire, needed to battle beasts and savages and fight for England—which was to defend all of civilization. Those who stayed at home must share the imperial spirit and, as well, protect the nation—according to Edwardian serials stories, it was under constant threat.

The serials' success in influencing boy culture gave them the power of an intense propaganda machine. Authors inculcated imperialism by manipulating the basic drives of boyhood (for action, adventure, and validation) and convincing the boys that they were "the central social actors of their day."[81] Serialized stories featured tales of fearless boys who triumphed in dangerous circumstances. Action-packed adventure stories and accounts of derring-do in imperial outposts, intrepid explorers, and lost expeditions stirred the blood and provided role models. Authors catered to basic myths of male self-sufficiency, good defeating bad, and the necessity of civilized Englishmen controlling uncivilized natives and dark continents. Heroism was presented as a natural expression of the innate superiority of the English.[82]

Novels and serials gave boys an appetite for adventure and an appreciation for resourcefulness, useful for those administering Britain's colonial outposts. But the demands of empire and nation kept giving rise to new social needs. The traumatic Boer War (1899–1902) woke up a complacent nation: the British Empire needed healthy, patriotic foot soldiers. That 40,000 rebellious farmers could tie up 450,000 British troops was disgraceful and demoralizing. The poor physical condition of the nation's fighting stock alarmed Rudyard Kipling and others, who in their writings portrayed Britain as a beleaguered island, vulnerable to inevitable attacks by enemies and in need of defenders.

Foreigners were seen as threats by many. The possible and actual invasion of England by Russians, Germans, and the French was a constant feature in boys' serials at the turn of the century; these stories portrayed foreign nations as bellicose and filled with jealousy and hatred for Britain. Sometimes the stories were obviously nonsensical, as when Chinese war balloons invaded the island, but on the whole they encouraged xenophobia and chauvinism. Harmsworth, probably the most influential jingoist, constantly warned of the threat of invasion. The fictional characters in his publications often acted out his own fears and beliefs. The famous fictional detective Sexton Blake, so beloved by boys at the time, was frequently pitted against the German high command, which was intent on invading England. Harmsworth's influence on consolidating popular opinion against Germany was such that he is considered to be a precipitator of World War I. The Germans saw him as a threat and, during the war, sent a warship to his country home in Kent to assassinate him. His gardener's wife was killed in the incident.

* * *

After the Boer War, by 1907, an unlikely new author and activist, Robert Baden-Powell (1857–1941), was perfectly positioned to command public attention and put forth his plan for transforming the nation's youths. The creator of the scouting movement and its all-but-sacred manual was a fifty-year-old unmarried inspector general of the cavalry whose biography is instructive. He had absorbed his social-climbing mother's ideals and sought fame and influence, though his love of power was masked by self-denial and Victorian earnestness. Baden-Powell flourished in Victorian and Edwardian England and left a legacy of robust narratives and a movement that supported the establishment.

The product of a famous public school (Charterhouse), he absorbed its values and set off to make his mark in the army. He functioned beautifully in the outposts of the empire, leading troops in Afghanistan, India, and Africa and writing books about his adventures as a scout and a spy. Biographer Tim Jeal paints a picture of a man who conducted his life as if it were a game and the world a playground.[83] In an era in which boys' fiction was saturated with tales of boy heroes leading lives of adventure in foreign lands, Baden-Powell was the iconic servant of the empire, a young man who had not outgrown the boyhood ideals of his leisure reading and schooldays. Baden-Powell was uncannily like the typical Henty boy. Certainly, he always had an eye for the main chance. Imperial service allowed him to stay in a state of perpetual boyhood and live an adventurous life.

During the Boer War (1899–1902), Baden-Powell emerged as the laconic, unflappable hero of the siege of Mafeking, and he would use his fame to rally the nation around the need for preparing boys to become men who could, if need be, defend their country and the British Empire. The motto of his training program was "Be prepared." The Boy Scouts sought to instill physical fitness, hardiness, loyalty, obedience—many of the virtues of the public schools. But the public school boys didn't need scouting—from the minute they entered school and its system of competitive athletics, they absorbed good form, honor, and how to play the game of life as a team sport. For those in state schools, however, scouting became the playing field on which to acquire these virtues. The difference, of course, was that the public schools produced leaders and officers. Scouting trained boys to follow, to serve as rank-and-file soldiers.

It was Baden-Powell's assertion that outdoor living counteracted the toxic effects of urban life. His scheme focused on fitness and character training as a solution to social ills, but the training was carried out without any acknowledgment of the systemic poverty or unhealthy and dehumanizing social conditions that had shaped Britain's spindly lower-class youth. It was a solution that dovetailed perfectly with the class-based conservative mind-sets of many Edwardians: the nation could pull its socks up without having to undergo painful social reform. Scouting would breed manly and loyal citizens who would defend the status quo. Ironically, Baden-Powell never seriously sought to enlist children on the cutting edge of poverty, street children, or those who had to work to live. He set out to train and inspire bored but respectable boys with a little time on their hands. Adults liked the ethical underpinnings of scouting. Boys liked the opportunity to act out the exciting feats of heroes that they had been introduced to in serial publications and novels; it was an invitation to romp and yet be put in touch with something larger than themselves.

Baden-Powell's books, including the scouting handbook, are replete with role models, real and fictional, that invoke courage and patriotism. They encouraged boys to relate to literary figures such as Kipling's Kim, as well as standard British heroes, often courageous military men, such as Admiral Nelson and Baden-Powell himself at the siege of Mafeking, or explorers such as Sir Francis Drake and Sir Ernest Shackleton. Baden-Powell posed Scouts as the new knights of England, heirs to a long legacy of honor, brotherhood, and chivalry.[84] Scouting fed the aspirations of boys by making them feel part of a line of manly men that stretched from King Arthur to Baden-Powell: the new knights were brave British soldiers and sailors, resourceful empire builders, and Boy Scouts.

Baden-Powell called the movement a "character factory." It was grounded in an ideology that demanded certain kinds of behavior. The Scout must be prepared in mind and body and promise to (1) be loyal to God and the King, (2) help other people at all times, and (3) obey the

Scout law. The Scout law required a boy to be trustworthy and truthful, useful and helpful (do good deeds daily); he must be a friend and brother to every other Scout, courteous, kind to animals, thrifty; he must smile and whistle under all circumstances and never complain or swear. Obedience to authority was integral to upholding the social system. The patriotism that Baden-Powell promoted was unconditional; dissent and critical thought were dismissed as irresponsible and disloyal. Being willing to die for one's country was represented as the most sublime form of self-sacrifice, and for boys, war was posed as the ultimate competition. The ideals of scouting were militaristic, not surprising given Baden-Powell's military career and the fact that by 1912, 247 of the 352 men that ran the Boy Scouts in Britain were serving or retired military men. [85]

Baden-Powell presented scouting in publications that captured the same audience as the boys' weeklies and popular adventure stories. Indeed, the original scouting manual first appeared in nine parts in the serial *Boys of the Empire*. The serial's savvy publishers promoted the work by promising readers a new and particularly jolly game, "The Game of Scout." [86] When it came out in book form in 1908 as *Scouting for Boys: A Handbook for Instruction in Good Citizenship*, it was replete with competitions and prizes. Boys were invited to pitch camp, do handicrafts, and play adventurously as explorers, generals, scouts, doctors, frontiersmen, and spies. The neckerchiefs and Stetson hats from camp life, inspired in part by Bill Cody's Wild West Show, and the woodcraft, tribal life, and ideals of self-reliance in the outdoors were entrancing.

Baden-Powell's fifty books and pamphlets and the Boy Scouts movement they supported have shaped the basic beliefs of millions of children. The Scout handbook has generally been overlooked by literary scholars, but its influence on sociocultural norms and its appeal to young readers make it more than the functional manual it is generally considered to be. The first edition of *Scouting for Boys* was viewed by Baden-Powell himself as a sacred text that initiated boys into a brotherhood: it was a thoroughly didactic introduction into scouting's ideology as well as an introduction to its philosophical principles and practices. [87]

Baden-Powell gave boys who lived at home their own code and compelling narratives and, thus, the sense that they could be part of "the club," even though they weren't in the public schools. In so doing, he became a prime literary influence in shaping the character of English boys. Baden-Powell pioneered a new style of writing for children — straightforward, colloquial, and eminently readable. By 1908, the words he used (*yarn, jamboree, posse,* and *palaver*) had a "humorous and dated quality" that was quirky enough to be memorable. [88] His "yarns" were short illustrative tales whose name invoked the notion of sailors' stories and those told over a campfire. They had a true-to-life folksiness that made them appealing to boys. "Every boy ought to learn how to shoot and to obey orders," he wrote in the original edition of *Scouting for Boys,* "else he is no more good when war breaks out than an old woman, and merely gets killed like a squealing rabbit."[89]

Scouting for Boys was organized around twenty-eight yarns and follow-up materials, including book suggestions, games, and practice exercises. Baden-Powell mixed exciting narratives with concrete information, everything that an Edwardian boy would want to know. He included first aid skills, animal care, camouflage, and tracking and stalking techniques and gave advice that ranged from how to deal with a dead body and identify criminals by their appearance, to why regular bowel movements were desirable and masturbation was not. When Kipling granted Baden-Powell permission to build a program for younger boys around *The Jungle Book*, Cub Scouts could play at being Mowgli. The titles of two of his books suggest that Baden-Powell saw himself as the wise Akela: *An Old Wolf's Favorites: Animals I Have Known* (1921) and *The Cub Book by the Chief Old Wolf* (1917). Kipling supported the organization by serving as a commissioner, writing the scouting song, and collecting some of his earlier sketches into *Land and Sea Tales for Scouts and Guides* (1923).

A product of the public school, military, and imperial postings, Baden-Powell's was an example of the boy-man so typical of the late Victorian and Edwardian eras. His moral imperative was success, but his emotional life had narrow parameters. Having emerged from youth with the sense that sex was unclean and marriage a fearful prospect, he finally married, but not until he was fifty—when it was important for his image and when he met a strong-minded woman. All his life, he remained a new kind of character, a boy-man—physically an adult but emotionally still a boy. Like other boy-men of his era, Baden-Powell remained preoccupied with boyish feelings and interests inculcated by public school life and his reading of adventure tales, medieval myths, and Hentyesque historical novels. The boy-man type that emerged from the public school experience and from this line of reading lingers on in English children's books and notions of Englishness. The code of manliness, despite awareness of some of its socially unacceptable aspects, still exerts an influence on British culture.

Throughout the later part of the nineteenth century, fiction for boys offered a form of Muscular Christianity and manly and stoic role models. After the Boer War, there was the scouting manual and its yarns that reinforced militarism and patriotism. Higher-toned serials, such as the *Boy's Own Paper*, featured stories by Ballantyne, Henty, Verne, and Doyle. A reader of *Boy's Own Paper*, Wyndham-Lewis, remembered his infancy as full of "tough, hairy, conquering Nordics plunging through trackless forests and lethal swamps, wrestling with huge apes and enormous cobras, foiling victims of Latin origin, crammed with experience and philosophy and knowing practically everything."[90] Boys gloried in tales of achievement and derring-do. Boys were assumed to be innately competitive and rebellious, and these characteristics and the "gamesomeness" of their antics were considered useful in tight situations and in defense of nation and empire.[91] Heroic adventure stories ensured that boys' magazines served as propaganda machines. By World War I, there was a close alignment among the ideals fostered by public school stories, "fearless tales of boyhood heroism in the penny dreadful, the fighting-fit spirit celebrated in many children's classics, and the narratives of imperial victories that preoccupied the popular press."[92] It was a recipe for disaster.

NOTES

1. Nuding, "Britishness and Portraiture," 238.
2. Nuding, "Britishness and Portraiture," 256.
3. Altick, *Lives and Letters*, 85.
4. Kumar, *The Making of English National Identity*, 189.
5. Houghton, *The Victorian Frame of Mind*, 305.
6. Backscheider, *Reflections on Biography*, 18.
7. Altick, *Lives and Letters*, 88–89.
8. Houghton, *The Victorian Frame of Mind*, 337.
9. Ashley, *George Alfred Henty*, 20.
10. Pears, "The Hero Gentleman," 222.
11. Barczewski, *Myth and National Identity*, 7.
12. Barczewski, *Myth and National Identity*, 29.
13. Barczewski, *Myth and National Identity*, 220.
14. Barczewski, *Myth and National Identity*, 13.
15. Pears, "The Hero Gentleman," 229.
16. Backscheider, *Reflections on Biography*, 8.
17. Pears, "The Hero Gentleman," 232.
18. Houghton, *The Victorian Frame of Mind*, 318.
19. Houghton, *The Victorian Frame of Mind*, 318.
20. Green, *Dreams of Adventure*, 205.
21. Green, *Dreams of Adventure*, 204–6.
22. Campbell, "Mythic Reflections."
23. Green, *Dreams of Adventure*, 220.
24. Parrinder, *Nation and Novel*, 77.
25. Green, *Dreams of Adventure*, 25.
26. Quayle, *Ballantyne the Brave*, 216.
27. Quayle, *Ballantyne the Brave*, 103–4.
28. Quayle, *Ballantyne the Brave*, 1.
29. Quayle, *Ballantyne the Brave*, 257.
30. Quayle, *Ballantyne the Brave*, 257.
31. Quayle, *Ballantyne the Brave*, 133.
32. Quayle, *Ballantyne the Brave*, 132.
33. Howarth, *Play Up and Play the Game*, 25.
34. Howarth, *Play Up and Play the Game*, 25.
35. Houghton, *The Victorian Frame of Mind*, 324.
36. Howarth, *Play Up and Play the Game*, 92.
37. Kumar, *The Making of English National Identity*, 219.
38. Parrinder, *Nation and Novel*, 304.
39. Parrinder, *Nation and Novel*, 86.
40. Green, *Dreams of Adventure*, 34.
41. Green, *Dreams of Adventure*, 125.
42. Singh, *Goodly Is Our Heritage*, 5.

43. Poon, *Enacting Englishness in the Victorian Period*, 6–7.
44. Ashley, *George Alfred Henty*, 50.
45. Ashley, *George Alfred Henty*, 76.
46. Arnold, *Held Fast for England*, 176.
47. Ashley, *George Alfred Henty*, 123.
48. Lord, *Duty, Honor, Empire*, 281.
49. Ashley, *George Alfred Henty*, 50.
50. Ashley, *George Alfred Henty*, 96.
51. Dartt, *G. A. Henty*, vii.
52. Arnold, *Held Fast for England*, 43.
53. Mackay and Thane, "The Englishwoman," 194.
54. Howarth, *Play Up and Play the Game*, 14.
55. Arnold, *Held Fast for England*, 36.
56. Arnold, *Held Fast for England*, 165.
57. Arnold, *Held Fast for England*, 165.
58. Arnold, *Held Fast for England*, 34.
59. Parrinder, *Nation and Novel*, 260.
60. Ashley, *George Alfred Henty*, xvi.
61. Altick, *Lives and Letters*, 7.
62. Ashley, *George Alfred Henty*, 316.
63. Pears, "The Hero Gentleman and the Hero," 217.
64. Quayle, *Ballantyne the Brave*, 302–3, 131.
65. Kumar, *The Making of English National Identity*, 190.
66. Arnold, *Held Fast for England*, 129.
67. Arnold, *Held Fast for England*, 77–78.
68. Ashley, *George Alfred Henty*, 244.
69. Castle, *Britannia's Children*, 174.
70. Geertz, *The Interpretation of Cultures*, 89.
71. Poon, *Enacting Englishness in the Victorian Period*, 136–7.
72. Ashley, *George Alfred Henty*, 306.
73. Altick, *The English Common Reader*, 31.
74. Quayle, *Ballantyne the Brave*, 129.
75. Haining, *The Penny Dreadful*, 29.
76. Bristow, *Empire Boys*, 12.
77. Bristow, *Empire Boys*, 44.
78. Haining, *The Penny Dreadful*, 342.
79. Turner, *Boys Will Be Boys*.
80. Bristow, *Empire Boys*, 40.
81. Bristow, *Empire Boys*, 48.
82. Carpenter, *Secret Gardens*, 16.
83. Jeal, *The Boy-Man*, 45.
84. Rosenthal, *The Character Factory*, 120.
85. Rosenthal, *The Character Factory*, 206.
86. Jeal, *The Boy-Man*, 367.
87. Rosenthal, *The Character Factory*, 161.
88. Jeal, *The Boy-Man*, 154.
89. Baden-Powell, *Scouting for Boys*, 9–10.
90. Turner, *Boys Will Be Boys*, 90.
91. Bristow, *Empire Boys*, 100.
92. Bristow, *Empire Boys*, 26.

FIVE

Romanticizing Childhood and England

And somehow this kind little heart, though it was only the heart of a child, seemed to clear all the atmosphere of the big gloomy room and make it bright-er. — Frances Hodgson Burnett, *Little Lord Fauntleroy*

As the momentum for social templates and indoctrination in manliness was cresting, a contrasting trend surfaced and drowned childhood in treacle and nostalgia. In 1885, Robert Louis Stevenson published a charming tribute to childhood, *A Child's Garden of Verses*. In this reverie of cozy nurseries, snug beds, and watchful nurses, the earnestness of the Evangelical and early Victorian era was replaced by sentimentality and gentle humor, and gone too were religious and educational agendas. Stevenson's poems reflected something lighter, an undercurrent of Romanticism surfacing in children's books that brought portrayals of childhood as a lost Eden and edged out didactic tones with an atmosphere of love.

The child speaker in Stevenson's poems sees good everywhere and reverently tells of the pleasures of childhood, with its toys and imaginative play. But it is often an adult speaking and reminiscing of childhood:

> It is very nice to think
> The world is full of meat and drink,
> With little children saying grace
> In every Christian kind of place.

The childhood that Stevenson writes of might be one we remember, or it might be one we wish we'd had. While in the final poem he invites the reader to look again at his or her childhood self through the windows of his book, for the most part, he acknowledges that childhood selves and states of mind are closed off to the adult; the child can't be lured back: "He has grown up and gone away, / And it is but a child of air / That lingers in the garden there." But in Stevenson's poems something of the childish condition of mind at that stage nevertheless persists, and by reading the poems, adults rediscover something of the comfort and security associated with the nursery. Stevenson is signaling an evolving element within the genre: an idealism in which the essence of childhood is honored and celebrated from an adult perspective.

The cherishing of childhood in this period had a whimsical quality (unlike the governing mood under Victoria). It resulted in poems like Stevenson's and stories that celebrated goodness, natural beauty, and innocence—values epitomized by the younger child. The child that readers sought to connect with had actually been introduced a century before by William Blake in *Songs of Innocence* (1789) in the form of the sprite—carefree, joyful, and artlessly good. For many late Victorians like Stevenson, an inward yearning for romance and beauty—concealed underneath outward acquiescence to social conventions—caused them to approach early childhood as an idyll.

Stevenson was using selective memorialization of those aspects of his early childhood that contrasted sharply with a family life that became, in his own words, "a pic-nic on a volcano."[1] He was a sickly only child, raised primarily by a loving nurse who was the pillar of his childhood days. Indeed, he dedicated *A Child's Garden of Verses* to this "angel of my infant life." In the preface, he invites children to find the book as kind a voice as his nurse's had been; he associated her with unconditional love and the joyous part of his childhood. This mattered because Stevenson's adolescent and adult life was often a struggle. His father's love, in contrast to his nurse's, was contingent on the compliance expected of young people by Victorian parents. Stevenson was supposed to honor his parents, to follow in his father's footsteps and mirror his beliefs and career. But as a young adult, he became a master at escaping from parental demands and hysterical responses to his nonconformity. Many of Stevenson's life choices were deliberately rebellious, although he did pursue a career in engineering, like his father, and then complied with his parents' wishes by studying the law. But he was, according to one biography, Claire Harman's *Myself and the Other Fellow* (2006), fiercely creative, hungry for experience, and aware of a duality in his nature: the coexistence of the passionate and imaginative with the rational within. His verses celebrated the imaginativeness of small children and their Blakeian sprightliness and placed them in an environment that was safe and nurturing.

In 1886, just a year after publication of *A Child's Garden of Verses*, delight in idealized Blakeian images of childhood intensified with the appearance of Frances Hodgson Burnett's novel *Little Lord Fauntleroy*. Like Stevenson's verses, it reflected rapidly changing ideas of childhood; it did so in the romanticized portrayal of one child, Cedric. Cedric was an innocent child whose beauty in form aligned perfectly with the era's characteristic penchant for reveling in the physical beauty of children. With his long blond curls, blue eyes, and rosy cheeks, Cedric was the apex of physical beauty. His mother let his curls grow long and dressed him in velvet and lace collars. It became the fashion to keep little boys' hair uncut and dress them in similar garments.

The boys themselves may have been the one market segment that Cedric did not win over. American newspapers printed reports of little boys responding to taunts with fistfights and exchanging their clothes with beggars when their mothers' backs were turned. English boys were more compliant. A familiar portrait of the young A. A. Milne shows him all dressed up in velvet and lace, Cedric-style, and glowering out from under his curls. The phenomenon of *Little Lord Fauntleroy* may have been a response on the part of Victorian parents to the austere way that they were brought up. For some mothers, dressing their sons like little Cedric may have been a way of keeping them dependent, doll-like, and within the feminine realm; a prelude to the inevitable loss of boys to public schools and boyhood preoccupations in general. It may also have been a protest against the grip of school and adventure stories.

In addition to his physical perfection, Cedric met a new standard for moral beauty. He was a nice child, thoughtful of others, and truthful and earnest. A case could be made that Burnett (and her readers) were still earnestly attached to goodness as an ultimate virtue in children but that Cedric's goodness was of a different order from the self-conscious virtue on display in moral tales. In Burnett's book, Cedric is portrayed as an unspoiled, poor, but gentile American child who suddenly learns that he is heir to an earldom. After he is taken to England to claim his birthright, Cedric's innocent loving kindness melts the hearts of everyone he encounters. In the story, the description of his extraordinary goodness offered by a visiting minister exemplifies the idealism of the day:

> It was not the boy's beauty and grace which most appealed to him; it was the simple, natural kindliness in the little lad which made any words he uttered, however quaint and unexpected, sound pleasant and sincere. . . . Nothing in the world is so strong as a kind heart, and somehow this kind little heart, though it was only the heart of a child, seemed to clear all the atmosphere of the big gloomy room and make it brighter.

Little Lord Fauntleroy delighted legions of readers, who couldn't help but think that the world was a better place simply because Cedric was in it. Cedric satisfied the late Victorian craving for light and goodness in a dreary world.

Whether late Victorians actually wanted to be like Cedric or not, they certainly wanted to believe in him very badly, and in his story even the lonely, ill-tempered grandfather was transformed by the boy's sweetness. This is a compelling image for love-starved Victorians, who wanted to believe that the goodness of a child could transform stiff and critical adults into loving supporters. Also compelling was the foiling of a plot to disinherit Cedric, which sets the scene for a happily-ever-after ending: he is loved, and the social status and wealth he inherits is somehow earned by his innate goodness. The story's ending was a relief from the grim cautionary tales and Yongeian accounts of spiritual soul-searching and the necessity of eschewing status and material success that many adults had been raised on. Reading about Cedric warmed chilly hearts and offered a more hopeful view of human nature. And with her optimistic and uplifting story, Burnett popularized notions of childhood as a period of inspiration and joy rather than a moral training camp.

Burnett followed up on the success of *Little Lord Fauntleroy* with *A Little Princess* (1905). Both stories were arrived at by virtue of her own life story, lifelong interests, and basic temperament. When she lost her father at an early age, the family emigrated from Birmingham, England, to poverty-stricken post–Civil War Tennessee. When her mother died as well, it was left to the teenage Frances to support her siblings (which she did by writing) and to bring them back to gentility from the brink of starvation. She spent her adult life writing to support an extravagant lifestyle and traveling back and forth between the United States and England, which was the setting for most of her novels.[2] England was the place that appealed most to her emotions and imagination. Leaving forever left her brokenhearted: "I refuse to let myself be homesick for England but in a locked back cupboard of my mind I beat my breast and slowly tear pieces of my hair out. England my soul requires."[3] Her choice to write romantic children's fiction may have been an indicator of her identification with the preoccupations, including sentimentality, of that place and era. It was all the more keen for having had her childhood foreclosed early and the trauma and misfortune that ensued.

Burnett wrote the story that would become *A Little Princess* in the rose garden at Maytham, her beloved home in England. There according to her letters, she lived a dream life, writing while sitting under a colorful umbrella, wearing a white dress and a large hat, and making friends with a robin that would come to take crumbs from her hand. The story first appeared in serial form as *Sara Crewe; or, What Happened at Miss Minchin's*, and it was so popular that it was turned first into a play and then a longer book titled *A Little Princess*. Burnett spares little in describing her main character's beauty and possessions: Sara Crewe was "a slim, supple creature, rather tall for her age, and had an intense, attractive little face . . . [with] big, wonderful eyes"; she is elegantly dressed in velvet, furs, and lace and has a gorgeous doll with golden hair and real eyelashes. This again aligned with the era's fascination with physical and surface beauty.

It is Sara's internal beauty that becomes most important as the story develops, and she loses her father and privileged lifestyle. Even when overworked and half-starved, she remains optimistic and compassionate toward others, and finally, when she finds a home and a new father, her triumph clearly stems from her generosity of spirit (though there is a little luck involved, too). For Burnett and her readers, meaning resides in the goodness of the child and his or her physical beauty, as well as in the lavish details that Burnett seems to have loved as much as her readers. In a letter to her son, she explained her rationale for the pretty scenery in her stories: "Children love detail. The garret and Melchisedec [a mouse] & Becky & Ermengarde [her friends] are so nice. And Sara standing on the old table with her head & body out of the skylight watching the clouds making islands & lakes at sunset & feeling as if she could climb up purple piles of cloud hills & gaze out upon primrose seas—ought to give you a quite queer uplifted feeling."[4] Burnett was romantic, drawn to luxury and nature, and adored beautiful things, including children. Throughout her adult life, she maintained the heart of a child and delighted in abundance: collecting dollhouse furniture, decorating her homes sumptuously, maintaining lovely gardens, and enjoying pretty clothes.

In spite of the burden of responsibility that she had to shoulder early in her life, Burnett had a streak of childlike optimism, and her writing expresses a buoyancy and fun. Her greatest desire was to be happy and to make others happy, too, and happiness was found in things, in prettiness, in sweetness. Her stories resonated with women of the late Victorian period who were struggling against their repressive upbringings and incessant domestic demands and interested in bringing beauty into their homes. Burnett seemed to be speaking to women as well as children through an interview in which she advised them to cope as she did, by striving to be happy and keeping their "pink lamps" lighted: "A pink lamp always makes everything look lovely," she told a journalist.[5] And in her stories, she gave children visions of living richly and of a world in which moral goodness and inner happiness were all of a piece with outer beauty and material prosperity. She also offered children an approach to life that promised reward for personal virtue—the choice of living generously and joyfully no matter what life brought them.

English readers were first introduced to the innocence and vulnerability of children by Charles Dickens. A half century later, Burnett was able to romanticize these qualities and elicit intense emotional reactions. Unlike Dickens, Burnett's had a weak social agenda, if any. She merely tapped into the desire for feelings and beauty that possessed many repressed Victorians. Anna Sewell, a very unlikely authoress, also mined the vein of Victorian sensibility. But she went straight for the conscience, and *Black Beauty* (1877) became an instant children's classic. It elicited great empathy and the awareness that being a good person demanded the practice of kindness to animals.

Sincere and passionate, the book was an indictment of the cruelty to horses so prevalent in Victorian times. The scale of the problem was vast, as there were hundreds of thousands of horses in London alone. Horses were handled cruelly and worked until they dropped. They were fitted with tackle that tormented them: the fashionable bearing rein pulled the horse's neck so high that it caused pain, damage to the windpipe, and a shortened life span. Sewell's account of the pitiful fate of horses was a call to action heard by many. One reader wrote to her: "You have so filled my mind with the thought of what these poor animals suffer from the bearing-rein, that I feel quite breathless as I look at some of them, and only my sex, and fear of the police, prevent my cutting the leathers and setting them free."[6] The novel's teaching potential was obvious, and groups interested in the prevention of cruelty to animals endorsed the book immediately. Worldwide, by 1910, several million free copies were distributed. A belief in the book's ability to teach kindness to animals was still evident in 1924, when a Texas cowboy was jailed for mistreating his horse: his sentence required him to read *Black Beauty* at least three times.[7]

Like many Victorians, Sewell could not escape her childhood and was trapped in the rigid social roles of her era. Born in 1820, she was the daughter of author Mary Sewell, who was the dominant influence in her life. Mrs. Sewell, a Quaker who dabbled in religious reform, sought to mold Anna into a "beautiful natural temple of the Lord."[8] She raised her daughter according to the Edgeworths' practical education, and the strong experiential component had the added intensity of a sternly moralistic agenda. Mrs. Sewell's love was both obsessive and contingent on her daughter's behavior. Sewell's training was so rigorous that even as a two-year-old, every hour of her day was accounted for. She had few toys and a bare-bones nursery; she was protected from vulgar and indulgent influences and schooled in self-denial. Mrs. Sewell set out to bend her daughter's tender mind to parental authority and defeat her faults— which we know from Sewell's diary: wastefulness, laziness, bad work, and giddiness.

Anna Sewell apparently could not subordinate her spirit without self-destructing. Her diary reveals that she was profoundly unhappy as a child and often felt guilty over her desire for worldly things.[9] Her mother's role in ruthlessly rooting out her flaws was internalized by Sewell, who grew into a rather unyielding spinster. Her niece described her as having a strong character, determined to uphold truth at any cost, even insisting on arranging bowls of fruit with blemishes facing out so that the fruit wouldn't appear better than it was. For Sewell, living up to her own high standards may have been an almost impossible task.[10] She was severe on herself to the point of emotional brutalization and was plagued with a recurring depression that she called "the Darkness." As an adolescent, Sewell developed a chronic limp, and she struggled with reconciling faith and pain, confiding in her diary, "I thank Thee, for my lameness. I am sure it is sent in love, though it be a trial. I should without it have too much pleasure in the flesh, and have forgotten Thee."[11]

For the most part, Sewell was irretrievably captive to her pseudo-Evangelical and Edgeworthian upbringing and then, as an adult, to Victorian norms. It was a time of rigid gender differentiation, when the family home was a prison for many middle-class women. They couldn't pursue ambitions or work outside the home; inside the home, dreaming or writing was difficult because women could find little time to themselves—it was very much the case that they had no room of their own, to paraphrase Virginia Woolf's words from almost a century later. Throughout Sewell's life, she was subject to fatigue and pain. One can only speculate whether Sewell (like other Victorians) used illness as a path to some pleasure and accomplishment.[12] Certainly throughout her life, illness provided an excuse for a small measure of independent social life and leisure—flare-ups led her to be sent to spas and visits away from her mother.

Most of Sewell's life was devoted to charity and domestic duties, but she did edit her mother's books. *Black Beauty*—Sewell's only personal writing project—was written during the last seven years of her life, when she was desperately ill and confined to a couch. She laboriously dictated sentences to her mother and lived five years longer than expected, until 1878, apparently to finish *Black Beauty*. The book represents the way in which Sewell, in her achievements, overcame the strictures of her upbringing and even her own ideas. She demanded that the choking rein be removed from horses, even though she couldn't see that child-rearing methods like those she was raised under were similarly cruel. Sewell ultimately "defers to her gender, to religion and Victorian propriety" and doesn't turn her protests about marginalized beings into conclusions and suggestions for action.[13] But jarring the public consciousness and fostering empathy for innocent and powerless beings was an important contribution. *Black Beauty* helped establish the principle that stories were a powerful means of eliciting, within society in general and children in particular, catharsis and identification with the plight and feelings of others. It linked Englishness with justice.[14]

Over time, children became the book's most passionate readers. They identified with the horse and took its side against cruelty. To do so felt manifestly good. The book is cathartic, eliciting anguish and grief that are strangely pleasurable. "Children like sad books," wrote Sewell biographer Susan Chitty, using an anecdote to make her point: "'Go on, I like it,' was the cry of a small boy of my acquaintance when his mother stopped in the middle of a chapter, alarmed by the deluge of tears the story was producing."[15] For over a century, child readers of this book have responded as if Anna spoke to them on some deeper, indefinable level: "It is read obsessively, as though it contained lessons which must be learned, no matter how painful."[16] *Black Beauty*'s passivity and unquestioning obedience don't sit well with some modern critics, but the book still has iconic status, and children still read it, cry, and feel emancipated by the story. The book testified to the cathartic power of literature and the beauty of stories that ring emotionally true and transmute sentimentality into an empathy that springs from the heart.

* * *

Burnett's two Romantic books were written in the last quarter of the nineteenth century, when the aesthetic movement was thriving in Britain. This was a loosely defined movement that gained a foothold in literature, fine art, textiles, wallpapers, furniture, and the applied arts in general. It arose from a new philosophy about art: that it not be useful in any practical sense but should exist solely for its own sake, for the sensual pleasure it could provide. Beauty was thought to be the most important thing in life. The impetus for these changes in outlook came partly from an impulse toward aesthetic appreciation that swept the nation in the 1860s. It was a response to author, art critic, and social thinker John Ruskin's writings on art and beauty. Ruskin taught the reading public to view art and architecture as expressions of human emotion, and he made art an important source of inspiration and pleasure.

Ruskin's notions were popularized by authors and illustrators who created images of innocent children for a segment of society that increasingly preferred Romantic idealism over dogma and favored sentimentality and innocent sensuality over emotional repression. The physical beauty of a child now mattered in a way that had been implicitly denied when focus was exclusively on the child's mind and conscience or ability to serve the family and nation. Readers of children's books were permitting themselves to look at child nature as the Romantics did all forms of nature, with the belief that meaning resides in all levels—not only beyond the surface of things. Cedric's long eyelashes, "darling little face," "graceful little body," golden flowing hair, and rosy cheeks were physical manifestations of inner sweetness. Sara Crewe's intense little face and wonderful eyes were an apt expression of her compassionate and generous nature. No longer did children have to be sheltered or taught or beaten into being good; they were the personification of goodness and beauty.

By the 1880s the aesthetic movement had a foothold in many households in England. Highly conscious of the uplifting potential of "art," a prosperous and secure middle class worked hard at cultivating taste and eschewing ugliness. New ideals of beauty were translated into a thriving arts-and-crafts movement, a growing interest in architecture and photography, reforms of clothing styles and home décor, and proliferating commercial products such as greeting cards and children's books. The beautiful child became a favored subject for artists. Sir John Everett Millais's portrait of his grandson bedecked in velvet and lace and blowing bubbles was first displayed in 1886, the year *Little Lord Fauntleroy* was published.

The painting was subsequently acquired, reproduced, renamed *Bubbles*, and circulated as an advertisement for Pears Soap. The *Bubbles* boy and Cedric became icons of Victorian sentimentality, personifications of the Beautiful Child so dear to late Victorian society.

The Victorian fixation on childhood owed much to earlier literary works—those of Wordsworth, Dickens, and Carroll, for example—that popularized the Romantic notion that childhood (and nature in general) was ennobling to the human spirit. Wordsworth was entranced with the spirituality of innocence and subscribed to the notion that children were uncontaminated by worldly experience. In "Ode: Intimations of Immortality from Recollections of Early Childhood" (1807), he looks back at youth as a time of dreamlike "glory and freshness," unimpaired vision, and closeness to God:

> Not in entire forgetfulness,
> And not in utter nakedness
> But trailing clouds of glory do we come
> From God, who is our home:
> Heaven lies about us in our infancy!

In *The Old Curiosity Shop* (1841), Dickens's Little Nell leads her infirm and morally weak grandfather by the hand in a flight from London and inspires him spiritually as well. Thereafter, there would always be a place in children's literature for "stories about children who teach adults how to live."[17]

Lewis Carroll writes in his preface to *Alice's Adventures Underground*, the first manuscript of what became *Alice in Wonderland*, about loving a child and experiencing the awe of being in the presence of "a spirit fresh from GOD's hands" on whom no shadow of sin has yet fallen: he saw "divinity in a child's smile." In a letter to the mother of one of the girls he photographed, Carroll wrote that coming in contact with innocence was good for one's spiritual life, as if proximity to children offered grace in the way religion does.[18] Authors and illustrators seemed driven by the Romantic belief that children were possessed of a magical intuitive spark that could rekindle childlike wonder, joy, and goodness in the adult. Their portrayals of children would foster a heightened awareness of human spirituality and imaginative powers that previous generations had lost touch with.

Portrayals of innocent children stood in stark contrast to the blighted landscapes of industrialized England, the repressive social atmosphere, and, as well, the potential for inner darkness that Victorians so feared.[19] The reverence that Victorians held for the child and child images stemmed from polarized notions of adult/child, corruption/innocence, and male/female that ran deep throughout English society.[20] In reaction to the moralist agenda of earlier generations, people no longer viewed childhood as a way station on the path to responsible adulthood. The world of grown-ups now seemed impossibly compromised, and child-hood had emerged as a better way of life.

The influential poet Walter De la Mare (1873–1956), who never ceased to lament the passing of his early childhood years, thought that growing up was a fiasco and that grown-ups were "diluted," not enriched by life.[21] He was not alone with these ideas. The attraction of the happy, innocent child in Victorian society lay in part in the image's contrast with an adult world that people saw as tainted by sexuality, compromise, hypocrisy, and emotional deadness. After all, lightheartedness and pas-sion had been all but expunged from their childhoods by Evangelical and rationalist influences, and as adults, these individuals had difficulty find-ing emotional satisfaction in adulthood. The challenge for this repressed, conformist society, attempting to respond to religious doubts and secular trends by effecting an aesthetic shift, was how to let the spark of imagina-tion be ignited without sending the passions out of control.

The elephant in the closet was sexuality. Generalized wariness of this most base human impulse created natural conditions for the idolizing of childhood to grow. Childhood was a magnet for the stifled passions of adults who had been schooled in asexuality. Investing their emotion in the sinless, natural state of children was a way to return to a safer, sim-pler world. Borrowing from the religious narratives of their youth, mid-dle-class Victorians created a myth of personal development: the Garden of Eden became childhood itself, a stage of life—life before Eve bit into the apple, blissful freedom before the onset of sin and guilt.[22] The end of childhood marked an entrance into the realm of sexuality that Victorian society could not openly accept. In negotiating the line between inspiring the imagination and stimulating sexual passion, it was safer to ignore sexuality and declare childhood as a place of absolute innocence. This resulted in a model of childhood that had no clear trajectory into fully functioning adulthood. And there are multiple examples from the Victo-rian era of men such as James Barrie and John Ruskin, who married yet were impotent, or Lewis Carroll, who sublimated his sexuality through worshipping young girls.

Women were expected to efface themselves. Charlotte Yonge, whose career spanned the length of the Victorian era, composed attractive pic-tures of women remaining in a state of dependence, like an extended childhood. For girls, family ties were expected to preempt personal aspi-rations, and personal fulfillment was to come from duty and obedience. Girls raised on Yonge became women for whom childhood and the sur-face beauty in things became an acceptable focus for yearning and emo-tionality, for these fixations didn't seriously challenge the prevailing mo-rality or the social status quo. It is only in the twentieth century that awareness has grown regarding how middle-class sentimentality about childhood in the Victorian era masked rigid and problematic gender differentiation and sometimes, in males, what would now be considered an unhealthily intense preoccupation with young girls.

We see this in the life of John Ruskin, mentioned earlier, whose writings as an art critic encouraged people to find pleasure in art. Ruskin was a precocious genius who became a towering figure in cultural and art circles as a young man and, over his lifetime, exerted a powerful influence on Victorian society's thoughts about nature, beauty, and childhood. In 1841, he wrote one of the first English literary fairy tales, "The King of the Golden River," a story about the exploitation of nature and a joyful, innocent boy who brings health to his valley. Ruskin was a Romantic whose emotional reactions to paintings and architecture shaped his desire to prevent the destruction of beautiful relics and places by the forces of industrialization and modernization. His impulse to preserve the past would be shared in years to come by many authors and illustrators for children, including Randolph Caldecott, Beatrix Potter, and J. R. R. Tolkien. Ruskin's life demonstrated the internal conflict brought on by the Victorians' efforts to unleash certain sentiments while continuing to suppress others.

The overprotected only son of a severe Evangelical mother and a father that idolized him, Ruskin was emotionally unstable and, in later life, prone to mental breakdowns.[23] He wrote his sole fairy tale at the request of a little girl, Effie, one of the girls whom Ruskin fell in love with as an adult. To his parents' distress, he later married the beautiful young Effie, but the union was never consummated. For some prominent Victorians like Ruskin, unsure of their sexuality and repressed to the point of impotence, childhood was an arena in which they could pursue alternate emotional satisfactions. Ruskin encouraged illustrator Kate Greenaway's infatuation with him as a way to feed what seems to have been an addiction to her drawings of winsome children. He asked her to send more and more, of girls wearing less and less:

> Will you — (it's all for your own good — !) make her [a drawing of a sylph] stand up and then draw her for me without a cap — and, without her shoes, — (because of the heels) and without her mittens, and without her — frock and frills? And let me see exactly how tall she is — and — how—round. It will be so good of and for you — And to and for me.[24]

He explained his fixation as an aesthetic impulse in the pursuit of natural beauty. It was in fact part of the distortion resulting from idolizing childhood at the expense of grappling with adulthood.

Lewis Carroll was another prominent Victorian who found inspiration in the presumed unspoiled nature of children. A bachelor, Carroll spent his lifetime in the company of young girls—talking, playing games, and laughing with them, holding on to the joy of youth by freezing their images in photographs. In his diary, he faithfully recorded and annotated sightings of any particularly beautiful young girls that crossed his path. The intensity of Carroll's devotion, like Ruskin's, went relatively unmarked in a sentimental and idealistic culture that was far more likely to judge love of the innocent child as healthy and admirable rather than as sinister.[25]

Carroll's Alice books were an ode to idealized girlhood from a man who sensed poignantly the fleeting nature of childhood. His mother's death coincided with his departure to Oxford, at the age of nineteen, and seems to have marked the end of his own delayed childhood, a blissful state whose loss he never ceased to lament:

> I'd give all wealth that years have piled,
> The slow result of Life's decay,
> To be once more a little child
> For one bright summer-day.[26]

In fact, Carroll found that he could stay in touch with the bright days of childhood by seeking out the company of young girls. Carroll begins *Alice's Adventures in Wonderland* with a poem that celebrates one golden afternoon on the river, when a real little girl, Alice Liddell, begged for a story and Carroll obliged—an echo of Ruskin's offering to Effie. Its final stanza reads as follows:

> Alice! A childish story take,
> And with a gentle hand
> Lay it where Childhood's dreams are twined
> In Memory's mystic band,
> Like pilgrim's withered wreath of flowers
> Plucked in a far-off land.

The story that follows is more than the fantastical romp it appears to be; it was also an elegy to lost childhood.

Scholars have suggested (with full irony) that all is not as it seems in *Alice's Adventures in Wonderland*: that it is not really the adventures of a child but an allegory for Everyman.[27] Alice represents anyone forced to live in a chaotic society; her innocent questions expose the cruelty and arbitrary nature of that society. In this respect, the book is about the bravery of children. It has been claimed by James Kincaid that Carroll himself could not imagine growing up—that he is the real child presence in the book, not Alice—and yet has Alice doing just that.[28] In *Through the Looking Glass*, which was written after the real Alice had grown up and married, Alice is the true protagonist, and in this story, she sheds childishness, leaving behind Carroll (it is supposed) in the form of the White Knight. The White Knight tells Alice that he will see her safely to the end of the woods, but then he must go back. The poem at the end of this second book is heartbreaking in its portrayal of the finality of their separation:

> Echoes fade and memories die;
> Autumn frosts have slain July.
> Still she haunts me, phantomwise
> Alice moving under skies
> Never seen by waking eyes.

Alice grown up ceases to be the little girl upon whom Carroll could, probably unconsciously, project himself. But the essence of her childhood haunts him. There has been a lot of speculation, based in part on the destruction of key pages of his diary, that Carroll may have approached her parents about eventually marrying the then twelve-year-old Alice. We do know that his contact with the girl was cut off.

Victorian society as a whole struggled with the idea of girls (and boys too) growing up. Devoting oneself to a celibate Yongeian life of serving one's family or else dying young (presumably with innocence intact) was a Romantic alternative to maturation in a society that couldn't easily accept adult sexuality. Victorian attitudes toward childhood reflect more than a superficial nostalgia or wave of emotionality brought on by romanticized portrayals of innocent babes. According to Catherine Robson's *Men in Wonderland: The Lost Girlhood of the Victorian Gentleman*, Alice may have represented for Carroll "the tenderest place of all"—his own remembered childhood.[29] Of course, this can be said of any adult's affection for a child, but that Carroll continued to seek out young girls throughout his life suggests that what he really sought was not Alice herself but the idealized, innocent child within that he had never let go of. And this may be key to the Victorian delight in children: by celebrating children and childhood, by placing them on a spiritual and aesthetic pedestal, adults could recover the security and simple joys of a childhood they never had or hadn't finished.

* * *

It was not just children that moved late Victorians and Edwardians. When many turned to their country as a source of emotional satisfaction, "England" and "Englishness" became passionately held mystical concepts and highly emotive words.[30] In *The Old Country* (1906), Henry Newbolt raved, "I love this Country. . . . It is to me everything that men have ever loved—a mother, a nurse, a queen, a lover, and something greater and more sacred still." Writers such as Newbolt were in the forefront of this trend, shaping and responding to an outpouring of love for the cultural legacies of the past and the beauties of the countryside. England evoked pleasant connotations of rustic Old England: villages, hedgerows, squires, country houses, and cottages—a distinctive heritage in which the soul of the nation lay.[31]

This structure of feeling seeped into and permeated the collective consciousness.[32] It provided a psychic balance wheel as middle-class society revolted against industrialization and urbanization and, after the humiliating Boer War, began to reject imperialism. Those who saw England as "industrial, over-capitalized, where the Struggle to Live is so sordid, and success means motor-cars and insolence" became absorbed in love of the countryside and its rhythms.[33] Hostility toward an artificial industrial society took a softly rustic and nostalgic cast in the form of rural myth making.[34] Just as early in the nineteenth century, radicalism had provoked an Evangelical focus on hierarchy clothed in notions of charity and mutual responsibilities, fears brought on by urbanization, unemployment, and intractible poverty reinforced conservatism, a yearning for everything and everybody to remain in their place always.[35] Mutual dependence was supported social harmony: "Each knew his place—king, peasant, peer or priest, / The greatest owed connection with the least."

In the country, traditional hierarchies seemed natural and fitting. Straightforward and wholesome country folk, commoners, and gentry were admired as the fonts of Englishness, the remnants of an ancient people. The hero of Kipling's *Puck of Pook's Hill* was Hobden the Hedger:

> His dead are in the churchyard—thirty generation laid.
> Their names were old in history when Doomsday Book was made;
> And the passion and the piety and the prowess of his line
> Have seeded, rooted, fruited in some land the Law calls mine.

Side by side with a reverence for common folk was adulation for the squire, around whom country life centered. The manly and Anglo-Saxon squire was the quintessential Englishman, and as seen in Henty's works, assuming that role was the ultimate goal of imperialists. Indeed, the goal of imperialists, industrialists, and anyone who achieved prosperity was a retreat to rural life and squirelike roles. Rudyard Kipling bought a old Sussex manor house in 1902 and wrote, "We discovered England . . . and went to live in it. England is a wonderful land . . . made of up trees and green fields and mud and the gentry, and at last I'm one of the gentry."[36] It was a retreat from both mercantile and Hentyesque military values.

As England's recent past came to be defined as unnatural and "inherently un-English," the ancient past as rooted in the countryside became a source of alternative values.[37] Morris dancing was revived as an anecdote to unhealthy urban environments. There was a tremendous desire for hearty naturalness, and the medieval era in particular was mined for rooted essences: the legends of medieval heroes King Arthur and Robin Hood were given great play. The English wanted "the England of the feudal times—of grey castle towers, and armored knights, and fat priests, and wandering minstrels, and crusades and tournaments; England in rush-strewn bowers and under green boughs."[38] According to Stephanie Barczewski's *Myth and National Identity in Nineteenth-Century Britain: The*

Legends of King Arthur and Robin Hood, a careful manipulation of the Middle Ages provided a portrait of a single nation with all its inhabitants marching together.[39] Notions of the medieval era as a time of unity, class harmony, workable simplicity, and hearty naturalness were favored by conservatives and liberals: the artist poet William Morris and the pre-Raphaelites gave medievalism Romantic expression in high culture.

Throughout England, people were assiduously collecting medieval remnants: folk culture, ballads, folk dances, and crafts. They were emotionally invested in the notion that ballads were the manifestation of a national literary genius in a primitive but robust form: according to A. T. Quiller-Couch, "rude these ballads are, but nothing in English verse has ever been racier, or more genuine, or closer to the core and marrow of England."[40] Ballads of Robin Hood were particularly popular and considered to be typically English. England's distinctive cultural heritage, the basis of its national soul, had to be both saved and appreciated. Ballads, folklore, and even place names were to be savored in a fashion similar to the epiphany felt many years later by author C. S. Lewis. He stood on a rural train platform, his ears tingling with cold: "Then the train came in. I can still remember the voice of the porter calling out the village names, Saxon and sweet as a nut—'Bookham, Effingham, Horsely train.'"[41] Echoes of Lewis's love of ancient place names can be heard in Penelope Lively's *The Wild Hunt of Hagworthy* (1971), which begins with a list of railway stations visited by Lucy on the way to her aunt's house: "Magical, infinitely familiar—Norton, Fitzwarren, Bishop's Lydeard, Crowcombe, Stogumber, Williton, Watchet, Washford, Blue Anchor, Dunster."

As academics and educators touted the English language as a font of national character, English as a subject was working its way into the curriculum, especially in nonpublic schools; it was a mode of democratizing and spreading the influence of the humanities. According to Brian Doyle, "English" eventually came to extend itself beyond disciplinary boundaries to encompass all mental, imaginative, and spiritual faculties: knowledge was less important than "cultivation of the mind, the training of the imagination, and the quickening of the whole spiritual nature."[42] English was viewed as an alternative to a classic education, as having the cultural authority previously invested in classics, with the added power of a "national dimension that yet somehow transcended nationality."[43]

* * *

The idealization of Englishness was cultivated in the pseudohistorical concept of medieval and "Merrie Old England" with its atmosphere of coziness, folk life, and rusticity, which was given form in Queen Anne–style buildings and images in children's books. For Victorians and generations of readers since, fictional portrayals of nature, the English countryside and past, and childhood have each sparked the communal imagination in a particular way and stimulated a spiritual response and a sense of emotional well-being. It is similar to the effect of tea, the national drink, one of the few beverages whose ingredients both stimulate and calm. Many authors and illustrators of children's books infused their works with nostalgic, often wistful visions of childhood and rural idyll, and their biographies attest to the enduring influence of early exposure to the country and nature. Memories of the countryside visited as a child sustained illustrator Kate Greenaway; her work is filled with delightful rural scenes and outdoor images that suggest she must often have been reminded of happier places than London. For author Kenneth Grahame, time spent on the river was nothing less than blessed escape from work responsibilities and an unhappy marriage. Greenaway, Carroll, Sewell, Potter, Barrie, Grahame, and, later, Tolkien and Lewis all created evocative literary worlds from their sojourns in the country. Often their "word paintings"—the Victorian term for descriptions of nature—were gentle, idealized re-creations of the lost haven of childhood, rich with longing for innocence and a sense of the authenticity and truth of the natural world.

The Romantic predilections of the late Victorian period may have taken some cues from Wordsworth, who wrote about childhood in *The Prelude* (1850). He felt that one's youth could be revisited in the same way that we can revisit beautiful places, and he found that recovering thoughts and emotions from his early years was invigorating: "So feeling comes in aid / Of feeling, and diversity of strength / Attends us, if but once we have been strong." Philosopher John Stuart Mill turned to Wordsworth's poems as an antidote to a depression that was brought on by his famously strict upbringing and education. Mill responded to both Wordsworth's subject matter (the rural objects and natural scenery that Mill also loved) and, more important, to something he called a "culture of feelings," encouraged by Romantics, in which spiritual and emotional responses were more important than rational or moralistic ones.[44] To Wordsworth and those influenced by him, a spiritual response to nature, as well as thoughts of childhood, were essential to restoring wholeness and peace of mind.

There are echoes of this notion in a letter that Charles Kingsley, author of well-known children's book *The Water-Babies*, wrote in 1863. He described the serenity and exhilaration experienced on a walk on the moors:

> with the hum of bees, and the sleepy song of birds around me, and the feeling of the density of life in myriads of insects and flowers strong upon me. And over all, the delicious sense of childhood and simplicity and purity and peace, which even a temporary return to the state of nature gives.[45]

Like Mill (and Stevenson and Carroll), Kingsley was raised by a rigid, demanding father. His father was a pious man whose religious beliefs

disallowed recreation, music, and theater. However, he was also a sportsman and naturalist, and Kingsley's mother loved the Devonshire countryside so much that she walked it extensively during her pregnancy,
willing her unborn child to see what she saw and to love it as well.[46]
They passed on a love of nature to their son. Like Stevenson, Kingsley
sought reprieve from social obligations in rural holidays justified primarily by sickness and exhaustion. Country life and long holidays were a
recurring feature in children's books of the late Victorian and Edwardian
eras. In much the same way that images of happy children appealed to
this emotionally locked-down population, pastoral scenes attracted repressed adult readers who felt that they lived compromised lives as
adults and were sapped by stressful urban lives.

Blake's and Wordsworth's sentimental idealizations of children and
nature came together in the picture book, a product of the aesthetic
movement of the nineteenth century. This medium evolved to feed a new
reading market—the child audience—but was actually designed to appeal to adults, its principal consumers. In one poem from *A Child's Garden
of Verses*, Stevenson celebrates what was becoming a familiar notion by
1885—the reading of picture storybooks as a treasured part of childhood.
Parents liked the books' sentimental depictions of beautiful children and
pastoral scenes and the fact that the books could serve as a tool for educating children in aesthetics—and values too but through visual elements
and gently uplifting plots and story lines.

Aggressively merchandised, especially at Christmas, picture books
were nevertheless taken seriously as an art form. New books were reviewed in art journals, and the genre was discussed at length in literary
magazines. Determined to make life more beautiful, late Victorians were
eager to purchase such beautiful objects. Picture books held even more
value because of people's awareness that beauty—like childhood and like
the English countryside—was rapidly slipping away. Religion, long a
source of comfort, beauty, and inspiration, was no longer an absolute
refuge. The market rose to meet demand for the beautiful, angelic child as
the texts and illustrations of new children's books expressed a yearning
for all things bright and beautiful that had less to do with God and more
to do with nostalgia for a simpler and more authentic way of life.

Late Victorian aesthetic ideals and formal training in the arts, sentimentality about children, the use of innocence as a source of emotional
uplift, and a penchant for linking children, the past, and rural beauty
came together in the works of Walter Crane, Randolph Caldecott, and
Kate Greenaway. According to Anne Lundin, these illustrators found a
new professional niche in illustrating for children's books and profoundly influenced public taste: their work provided the prototype of the modern children's picture book.[47]

The work and reputation of Walter Crane, a decorative book artist, are
probably the least familiar to us of the three. Most famous for *The Baby's*

Opera (1877), he refused primary identification as an illustrator for children and never achieved the iconic status of Caldecott and Greenaway. (A measure of Greenaway's influence is the Kate Greenaway Medal, awarded annually since 1955 for the most distinguished children's picture book published in Great Britain. The equivalent American award, the Randolph Caldecott Medal, likewise honors its namesake.)

From Crane we have timeless, folkloric images and artistic details, such as illuminated capitals and scrollwork. And we have ideas about illustrating children's books that appear to have influenced both Greenaway and Caldecott. Crane wrote that graphic art should be beautiful and should address an impressionable quality of mind that he called "child-like": a fresh direct vision and quickly stimulated imagination that should be maintained not only in art but throughout life.[48] He felt that in children's illustrations, the imagination can roam freely; the reader can find humor, pathos, a sense of wonder and romance, and (perhaps most important) access to the heart of a child, "a heart which, in some cases, happily, never grows up or grows old."[49]

Caldecott's illustrations were livelier than Crane's. He was famous for his pictorial storytelling style, wit, and folkloric portrayals of eighteenth- and early-nineteenth-century England. Historian of children's literature F. J. Harvey Darton wrote, "You always feel that Caldecott is not thinking of a picture, but of folk and lovable dogs and horses and flesh-and-blood hybrids like his fellow-Englishmen."[50] Caldecott really delivered on Crane's ideal of a fresh childlike vision and backed it up with the evocative force of folklore and nostalgia for an England that no longer existed.

While Caldecott never lost sight of the story, for Greenaway, the images were enough. As a child, Greenaway was attracted to visual detail and often tried to learn what a story was about, not by reading, but by looking at the pictures.[51] As an adult, she was dedicated to the aesthetic movement and famous for her distinctive style. According to Darton, "her light and gentle fancy made her text and fidelity to it of secondary importance. The book she illustrated, whatever it was, was Kate Greenaway's."[52] In books such as *Under the Window* (1878), *Mother Goose* (1881), and *Marigold Garden* (1881), Greenaway conveys the yearning for lightness of being and joyfulness that underlay the era's sentimental ideals as they sought aesthetic expression. Ina Taylor sums up the Greenaway world as "nearly always May," her illustrations a depiction of a time when trees are in blossom, roses scent the air, and children in muslin frocks rush outside to play.[53] Her redolent images of the English countryside, thatch-roofed cottages, and children quaintly dressed in pretty, vaguely eighteenth-century bonnets, smocks, and breeches attracted cult-like fascination from readers. Greenaway designed and sewed beautiful clothing. After becoming famous for her picture books, the illustrator's entrancing visions went on sale, creating a vogue for Greenaway-inspired children's clothing that raged throughout the 1880s and 1890s. Her images, with their timeless notions of English childhood, also appeared in the form of needlework, greeting cards, calendars, ceramics, and wallpaper. They still sell and have found a permanent place in the popular culture of childhood.

Greenaway offered Victorians aesthetic satisfaction and imaginative refuge in a compelling secondary world, the garden of childhood. Like that of many late Victorians, Greenaway's work was influenced by a lifelong passion for pastoral England. Her fondest memories of childhood were of visits to a rural village called Rolleston, a sort of Eden where she was affectionately cared for by a farm family and grew to love flowers and gardens. Greenaway used the inspiration of these years to create lyric landscapes of childhood, fantastic wonderlands of apple blossoms and droll children in pinafores.

Greenaway is particularly known for her association of the child with the natural world, albeit a romanticized one. Her juxtaposition of children and the natural scene wasn't just coincidental. Her pictures were infused with images of childhood and rural Arcadia that evoke the piper in William Blake's *Songs of Innocence*:

> Piping down the valleys wild
> Piping songs of pleasant glee
> On a cloud I saw a child.
> And he laughing said to me . . .
>
> Piper sit thee down and write
> In a book that all may read —
> So he vanish'd from my sight.
> And I pluck'd a hollow reed
> And I made a rural pen,
> And I stain'd the water clear,
> And I wrote my happy songs,
> Every child may joy to hear.

Greenaway picked up on Blake's "rural pen" but tamed his vision. Her landscapes were lyrical, their beauty lying in an order and security in which "nothing is allowed to run wild and threaten the tranquility."[54] Her children testify to Blake's vision of childhood as innocent and happy, but they have a wistful, stylized quality too. Her images elicited adoring reactions, a heady sentimentality. Its narrow vision of the beautiful static child retains a kind of sentimental appeal that is revisited, periodically, in modern children's books.

Through Crane's, Caldecott's, and Greenaway's books, readers were invited to celebrate innocent childhood, Englishness, and a better world that still lingered, supposedly, in the countryside. It was a form of social memory. These illustrators' work helped jaded adults recover their innocence by providing, as Lundin writes, a "kind of [Proustian] madeleine redolent of innocence and sophistication, the archaic and the avant-garde. An unsullied now."[55] Late Victorian picture books shared a tendency to evoke an imagined Arcadia of preindustrial England. They conjured up a compelling alternate world that allowed readers to deny, at least for the moment, the sordidness of urban living and their cramped lives as adults.

The images of Crane, Caldecott, Greenaway, and Burnett invited readers to delight in childhood and all its trappings: beautiful tots, jovial squires, lovely gardens, tranquil villages, and the whiff of a gentler yesteryear. They were also speaking to the child within each reader, regardless of age, who yearns for a safe, happy world to offset the gray tones of the real world. In reading these works, one could still believe, for a moment anyway, in lost heirs and orphaned princesses finding love and security and childhood as an idyll. The world of these sentimental Romantic authors and illustrators is one of happiness in the moment and beauty, childhood as a secondary world, an Eden to which the reader can escape via the imagination. Unlike those who wanted to save, teach, or control children to guarantee a certain future for them, these artists simply wanted to revel in childhood as a safe zone, a place of aesthetic inspiration, happy endings, and emotional comfort. For them, childhood was a time of uncomplicated joy, when there is freedom and oneness with the natural world and where youth can, as Blake wrote, run down a green plain leaping and laughing "and wash in a river, and shine in the Sun." Or, as Wordsworth so famously wrote, "to be young was very heaven." These authors and illustrators put into effect the visions of the Romantics and claimed early childhood (and adolescence inasmuch as it is free and happy) for their standards and principles.

NOTES

1. Harman, *Myself and the Other Fellow*, 95.
2. Thwaite, *Waiting for the Party*, 150.
3. Gerzina, *Frances Hodgson Burnett*, 253.
4. Gerzina, *Frances Hodgson Burnett*, 238.
5. West, "'There Is No Devil,'" 252.
6. Bayly, *The Life and Letters of Mrs. Sewell*, 275.
7. Chitty, *The Woman Who Wrote "Black Beauty,"* 235.
8. Chitty, *The Woman Who Wrote "Black Beauty,"* 60.
9. Chitty, *The Woman Who Wrote "Black Beauty,"* 104.
10. Gavin, *Dark Horse*, 110.
11. Bayly, *The Life and Letters of Mrs. Sewell*, 248.
12. Pickering, *Creative Malady*.
13. Ferguson, "Breaking in Englishness," 34–52.
14. Ferguson, "Breaking in Englishness," 39.
15. Chitty, *The Woman Who Wrote "Black Beauty,"* 245.
16. Lansbury, *The Old Brown Dog*, 97.
17. Gerzina, *Frances Hodgson Burnett*, 122.
18. Wullschläger, *Inventing Wonderland*, 21.

19. Smiley, *Charles Dickens.*
20. Robson, *Men in Wonderland,* 31.
21. Whistler, *Imagination of the Heart,* 26.
22. Robson, *Men in Wonderland,* 8.
23. Hilton, *John Ruskin.*
24. Engen, *Kate Greenaway,* 93–94.
25. Brooker, *Alice's Adventures,* 37.
26. Wullschläger, *Inventing Wonderland,* 32.
27. Carpenter, *Secret Gardens,* 62.
28. Kincaid, *Child-Loving,* 196.
29. Robson, *Men in Wonderland,* 51.
30. Houghton, *The Victorian Frame of Mind,* 9.
31. Kumar, *The Making of English National Identity,* 199.
32. Poon, *Enacting Englishness in the Victorian Period,* 6.
33. Wiener, *English Culture,* 61.
34. Wiener, *English Culture,* ix, 7.
35. Wiener, *English Culture,* 42.
36. Wiener, *English Culture,* 57.
37. Barczewski, *Myth and National Identity,* 105.
38. Barczewski, *Myth and National Identity,* 6–7.
39. Barczewski, *Myth and National Identity,* 7.
40. Barczewski, *Myth and National Identity,* 233.
41. Sibley, *Through the Shadowlands,* 36.
42. Doyle, "The Invention of English."
43. Doyle, "The Invention of English," 98.
44. Sanders, *Charles Dickens,* 90.
45. Chitty, *The Beast and the Monk,* 68.
46. Chitty, *The Beast and the Monk,* 25.
47. Lundin, *Victorian Horizons,* 3.
48. Lundin, *Victorian Horizons,* 110.
49. Rose, *The Edwardian Temperament,* 187.
50. Darton, *Children's Books in England,* 277.
51. Engen, *Kate Greenaway,* 27.
52. Darton, *Children's Books in England,* 278.
53. Taylor, *The Art of Kate Greenaway,* 8.
54. Taylor, *The Art of Kate Greenaway,* 8.
55. Lundin, *Victorian Horizons,* 3.

SIX

Being Playful and Emotionally Alive

A book of Youth—and so perhaps chiefly for Youth, and those who still keep the spirit of youth alive in them.—Kenneth Grahame

It is curious, too, that many of our most interesting games happened when the grown-ups were all away.—E. Nesbit

The prelude to idealization in children's literature was fear and discontent; its aftermath was often tedium. By the end of the nineteenth century, the upper and middle classes sought distraction from religious and philosophical schemas—including static notions of the Beautiful Child. A rebellious Romantic impulse was bubbling up in public thinking about childhood and life in general. Instead of using stories to, on one hand, control and socialize children or, on the other, worship their innocence, a restless core of writers and readers wanted to free children (and their art) from the confines of Victorian society's expectations. Reliving childhood through playing at it and giving children permission to be mischievous and imaginative were steps toward throwing off the social fetters that had bound Victorian society. It was a playful, mildly antiauthoritarian impulse that opened the door to irony.

Stories began to emerge in which children looked at adults and found them lacking. An early example of subverting notions of adulthood had been introduced midcentury in the works of Lewis Carroll (1832–1898). Carroll struggled within the harness of religion his entire life and, in *Alice in Wonderland* (1864), rejected moralizing altogether. The book celebrates the liberty of thought and pleasure itself and is a zany spoof of contemporary manners. The underground world of the rabbit hole is commonly thought to illustrate the arbitrary nature of the human world and its authority structures and social norms. Like Carroll in Victorian England, Alice is surrounded by a confounding society, and the book stands as a kind of maverick salute to the gallantry of childhood prevailing against a repressive and punitive world.

At the time of its publication, Carroll's book was read simply as a dreamlike fantasy, something apart from the business of daily living. Children's writers after Carroll persisted in their task of imparting social and religious templates, although Romantic impulses found outlet in adoring portraits of children and a penchant for heroic adventures. It was not until the Edwardian era that children's authors fully developed the idea that the innocent play and pleasure of childhood had value in their own right. In their hands, the "child" became a model of a certain life-style: lighthearted and playful, robust and authentic. The mood of the epoch was expressed through a quality of escapism that surfaced in children's books.

Edwardian children's literature was about living in the moment. Play itself was "an acceptance of a code of rules and a dimension of behavior wholly distinct from those of ordinary life."[1] The setting for play was real life, the outdoors and home; and the impulse to play was portrayed as instinctive and healthy. In tales by Beatrix Potter and Rudyard Kipling, the animals lived according to their true natures rather than by social templates. E. Nesbit wrote of escapades by siblings and wild but safe magic, accessed from the solid base of home and family. Kenneth Grahame's *The Wind in the Willows* showed Toad answering the call of his wild side but also suggested that real bliss can be found in much simpler ways: lying around at home, messing around in boats, and discovering the magic of nature. New books invited children and adults to escape into small adventures and imaginative play. Edwardian children's authors seemed entranced with childhood as a Romantic way of life, sans responsibility and adult demands. In *Peter Pan*, James Barrie juxtaposes everyday life and a fantastical Never Never Land and explores the alluring notion of playing forever as an alternative to growing up.

* * *

The new qualities that were rapidly gaining social and moral value—spontaneity, playfulness, surrender to the imagination, and a paradoxical authenticity—lived in the king who gave his name to the era. When Edward VII (nee Albert Edward) succeeded Queen Victoria in 1901, a new role model and social tone were set in place. Edward's tenure as heir apparent had spanned almost sixty years, and his adult years were one long reaction to a stifling childhood. His father, Albert, had designed a highly programmed life and rigorous educational program for Bertie, as he was known to his family.[2] Bertie was kept in isolation from other children and schooled in the value of duty so favored by his parents. But he couldn't meet their expectations. His father regularly boxed his ears for minor infractions, and both parents despaired of his character and potential.

After her husband Albert's premature death in 1861, the grieving Victoria shunned society and put Victorians into a long period of mourning. She held up Albert as a model of the proper English citizen, and her rectitude and earnestness came to characterize the repressive era that bore her name. In stark contrast, Bertie turned his back on restraint and embraced pleasure, living a luxurious and sybaritic life and gaining a reputation as a playboy. While Victoria despised her son as irresponsible and self-indulgent, Bertie as crown prince and then king was popular with the English people.

The Edwardian era was preceded by the fin de siècle nineties, known for its lightness of mood, and followed by the Great War, which began in 1914. The dark trauma inflicted by the war would make the previous two decades, in retrospect, a golden era. The Edwardian age saw an extraordinarily privileged upper class maintaining a lifestyle of indulgence and conspicuous consumption, in stark contrast to the dire poverty of the lower classes. The middle class was mainly comprised of conservative, respectable people who were determined to hold onto their status and property in the face of the Boer War, external threats from Europe, and social discontent. A small but enthusiastic faction of freethinkers among the middle class, including socialists and suffragettes, put forth new ideas.[3] During Edward's reign, women wore white lace and big hats and went to garden parties and on boating excursions; suffragettes threw away their corsets, donned bloomers, and rode bicycles. Boy men, with an ethos shaped on the playing field, administered the empire. Leisure sports were the craze, and cricket became a ritual that celebrated the love of beauty, grace, and youth that was a legacy of the Romantics.

The stories of Beatrix Potter (1866–1943) came onto the scene on the cusp of the Victorian and Edwardian eras. Her aesthetic combined Romanticism and a reverence for old England. Young Beatrix had filled her diary with accounts of her grandmother's reminiscences, and regency details found their way into her little books—most notably, in the swords and wigs of *The Tailor of Gloucester*. Her stories were full of Edwardian irony and mild derision of Victorian sentimentality and manners. Potter mocks gentility in *The Pie and the Patty-Pan* by having a cat and a dog sitting down together to tea. In *The Tale of Tom Kitten*, Tom and his sisters refuse to behave for their socially conscious mother's tea party and end up disgracing her. Potter hated social pretensions and refused to shield young readers from reality. "Though her endings are happy ones," writes MacDonald, "they do not deny the existence of pain and death, and do not skirt the enmity between various animal species, or between animals and human beings. Big animals eat little animals; humans eat all kinds of creatures."[4] While they talk and wear clothes, Potter's animals act according to their natures.

   Like Edward VII and numerous others who were raised by Victorians, Potter was choosing to define herself in reaction to her parents and their way of life. Her parents lived a life of stultifying routine and upper-middle-class propriety and kept Potter away from school, isolating her from other children except her brother. Oblivious to Potter's needs as a child or person, her parents prolonged her dependency and twice opposed her desire to marry. Potter later described her early life as "unloved" but "not unhappy," for in her forced solitude she found space for experiment and originality. She occupied herself for hours by reading, studying natural history, and memorizing Shakespeare's plays and long passages from the Bible. Her nursery was home to rabbits, bats, hedgehogs, birds, lizards, and toads, which she studied and drew obsessively. According to her journal, rabbits were particular favorites; she liked their innate playfulness. Beatrix even taught her rabbit, Peter, to ring a little bell and drum on a tambourine. Her study of animals and her appreciation of their personalities provided the basis for her tales of endearing, mischievous, and self-involved characters.

   Yearly vacations in the country provided a blissful antidote to Potter's repressive life at home. She emerged from childhood convinced of the benefits of rural life, with its rhythms of a distant past and its simple, unchanging ways. She was a stalwart young woman who, despite her Victorian upbringing, refused to remain stunted and obedient. Driven by the urge to create, she groped for something that she could do that would make money and give her a measure of independence. She found it in writing and illustrating children's books. Ultimately, in her late forties, Potter embraced country life as a local: she married a country solicitor, lived as a Lake Country farmer, and quit writing.

   Potter's stories were event-filled tales, full of predators, consequences, and black comedy. Despite the pretty pastel images of gardens and cozy kitchens and the fantasy element of talking animals, her world had a fable-based ring of truth. Potter didn't sanitize life, and danger and mortality are unsentimentally presented as facts of life: if one is too innocent or rash, one may make a meal for someone else.[5] When Peter Rabbit disobeys his mother, he almost ends up like his father—served up in a pie by Mrs. MacGregor. Squirrel Nutkin reaps the consequences of impertinence by losing his tail. Jemima Puddle-Duck narrowly escapes disaster when she confides in a courtly and handsome fox. A synthesis of realism and fantasy, Potter's tales are also drily funny: Pig Robinson's aunts "led prosperous uneventful lives, and their end was bacon." Consequences and punishment lose their sting when handled with humor, with matter-of-factness, and without drama and moral purpose.

   In *The Tale of Peter Rabbit* (1903), naughty Peter seems archetypal boy and rabbit at the same time. Potter's array of fallible characters gave significance to the idea that living beings play the game of life according to inherent predispositions and that they are not and can never be perfect. While sometimes used as cautionary tales, *Peter Rabbit* and other Potter books are not primarily about lessons. They are simply about animals living according to their nature. Potter provided children with a model for accepting themselves and living in freedom—and then gave herself permission to live that way, too. Her books expressed and advanced a shift in children's literature in which authors were writing against constructions of childhood laden with adult religious and philosophical ideals. Romanticism persisted, but the movement's static worship of beauty and idealization of childhood were giving way to fiercer and more dynamic notions. Childhood was becoming full of color and life, a state separated from and contrasting sharply with adulthood.

* * *

By the turn of the century, more and more people were favoring the Romantic notion of untethered children who lived with emotional intensity, as Wordsworth described in his *Prelude*: "A race of real children, not too wise, / Too learned, or too good, but wanton, fresh, / And bandied up and down by love and hate; / Fierce, moody, patient, venturous, modest, shy, / Mad at their sports like withered leaves in winds." Kenneth Grahame expressed this vision of children as innately joyful in his reminiscences about an Arcadian childhood, *The Golden Age*, published in 1895. He celebrated the child's exuberance and connection with nature: "Earth to Earth! That was the frank note, the joyous summons of the day . . . boon nature . . . earth effluence. . . . I ran sideways, shouting; I dug glad heels into the squelching soil; I splashed diamond showers from puddles with a stick; I hurled clods upward at random." Edwardians idolized Grahame and his idea of an intoxicatingly free childhood.

In his essays, Grahame portrayed children (and adults as well) in a new way: with humor and without sentimentality. He aimed at adults, writing semiautobiographically of children living with gusto. He had lived out this possibility after his mother died when he was five, and his upbringing was entrusted to a group of unimaginative aunts and uncles whom he dubbed "the Olympians." Distant and aloof, they provided for his physical needs but were unengaged in his life and their own. Grahame sharply contrasts their colorless, boring lives with the rich life that he and his siblings enjoyed outside: "This strange anaemic order of being was further removed from us, in fact, than the kindly beasts who shared our natural existence in the sun."[6] Grahame lamented that his aunts and uncles

> never set foot within fir-wood or hazel-copse, nor dreamt of the marvels hid therein. The mysterious sources—sources as of old Nile—that fed the duck-pond had no magic for them. They were unaware of Indians, nor recked they anything of bisons or of pirates (with pistols!),

though the whole place swarmed with such portents. They cared not
about exploring for robbers' caves, nor digging for hidden treasure.[7]

They were adults in the Victorian sense, seemingly without a vital inner
life: serious and dutiful rather than spontaneous and expressive. The
grown-up Grahame speaks for his peers in lamenting the lost Arcadia of
childhood and pondering whether, perhaps inevitably, he too had become an Olympian.

Grahame's life mirrors the dynamics that he set up in his essays. Despite the emotional neglect of his early years, Graham enjoyed the freedom of his childhood. He spent hours by the river and roaming the
countryside; at school (St. Edwards in Oxford), he was allowed to wan-
der the streets and surrounding areas at will. But the freedom came to an
abrupt end when his desire to attend university was thwarted by an
uncle who sent Grahame to London to work in a bank. As his biographer
wrote, "he went to London as a mid-Victorian who knew where his duty
lay, but also as a disgruntled adolescent."[8] As he worked his way up to
the top position in the Bank of England, Grahame retained his youthful
zest for life. He achieved success and popularity for his essays, *The Pagan
Papers* (1893), and two collections of short stories: *The Golden Age* (1895),
and *Dream Days* (1898). He savored his bachelor life, long weekends in
the country with his friends, and a home filled with toys. Grahame im-
pressed those who met him as being curiously childlike, looking like a
startled fawn or like a St. Bernard, too big for the city.[9]

The Edwardian notion of adulthood as a diminished, foreclosed existence that Grahame had publicized caught up with him in the end. With
his marriage in 1899 came adult responsibilities and the constrictions of
living in tandem. It is significant that even on his honeymoon Grahame
preferred sailing with his friends to spending time with his bride. A year
later, the couple had a child, Alistair. Born with disabilities and spoiled
by his parents, Alistair developed into a difficult child. For ten years,
Grahame wrote nothing. He did, however, tell his son stories and write
him a series of letters about a mole, a rat, and a toad. The toad, who father
and son agreed was like Alistair in many ways, became the chief character in a manuscript that appeared in 1908 as *The Wind in the Willows*.[10]
The book confounded expectations: unlike his acclaimed earlier works, it
was a fantasy about animals ostensibly for children rather than a semiautobiographical reverie about children for adults.

Grahame himself thought of the book simply as a series of animal
tales. His love for his characters is evident in his charge to illustrator E. H.
Shepard: "I love these little people. Be kind to them."[11] It is probably safe
to say that Toad's frenetic escapades, which dominate the later chapters
of the book, are what appeal most to children about *The Wind in the
Willows*, and in this fiercely Romantic sense, it is firmly Edwardian. It
calls to the reader's wilder impulses. But the book also builds on the

notion of nature as a refuge, an Eden for adults. Grahame pitched the book to publishers as "A book of Youth—and so perhaps chiefly *for* Youth, and those who still keep the spirit of youth alive in them: of life, sunshine, running water, woodlands, dusty roads, winter firesides; free of problems, clean of the clash of sex; of life as it might fairly be supposed to be regarded by some of the wise small things" that live in the grasses and woods.[12] The early chapters that celebrate the riverside pleasures so dear to Grahame's heart seem to have been written, perhaps unconsciously, for himself and like-minded adults.[13] They reveal Grahame's longing for the freedom of childhood and the simple pleasures of bachelor life—affectionate friends, good food, simple amusements, and the idyllic Arcadian world. This reinforced the theme, also Edwardian, of adulthood as problematic.

Grahame probably never imagined the high levels of literary interpretation that would be brought to bear on his humanlike animals and their environment. The book has been lauded as an allegory of the human psyche[14] and a psychological treatise on the development of imagination.[15] Grahame, like many Edwardians, was as preoccupied with the imagination as he was with childhood. He seemed to pose play as arising from a realm of inner activity (fantasy or the imagination) that functions to nourish adults and connect them to their child selves. His compelling portraits of play thus found their mark with child and adult audiences.

It is significant that two of the most important Edwardian children's authors, Kenneth Grahame and Beatrix Potter, quit writing relatively early. *The Wind in the Willows* was Grahame's only novel, and he wrote very little after this. He had always resisted those who wanted more from him, responding that he was "a spring not a pump."[16] He may have stopped because he could no longer keep in touch with childhood and the wellsprings of his being. Potter, however, may have ceased writing because writing for children was no longer necessary financially or as an emotional outlet: her adult life was full. In both cases, they may have bought into the Edwardian notion that the imagination was somehow the sphere of youth. When they no longer could retain their youthful spirit, relate to prevailing notions of childhood (as mischievous, gay, and irresponsible), or find refuge in childhood preoccupations, they put youth and writing behind them.

* * *

Edith Nesbit (1858–1924) fleshed out the emerging Edwardian vision of childhood by writing stories of real children who lived in the everyday world. The narrator was often a child, and the audience was unmistakably children. Attachment to home and family was taken for granted, and often a specific house in the suburbs of London provided the backdrop for imaginative games and magic. Her first children's book, *The Story of the Treasure Seekers,* came out in 1899, one year after Grahame's *Dream Days* (1898) and four years before Potter's *The Tale of Peter Rabbit* (1903). It began with this disclosure:

> There are some things I must tell before I begin to tell about the treas-ure-seeking, because I have read books myself, and I know how beastly it is when a story begins, "Alas!" said Hildegarde with a deep sigh, "we must look our last on this ancestral home"—and then someone else says something—and you don't know for pages and pages where the home is, or who Hildegarde is, or anything about it. Our ancestral home is in the Lewisham Road. It is semi-detached and has a garden, not a large one. We are the Bastables.

And so begins the Bastable children's quest to restore the family's for-tunes, at low ebb after their ill father's partner absconded to Spain.

Nesbit's books invoked the stories and serials that children were rou-tinely exposed to through their reading. Thus, the six Bastable siblings dig for buried treasure, try to rescue Gentlemen from the deadly peril of Highwaymen, catch burglars for a reward, and, more mundanely, sell homemade cold medicine and poetry. The children in *The Treasure Seekers* and Nesbit's subsequent books were qualitatively different from the fa-miliar child characters of earlier children's books. The focus was on hav-ing fun and living in the moment, rather than being prepped for the future. Nesbit's children were high-spirited believable human beings who played and had exciting adventures in and around their homes. In later books, she kept the everyday background yet introduced magic, fantastical creatures, and time travel.

For the most part, Nesbit was concerned with entertaining, not with pursuing nostalgia. She returned to her own childhood for imaginative stimulus, claiming that writing was a task simplified by her ability to remember exactly what it was like to be a child. It has been suggested that she remained a child all her life. According to her biographer, the adult Nesbit retained "all the caprices, the little petulances, the sulks, the jealousies, the intolerances, the selfishnesses of a child; and with them went a child's freshness of vision, hunger for adventure, remorse for unkindness, quick sensibility, and reckless generosity." [17]

Her childhood was a time of bad school experiences, night terrors, and grief at the loss of her father when she was four; yet, she was rescued by the support of an adoring mother, the satisfactions of reading, and tomboyish play with her brothers. It has been suggested that Nesbit was basically unhappy as a child and that unhappiness at some point in child-hood is the best possible training for any children's author. [18] Whether this is the case or not, Nesbit spared the children in her books anything like the trauma in her own life. For them, she created a gloriously carefree childhood where nothing was too wonderful to happen. There was no imperative for growing up and no sense of childhood as a paradise lost.

The playful, sometimes edgy element in Nesbit's books was the product of a volatile woman whose life force allowed her to weather grinding poverty as a young mother and turn to writing as a means of keeping her family's head above water. With success at the age of forty, expressing her playful side became a sort of performance art. She became a Bohemian with socialist leanings, who smoked, swam, boated, rode bicycles, and hosted fun parties.[19] Life never sobered her up as it did Grahame, and she had little recourse to nostalgia.

Nesbit's characters are natural and realistic. With the *The Treasure Seekers*, the question of voice would emerge as central to the genre's evolution. It has been dubbed the first truly modern book for children, because there is a genuine sense of the child's voice.[20] Oswald Bastable was alternately knowing and naïve, and the story is told through his colloquial and natural language and lively dialogues with his brothers and sisters. His sentiments ring true because, like most children, he values honesty, courage, and imagination over excessive piety.[21] The sibling banter is spontaneous and irreverent, and the natural realism of Nesbit's child characters was a radical new development. While in later works Nesbit ultimately abandoned the voice of a child narrator, she maintained a natural and direct style and a habit of describing events concretely yet with great imaginative power. Even with adult narrators, the tone didn't change, and neither did the reader's ability to join in Nesbit's fictional adventures.

To keep the children front and center in all her books and allow for the free play of their imaginations, adult characters had to be sidelined. In *The Wouldbegoods*, Oswald explains that good times with grown-ups are pleasurable and safe, but "not so interesting as the things you do when there is no one to stop you on the edge of a rash act. It is curious, too, that many of our most interesting games happened when the grown-ups were all away." Some adults were acceptable playmates, however. Oswald liked the neighbor boy's uncle because "he always talks like a book, and yet you can understand what he means. I think he is more like us, inside of his mind than most grown-up people. He can pretend beautifully." There was the recurring notion that children had unique access to the imagination in a way that most adults did not.

For imagination to have free rein, adults have to either join in or get out of the way, and Nesbit was one of the first children's authors to explicitly recognize this. She cleverly created families of children whose parents were swept up by domestic troubles, beleaguered by bill collectors, or away on trips. In *The Story of the Amulet*, the father is in Manchuria reporting on the war, "and Mother, poor dear Mother, was away in Madeira, because she had been very ill." Nesbit, in loco parentis, never allowed the children to be in real danger. The parents in Nesbit's books—though absent or distracted by misfortune—love their children dearly, and behind the exhilarating adventures and freedom, there is always the safe haven of home and hearth. Nesbit's parents did not stifle their children.

This was a new take on adult-child relationships. Nesbit abstained, for the most part, from sentimentality. She opposed authoritarianism and self-conscious moralizing and, through her characters, said so to her readers: "You are intelligent children, and I will not insult you with a moral. I am not Uncle Thomas. Nor will I ask you to remember what I have said. I am not Aunt Selina." In Nesbit's books, the mistakes of adults are told with a comic, often ironic tone. She always advocates for the child and deflates adult pretensions without rancor or bitterness. In Nesbit's books, adults (and society) are never portrayed as evil. This, of course, is in marked contrast to Dickens's portrayals of children victimized by cruel adults and Evangelical, Edgeworthian, and Yongeian authors' depictions of life as a serious business, a succession of high-stake trials and choices.

Hard times in Nesbit's books simply provided the opportunity for exciting new experiences and then a return to abundance. In *The Railway Children*, the father is imprisoned on false charges, and the children lose all the accouterments of ordinary suburban life: pretty clothes, a lovely nursery with heaps of toys and a Mother Goose wallpaper, a kind and merry nursemaid, and a dog called James. While losing their father is devastating, their resulting poverty, a move to the country, and their mother's distraction open the door to wonderful adventures. The children's exuberance and pleasant personalities attract good things (including a beneficent grandfather figure), and because this is a Nesbit story, in the end they get their father back and everything turns out all right.

The relative autonomy of her lively child characters and their engagement in imaginative adventures of their own making has led to Nesbit being characterized as subversive.[22] Certainly, she was detached enough from the establishment to poke gentle fun at it. Nesbit invites children and adults to enjoy the irony of male rituals and assumptions of male superiority. In one of Oswald's narratives, Nesbit writes, tongue in cheek, that the character Dicky "smoked the pipe of peace. It is the pipe we did bubbles with in the summer. . . . We put tea-leaves in it. . . . The girls were not allowed to have any. It is not right to let girls smoke. They get to think too much of themselves if you let them do everything the same as men." Nesbit had male and female characters and didn't reinforce female subservience.

Nesbit, like Dickens and other authors before her, criticizes society by presenting it through the innocent eyes of children, but her criticism is generally a subtext and is lighthearted and playful in comparison to that of her predecessors. In *The Story of the Amulet*, Nesbit has the time-traveling queen of ancient Babylon visit modern Edwardian England.

"But how badly you keep your slaves. How wretched and poor and neglected they seem," she said, as the cab rattled along Mile End Road.

"They aren't slaves; they're working people," said Jane.

"Of course they're working. That what slaves are. Don't you tell me. Do you suppose I don't know a slave's face when I see it? Why don't their masters see that they're better fed and better clothed?. . .You'll have a revolt of your slaves if you're not careful," said the Queen.

"Oh no," said Cyril; "you see they have votes—that makes them safe not to revolt. It makes all the difference. Father told me so."

She mocks tradition, again gently, in a story in *The Book of Dragons* (1899), when a little boy leaves open "The Book of Beasts" and the creatures come alive, escape, and threaten all of England. When the children rush to enlist St. George in the fight, he starts to draw his sword, but then hesitates at the idea of fighting *many* dragons and ultimately refuses to fulfill his role as the traditional defender of England. He tells the children: "It's no good. . . . They would be one too many for old George. You should have waked me before. I was always for a fair fight—one man one dragon was my motto." There is good-natured irony in the book's conclusion as well: it is England's bad weather, not chivalrous heroism, that defeats the dragons.

But Nesbit occasionally pulls aside the curtain that she describes as hanging forever between the world of magic and the real world and introduces a magic that could be wild and biting. In *The Enchanted Castle*, an unwise wish is granted by a magic ring, and the audience for the children's play (seven figures made up of broomstick, blankets, umbrellas, and handmade masks) comes to life as Ugly-Wugglies, businessmen on their way to work in the city. Jimmy joins them when he greedily declares, "I wish I was rich," and this wish is granted:

By quick but perfectly plain-to-be-seen degrees Jimmy became rich. . . . The whole thing was over in a few seconds. Yet in those few seconds they saw him grow to a youth, a young man, a middle-aged man; and then, with a sort of quivering shock, unspeakably horrible and definite, he seem to settle down into an elderly gentleman, handsomely but rather dowdily dressed, who was looking down at them through their spectacles and asking them the nearest way to the railway station. . . .

"Oh, Jimmy, don't!" cried Mabel desperately.

Gerald said: "This is perfectly beastly," and Kathleen broke into wild weeping.

The magic is ultimately undone, and everything turns out all right in the end, but through recourse to magic, Nesbit gave children access to what had once been available to them only in folk and fairy tales: primitive fantasies, survivable terrors, and catharsis. Nesbit was a master at providing scenarios in which the child characters (and readers) could venture out imaginatively and then return to the safety of home and real life.

Both Potter and Nesbit painted a world where small characters lived out their lives according to their inherent natures with innocence and playfulness. Relatively unconcerned with teaching the child how to grow up, authors invoked the imagination freely. Imaginative play was portrayed as a natural part of existence—of childhood—and as an auxiliary to reading. Kipling's *The Jungle Book*, which came out in 1893, was seized on as a sort of "rightful heritage" by imaginative children who immediately began to perform the tales, to "play Jungle."[23] Its author had grown up acting out stories that fired his imagination. In Kipling's autobiography *Something of Myself*, he recounts,

> When my Father sent me a *Robinson Crusoe* with steel engravings I set up in business alone as a trader with savages. . . . My apparatus was a coconut shell strung on a red cord, a tin trunk, and a piece of packing-case which kept off any other world. Thus fenced about, everything inside the fence was quite real, but mixed with the smell of damp cupboards. If the bit of board fell, I had to begin the magic all over again. . . . The magic, you see, lies in the ring of fence that you take refuge in.[24]

As a child, Kipling often took refuge in reading. When he was six, his parents, who were stationed in India, sent him back to England to be educated, and Kipling clashed violently with Mrs. Holloway, the Evangelical with whom he boarded for five years. A literal-minded disciplinarian, Mrs. Holloway took her in loco parentis role seriously, taught Rudyard about hell, and punished him severely for telling "lies," even forcing him to parade through the streets wearing a placard with "Liar" written on it. The adult Kipling wrote wryly that being forced to give a lot of attention to his lies may have inspired his later literary efforts.[25] Intermittent misery may also have fueled a powerful imagination. Reading became his refuge, and through writing he offered that refuge to other children.

Kipling had a special feel for children. *Just So Stories* (1912), with much intoning and embellishments, was first tried out on his own children. In love with imaginative play, Kipling despised the cult of athletics that gripped the public schools at the turn of the century. He had suffered for being unathletic at school, and in his *Stalky* stories, he took on many of the most cherished ideals of the public schools as ossified in the fifty years since *Tom Brown's Schooldays*. He mocked the ethos of "playing the game" with its blind allegiance, elitism, and self-conscious public school morality. His schoolboys, unlike Tom Brown and Eric, were witty, irreverent rascals full of scams. They enacted school life as a charade rather than a stylized, rule-bound sporting event. Readers adopted the term *Stalky* for a type of waggish game-type behavior in which advantage was seized by trickery. This game tactic was used to outwit the natives in the outposts of empire.

Kipling's narrative and artistry were so compelling that in 1907, he became the first English-language recipient of the Nobel Prize in Literature. Kipling played with logic and language in a way perhaps not seen since the Alice books. He was second only to Carroll in his rich and playful wordsmithing and nonsensical phrases:[26] the Elephant's Child was possessed of "'satiable curtiosity"; tree trunks were "'sclusively speckled and sprottled and spottled"; "the Tabus of Tengumai . . . were all Bobsulai." Kipling's *Jungle Book* read like fables that provided rules to keep the individual, family, and community safe. His stories gripped the imagination and had the extraordinary potency and universality of folklore. One child reader, J. M. S. Tompkins, later described his boyhood self as gripped by *The Jungle Book*, feeling in it connection with "something wild and deep and old."[27]

* * *

Many Edwardian authors considered play to be liberating and invited readers to experience works that encouraged a "summer-holiday self," a magic, ecstatic mode of being that gained vividness from its distinction from the commonplace and familiar.[28] Others were convinced that "doing something for the intrinsic enjoyment of the thing . . . is one of the ultimate ends of art and perhaps of human existence."[29] Reading joined physical activity as a form of play, both thought to involve the imagination.

In 1883, a book appeared that broke the mold. It had no morals, and while it was an adventure novel, it did not celebrate imperialism or the code of manliness. Its grip on the imagination was so powerful that it became a classic. Like other classics, it conforms and serves as an outlaw. Classic children's books not only foster prevailing mind-sets but introduce complexity and nuance. *Treasure Island* (1883), an iconic tale of adventure, conveys the romance of boyhood in an unparalleled way: Jim Hawkins illustrates daring, "yet does so with a delightful, rosy good boyishness, and a conscious, modest liability to error."[30] Yet, while evoking in full measure the lure of heroism and exhibiting the full capacity of successful make-believe, Stevenson shares the dark side of adventure.

Adventure came calling when young Jim saw an old pirate come plodding up to the door of his parents' inn, his sea chest following behind him in a handbarrow. He was "a tall, strong, heavy, nut-brown man; his tarry pigtail falling over the shoulder of his soiled blue coat; his hands ragged and scarred, with black, broken nails; and the sabre cut across one check, a dirty, livid white." Jim watched him looking around the cove, whistling to himself, and then breaking out in that old sea song that he sang so often afterward: "Fifteen men on the dead man's chest—Yo-ho-ho, and a bottle of rum!"

Nothing is the same after the old pirate takes up residence in the Admiral Benbow, and in all his fancies, Jim could never have imagined anything as strange and tragic as his subsequent adventures in pursuit of treasure. But Jim is a boy after all, though the story is told in retrospect by the adult Jim, and fierce scenes of action are punctuated by reveries of home. The spellbinding yarn is geared to young sensibilities, and according to Henry James, "it is all as perfect as a well-played boy's game" with the action kept at a critical pitch.[31] From the first, the boy reader is assured that Jim and his close friends will survive. The violence is rarely explicit, and Jim sails through without physical wounds. Yet evil is confronted and demystified: Jim hears the voice of Blind Pew as "cruel and cold and ugly," and the brutish life of the pirate is manifest in their scars and maimed limbs. And Jim learns some hard lessons about blood money and "the human cost of growing up in a world where it can be very hard to tell the respectable citizens from the pirates."[32] He finds out a lot about human nature and his own but returns not as a triumphant hero but seasoned and haunted. The book concludes with an older, wiser Jim plagued forever by dreams of that "accursed island" in which he hears the surf booming on the coasts and the voice of Captain Flint ringing in his ears: "Pieces of eight! Pieces of eight!"

Stevenson was young himself, thirty years old when he began *Treasure Island* in 1881. He had just broken free from his parents, survived a harrowing trip to California, married a Bohemian divorcee, and squatted in Silverado (a mining camp) for his honeymoon. Play was very important to him. This was a man who, with his twelve-year-old stepson, Lloyd Osbourne, staged war games with six hundred lead solders. One day, in a heavy rain in Scotland, Lloyd was making a map, and Stevenson leaned over his shoulder, drew an X on an island, and labeled it "Treasure Island." He had longed to write exciting, action-filled stories, and now, with suggestions from his family, he wrote three chapters in a few days. This was the first full-length narrative he had ever written.

Stevenson's love of romance novels was congruent with this period. Victorians were turning to the romance and adventure as a relief from the earnestness and strict behavioral expectations that constrained their lives. *Treasure Island* was consciously written to appeal to the Romantic nature, the thoughts and dreams of human beings in general and children in particular. A rebel with a passionate appreciation for youth,[33] Stevenson thought that loving romance was part of being human, and the craving for adventure in exotic lands began in childhood and persisted throughout life. He believed that every child "has hunted gold, and been a pirate, and a military commander, and a bandit of the mountains; but has fought, and suffered shipwreck and prison, and imbrued its little hands in gore, and gallantly retrieved the lost battle, and triumphantly protected innocence and beauty."[34] At the beginning of *Treasure Island*, Stevenson very consciously issues an invitation to the childish pleasures associated with sailor tales of "schooners, islands, and maroons / And Buccaneers and Buried Gold, / And all the old romance, retold / Exactly in the ancient way."

However, Stevenson was also setting out in uncharted territories. And he knew it. According to biographer Claire Harman, Stevenson thought that his tale, despite borrowing from familiar pirate motifs, was "as original as SIN." [35] *Treasure Island*'s novelty lay in its absence of dogma, moralizing, and theories of education and politics and its ability to plug in to the concerns of boys on the edge of maturity, when the innocence of childhood is exchanged for knowledge of the human condition and a more nuanced sense of good and evil. The book is also an antiadventure book, an exercise in moral ambiguity that questions existing values. [36] Stevenson, according to his stepson, was against keeping children in ignorance, raised as he had been raised: he wanted children to know what the world was like, in all its baseness and treachery, to be "armed for taking his part later in the battle of life." [37]

Stevenson's book signaled a new, perhaps premature maturity in children's books. In 1887, the teen years were still seen as sort of an extended boyhood. Stevenson was before his time in that he wrote for a new stage of development that was neither childhood nor boyhood but adolescence. However, the modern notion of adolescence (indeed, the term *adolescent*) didn't even appear on the scene until 1904. Children's literature had yet to split in two, with children's and young adult literature forming discrete categories. And yet here we have Stevenson writing about the child hero as one who doesn't conduct himself spotlessly, the norm for boy heroes of the late Victorian era. Simplistic notions of good and bad weren't in effect in Jim's world. Indeed, Stevenson's notion of adventure was like that of the boy in John Masefield's *Martin Hyde: The Duke's Messenger*, first published in 1909. He is caught up in war and spying and concludes that the adventurous life is one of "sordid unquiet, pursued without plan, like the life of an animal. Have you seen a dog trying to cross a busy street? There is the adventurer. Or the rabbit on the cliff, in his state of continual panic." [38]

In some ways, *Treasure Island* is strikingly modern, and its echoes can be heard, much later, in Tolkien's *The Hobbit*, when Bilbo realizes that he is embarked on a "bitter adventure." Bilbo encounters treachery and greed just as Jim did; both are unlikely heroes who achieve despite fear and human frailty, and both want to go home and live quietly. Both Tolkien and Stevenson question conventional heroism. And yet both hold out the notion of proving oneself, peeping over the edge, and returning home different. *Treasure Island* provides the satisfaction of a romance while serving as the precursor of the classic hero's quest that is a defining feature of much of modern adolescent literature.

Stevenson was laying down the roots of the notion that youth involves a period of testing and that growth is gained experientially and independently, not by mastering codes of behavior or religious doctrine. His book was set in a more robust England of the eighteenth century, and Jim was hardly the product of middle-class nineteenth-century Victorianism. Unlike Stevenson and others, he did not have to break the grip of filialness to be free enough to develop into his own person. The reader is likewise freed from imposed innocence/ignorance and didacticism and able to explore, through story, the confusion and inconsistencies of human existence and the way that characters tend to respond to events according to their particular nature. Jim's defiance of authority and rule breaking is explorative rather than purely impulsive. According to Susan Gannon, Stevenson invites the reader to question the values that make for success in the world and ponder the moral dilemma of treasure and the pervading moral ambiguity of "coincidence in support of opportunism" that leads to success.[39] *Treasure Island*, she writes, provides experience, honestly rendered.

Treasure Island introduced the notion of the Romantic adventure as a quest, no less exciting, in which something is learned. While it wasn't primarily written to serve as a means of questioning the universe or as a model for youthful development, in a burst of creativity, Stevenson introduced the idea of an autonomous boy hero who had all the knowledge he needed to control his fate: Jim as a modern adolescent. His adventure involves heavy doses of reality, and he has to come to grips with the fact that maturation involves disillusionment with authority and prevailing value systems. Jim's fate, to be a damped-down adult, was in line with the late–Victorian era idea that youth is great and adulthood anticlimactic, but the book paved the way for subsequent twentieth-century notions that the task of adolescence is maturing through tests and self-discovery and by defining oneself by butting up against establishment values rather than simply internalizing them.

* * *

Children's literature had entered a new era. The conscious use of stories to socialize (as in Yonge and domestic novels) and indoctrinate (as in Henty, adventure, and public school stories) had crested. In the twentieth century, imagination would be activated for pleasure but also to explore universal concerns, most notably the issue of growing up. The roots of this focus on the child (its pleasure and then autonomy in choice making) lay, of course, in Newbery's stories. Almost a century later, in his Alice books, Lewis Carroll chronicles a child's negotiating the terms of childhood and portrays the period as a time of disappointment, fear, and rejection. Childhood, to Carroll, is like a "dark corridor,"[40] and painful and damaging experiences are a natural cost of passing through. He ultimately points the way to life on the other side by letting Alice resist silliness and grow up. But Carroll's dark vision of childhood was rejected by Victorian Romantics for whom childhood was a focal point for sentimentality and nostalgic reveries. They read the Alice books as funny and dreamlike fantasies. Side by side with tales of boy heroes triumphing in the game of empire, Burnett's and Greenaway's visions of childhood as innocent and blissfully gay would dominate until late in the century, when some adults began to wonder whether childhood, with its special access to the imagination and play, was not in fact a better way of being; for adulthood, with its curtailment of imagination and renunciation of play, left humans undeniably diminished.[41]

While in *Treasure Island*, Stevenson showed the costs of adventure and growing up, it was mainly read as rousing adventure without an ounce of moralizing. James Barrie took the era's preoccupation with childhood, growing up (or not), and imaginative play to its logical conclusion in *Peter Pan*. The work was formidably great, almost fearsome in its impact. It plugged into the notion of play as an essential, transcendental, and irrational dimension of experience in which one was possessed of higher awareness.[42] On stage, the play swept audiences away. Children were hauled screaming from the theater because Captain Hook captured the essence of their fears and desires.[43] Adults and children alike instinctively clapped their hands to show that they believed in fairies. Barrie brought animals, heroes and villains, pirates, wild Indians, and fairies alive all at once, overcoming rationality and confronting viewers with the option of playing eternally as an alternate way of life.

The character Peter Pan was modeled on Barrie himself, and long after the play was written, the author wrote in his notebook that he finally understood the true meaning of *Peter Pan* as a "desperate attempt to grow up but can't." Barrie was neither child nor adult, sexless, and ultimately lonely. As an adult, he met a family, the Llewelyn Davies, and his fierce games with the sons (Peter, George, Jack, and later, Nico and Michael) made him feel joyous, exuberant, and in touch with childhood. He was enthralling to the boys because he could transform himself into a child and even outdo them imaginatively. His notebooks reveal that he lived his life on two levels, simultaneously playing with the boys and observing them.[44] The sparks the boys struck within him were channeled directly into *Peter Pan*. His intensity may have stemmed from Barrie's childhood, when he lived in the shadow of a favored older brother; he was also of extremely short stature. It has been proposed that themes of becoming visible emerged from these circumstances. Barrie wrote quirky, amusing pieces that betrayed a shape-changing kind of empathy. Writing *Peter Pan* allowed him to explore his preoccupation with youth—a typical one for his era—and his own inability to grow up.

According to James Kincaid, the tension in many children's stories is the same: "an urgent need for the child, the elusive child-forever, is played off against all the sensible, Freudian-ironic, and undesirable factors that erase distance, make the child manageable, catchable, and thus just another grown up-soon-to-be."[45] *Peter Pan* shows the consequences of staying in that tunnel of permanently choosing fantasy over reality and eternal youth over growing up: the result is a shallow existence and stunted development. By the story's end, Peter is an un-Romantic child: he is egotistical and heartless, his innocence ignorant and his gaiety irresponsible.[46] It is an interesting contrast to Alice, who is un-Romantic because she chooses sobriety and maturity.

Peter Pan was an extravagant theatrical tour de force that could be approached as mere entertainment, a swashbuckling dream of pirates turned into a sentimental play, except for the fact that Barrie was actually mocking the popular taste for pretty stories and sentimentality[47] and exposing the notion of "the imaginary perfection of childhood"[48] by portraying its natural conclusion in the character of Peter Pan. *Peter Pan* was a profound response to the Edwardian penchant for making childhood a form of escape from troubling realities, such as shaky religious beliefs or social injustice. With an almost eerie insight, Barrie slipped in and out of the fantasy so tempting to Edwardian society: of choosing childhood as an alternative to adulthood.

With World War I came another option—that of choosing death as a glorious sacrifice. Public school stories (serial or fully developed), tales of the empire and dark continents, and Baden-Powell's yarns built on the notion that children could be socialized through reading. For boys, socialization was facilitated by an undercurrent in Victorian and Edwardian culture that idealized manliness, militarism, and obedience and celebrated adventure.[49] Boys were thrilled by the sheer excitement of the worlds they were exposed to through stories. The public school was an exotic arena in which older boys held godlike status and powers; the empire was a place for proving one's mettle. The hook in boys' stories was the vicarious experience of heroism and the sense of being really, truly important. The payoff for society was a generation of youth who didn't question the established order and pledged themselves to serving the nation and, when necessary, dying for it. To paraphrase James Barrie, to die was an awfully big adventure—and this made war the biggest adventure of all.

The intense identification with England and the emotional investment in Englishness that was a part of the content and tone of school stories and historical fiction contributed to nationalism, to imperialism, and, ultimately, to ideals that fed the carnage of World War I. By the end of the century, England's fascination with the manly Christian gentleman whom Hughes had introduced and Henty had developed into a type was overlaid by the notion of beautiful young public school boys for whom boyhood was the glorious prime of life and adulthood, inevitably, an anticlimax. In this kind of an imagined world, dying becomes an almost sublime alternative to growing old.[50] With loyalty and patriotism held as supreme virtues, the deaths of young men in war became a beautiful thing, not wasteful and tragic: these men died unsullied and at their peak. As a headmaster of Harrow put it to a group of students, "to die young . . . [with] unattained hopes and aspiration, unembittered memories, all the freshness and gladness of May—is that not cause for joy rather than sorrow?"[51] The idealization of death in school stories was transferred to the setting of the trenches—to real life. Young World War I soldiers wrote letters home that expressed a belief in the self-sacrifice of war as an escape from the triviality of life. According to one, "even if you do get killed, you only anticipate the inevitable by a few years in any case, and you have the satisfaction of knowing that you have 'pegged out' in the attempt to help your country. You have, in fact, realised an ideal."[52]

With difficulty coming up with a vision of themselves as adults and caught up in the patriotic frenzy, young men willingly, even gaily, marched off to "play the game" in the trenches—and to die. The statistics are heartbreaking: 1,159 of the 5,588 old Etonians who served in the war died, and 1,469 were wounded. Five out of every nine men who fought in the trenches were killed, wounded, or missing.[53] Officers lasted on the average three weeks. The codes (being a soldier meant playing the game as a loyal team member) and ethos of prewar Englishness (the logical extension of Romantic patriotism was dying for England) that boys had absorbed through reading (and from society and English culture) had set them up to serve as cannon fodder. We can now see the end result, the slaughter, as an aberration of nationalism and the betrayal of youth.

NOTES

1. Coe, *When the Grass Was Taller*, 293.
2. Hibbert, *Queen Victoria*, 187.
3. Priestley, *The Edwardians*.
4. MacDonald, *Beatrix Potter*, 132.
5. Lane, *The Magic Years of Beatrix Potter*, 157.
6. Grahame, *The Golden Age*, 7.
7. Grahame, *The Golden Age*, 5.
8. Kuznets, *Kenneth Grahame*, 5.
9. Chalmers, *Kenneth Grahame*, 50–51.
10. Kuznets, *Kenneth Grahame*.
11. Green, *Kenneth Grahame*, 346.
12. Chalmers, *Kenneth Grahame*, 145.
13. Philip, "*The Wind in the Willows*," 299–316.
14. Carpenter, *Secret Gardens*, 160.
15. Tucker, *The Child and the Book*, 4.
16. Kuznets, *Kenneth Grahame*, i.
17. Moore, *E. Nesbit: A Biography*, 208–9.
18. Streatfeild, *Magic and the Magician*, 28.
19. Briggs, *A Woman of Passion*.
20. Moss, "E. Nesbit's *The Story of the Treasure Seekers*," 188.
21. Moss, "E. Nesbit's *The Story of the Treasure Seekers*," 192–93.

22. Lurie, *Don't Tell the Grown-Ups*, 102–3.
23. Green, *Kipling and the Children*, 123.
24. Kipling, *Rudyard Kipling*, 8.
25. Kipling, *Rudyard Kipling*, 6.
26. Green, *Kipling and the Children*, 180.
27. Tompkins, *The Art of Rudyard Kipling*, 56.
28. Coe, *When the Grass Was Taller*, 17.
29. Rose, *The Edwardian Temperament*, 164.
30. James, "Robert Louis Stevenson," 154.
31. James, "Robert Louis Stevenson," 154.
32. Gannon, "Robert Louis Stevenson's *Treasure Island*," 243.
33. James, "Robert Louis Stevenson," 131.
34. Stevenson, "A Humble Remonstrance," 94.
35. Harman, *Myself and the Other Fellow*, 227.
36. Carpenter, *Secret Gardens*, 108.
37. Osbourne, *An Intimate Portrait of R.L.S.*, 39–40.
38. Masefield, *Martin Hyde*, 158.
39. Gannon, "Robert Louis Stevenson's *Treasure Island*," 252.
40. Cohen, *Lewis Carroll*, 138.
41. Chaney, *Hide-and-Seek with Angels*, 237–38.
42. Coe, *When the Grass Was Taller*, 295.
43. Wullschläger, *Inventing Wonderland*, 128.
44. Birkin, *J. M. Barrie and the Lost Boys*, 84.
45. Kincaid, *Child-Loving*, 278.
46. Chaney, *Hide-and-Seek with Angels*, 374.
47. Carpenter, *Secret Gardens*, 186.
48. Chaney, *Hide-and-Seek with Angels*, 25.
49. Rose, *The Edwardian Temperament*, 113.
50. Quigly, *The Heirs of Tom Brown*, 248.
51. Quigly, *The Heirs of Tom Brown*, 142.
52. Rosenthal, *The Character Factory*, 103.
53. Richards, *Happiest Days*, 13.

SEVEN

Small Adventures and Happiness

Let youth be happy, or as happy as possible. . . . Every day of happiness, illusory or otherwise . . . and most happiness is illusory—is so much to the good. It will help to give the boy confidence and hope.—Charles Hamilton (Frank Richards)

The First World War was so traumatic that the existing mandates for children—imperialism and jingoistic patriotism, as well as passive domesticity for females and the code of manliness for males—could not stand. As children's writers began to distance themselves from missionary nationalism and the self-sacrificial duty-bound notions that had possessed prewar stories, the grip of ideology on children's literature loosened. Of course, stories still continued to play the role that children's literature usually plays in acculturation, but British society had begun to question the necessity of controlling childhood and manipulating children's reading to foster conformity and serve the nation. In the interwar period, children were allowed to enjoy the lack of obvious social fetters, and twentieth-century children's books would now please children first and adults second.

Adventure was king: either small and realistic adventures or wild and escapist ones. Serials and pulp fiction became formulaic, and hacks churned out exciting plot-driven stories, written to specification. Adventures were amusing and undemanding with a formulaic nature that appealed on the basis of stability. Characters were types that didn't have to be lived up to, or they were eccentrics that were a source of amusement rather than inspiration. In serials, the humor was broad; in books such as those of Milne and Ransome, it was gentle and low-key. Irony was now a common feature in children's literature.

The Edwardian penchant for entertainment and playfulness had come to dominate the world of twentieth-century children's fiction. Mass market writers generally borrowed backward and served up dishes with tried-and-true elements and an emphasis on escapism. As notions of national character kept evolving in light of post–First World War moods, the pulse of traditional Englishness in memorable children's stories weakened; or, perhaps it would be more accurate to say that identification with the nation was no longer in the forefront, and pre–First World War chauvinism was damped down (though not dead). Images and values seemed ossified, and literary-minded adults despaired of the quality of books offered to children. It was a period when publishers were unwilling to rock the boat (of profit) by taking a chance on original works. Nevertheless a few praiseworthy ones made it into print: A. A. Milne and Arthur Ransome provided a rooted cultural essence and contemporary sensibility. They offered a different kind of paired stability and escapism from the serials and mass-market children's fiction and brought into the genre of children's literature strong and compelling portrayals of holidays and place, friendship, family codes, and an evolving Englishness that matched current social ideals and seemed timeless. In interwar serials and books, the focus was on the child being happy. Enid Blyton was in the forefront of trends toward pleasing children by giving them what they want, and in the fifties, she was a victim of the professionalization of children's literature (the development of standards, awards, review sources) and critics who found her relentless merchandising and retro values offensive and potentially detrimental to children. They were out of alignment with contemporary social ideals.

* * *

It has always been difficult to control the genie of imagination, a goal of didacts and propagandists. As discussed in chapter 4, there was a concerted effort to break the grip of wildly imaginative, grotesque, and violent penny dreadfuls in the second half of the nineteenth century. These appealed to the working class and to children who loved their wildness and outlaw characters. Young Robert Louis Stevenson was addicted: "Eloquence and thought, character and conversation, were but obstacles to brush aside as we dug blithely after a certain kind of incident, like a pig for truffles."[1] Highwaymen and criminals were celebrated and heroines flogged and ravished, the women often as wild as the men: "In the doorway, in her nightdress, which revealed all the beauties of her buxom form, stood Mary Kelly, a pistol in each hand."[2] The wild underbelly of Victorian life was exposed for all to read about, and alliances formed to counter the publications' supposed contaminating effect on children.

After 1855, a series of somewhat more respectable blood-and-thunder magazines came into being, including *Boy's Own Magazine* (1855), *Chatterbox* (1866), and the *Boys of England* (1866). Healthy action replaced portraits of vice, as these and other new publications catered specifically to middle-class young people. Sex was taboo, violence still permitted. Up until World War I, the ideological basis of boys' stories was imperialism, nationalism, and patriotism; the type to be fostered was the manly boy. But the respectable boys' serials had also laid the ground for unfettered adventure (or, at least, adventures without an overt ideological message). New heroes in serials included detectives or inventors. The darling of fin de siècle England was the serial detective story, and several hundred titles were in production by the turn of the century. Sherlock Holmes first appeared in the *Half Penny Marvel,* and soon the detective Sexton Blake evolved into a national hero and was busy pondering his cases at home in Baker Street or traveling the nation and globe, fighting evil gangs and obsessive criminals. In Blake, we have the model of an amateur who accepts payment from only those who can afford it and will not work for anyone who dishonors Britain. He thrived on foiling threats to national security. Overall the emphasis was on thrills. *Boys Will Be Boys* author E. S. Turner gives the flavor of Blake's exploits by referencing a *Marvel* story in which Blake is fighting hand to hand in the basket of a balloon drifting over the channel; when he cannot break the grip of the villain, he shoots the silk of the balloon and wakes up on a steamer. To mystery writer Dorothy Sayers, Blake was a "legendary hero of Britain," and detective blood-and-thunders were "the nearest approach to a national folk-lore, conceived as the centre for a cycle of loosely connected romances in the Arthurian manner."[3] One hundred authors wrote more than four thousand adventures featuring the intrepid and eccentric detective, and he was featured until 1933.

By the onset of the First World War, serials targeting young people were ubiquitous, with circulation for some issues topping one million. Publishers kept putting out "improved" papers and trying to reinvigorate national pride and public morale.[4] Alfred Harmsworth's serials for boys were part of a newspaper empire in which pioneering tabloid journals sought to provide amusement without vulgarity. Sensationalism would be a popular feature of the postwar years as boys fought against nature in the form of blizzards, ravenous rats, international anarchists, and evil figures such as the Black Panther. Boys identified with all-powerful characters such as G-men, air aces, master spies, explorers, and pugilists. While violent scenes abounded, they came across to George Orwell as relatively harmless and unconvincing, especially in contrast to American images:

> In the Yank Mags you get real blood-lust, really gory descriptions of the all-in, jump-on-his-testicles style fighting, written in a jargon by people who brood endlessly on violence. A paper like *Fight Stories,* for instance, would have very little appeal except to sadists and masochists. You can see the comparative gentleness of the English civilization by the amateurish way in which prize-fighting is always described in the boys' weeklies.[5]

Boyish desires were catered to and wish fulfillment, escapism, and feelings of potency delivered via compelling adventure stories, school tales,
science fiction (death rays, robots, and invisible men!) and historical fiction. Boys' day-to-day interests and needs were addressed through col-
umns of editorial advice and support for hobbies and interests.

Interwar serials for boys carried cheerful patriotism, a wistfulness
about empire, and lashings of xenophobia and ridicule of foreigners.
While there were fewer heroes "fettered by the white man's burden or
imperative of consolidating the Empire," foreigners were nevertheless
victims of "old stereotypes recycled in new settings."[6] There was plentiful use of racial and national stereotypes, all the better to foreground
British superiority and maintain imperialistic attitudes. As Geoffrey
Trease saw it,

> the British must always win. One Englishman equals two Frenchmen
> equals four Germans equals any number of non-Europeans. A "loyal
> native" is a man, dark of skin and doglike in devotion, who helps the
> British to govern his country. A "treacherous native" is one who does
> not.[7]

Racism was not as adamant as in 1853, when Dickens said, "A savage is
something highly desirable to be civilized off the face of the earth,"[8] and
Harmsworth-like chauvinism was a casualty of the First World War.
However, in children's postwar publications, the empire was declining,
but racism was not. Latent imperialism took the form of portraying the
world as an international playground. The girl aviatrix, a new character,
flew the world on various missions; boys continued to test themselves
against villains and wild animals in far-flung venues, especially the Wild
West and the frozen north. In general, their relationships with "natives"
were less polarized than in Victorian times (American Indians were no
longer shot on sight); however, they confirmed existing stereotypes.

Children were taught that nationals of other countries were either
strange (possibly sinister) or silly.[9] Foreigners at school were derived
types, such as Hussi Rangit Lal Khan, "a dusky son of India with typical,
characteristic features," and Yung Ching, "a typical Chinese boy of the
upper class, thoroughly westernized, very tricky and pretending to be
innocent . . . very deep."[10] Examples of Babu and pidgin English
abounded—"Me tellee whoppee. Me solly. Only jokee"—and as a send-
up of Germans: "Vell, Bulstrode, I tink you vas vun bully and a prute."
When Baron von Schitzenhauser visits the Wild West, he begins to ex-
claim "Py yiminy!" and explains, "Aber I ain't afraid uff Indians. I tondt
vandt any such exberiences ag'in as vot I haf had. Nodt in dot vay,
eenhow."[11] Names were also plumbed for entertainment value: the detective Sexton Blake had a young Chinese assistant named "We-wee";
Littlecote students traveled the world with an oriental tutor, Chunder
Loo; Greyfriars School had two brothers, Wun Lung and Hop Hi. When

accused of making foreigners "funny," author Frank Richards unabashedly replied that they were funny—an attitude that many of his contemporaries agreed with. Camp accents and tongue-in-cheek names introduced comic relief and were not considered inappropriate in a Britain in which foreigners were looked down on as "unseemly"—their boots too small, their foreignness evident in their clothes and comportment. Even Agatha Christie's Belgium detective, Hercule Poirot, was patronized and underestimated because he minced around and had a showy mustache and an accent.

There were familiar stereotypes (gender, class, race), homogenization of culture, and sense of datedness in the serials and mass fiction that children consumed so avidly. And yet, there was vitality and humor, and children adored the over-the-top characters and adventures. Serials catered to "the English propensity not only to tolerate but positively to encourage eccentricity. . . . The mere presence of such odd folks among them is a testimony to the community's gentleness, tolerance, and humor." [12] The British have a tradition of celebrating oddness (think Carroll and Lear) and, especially from the Edwardian era onward, bringing humor and irony to bear (thank you, Nesbit). Most readers could find some character to laugh about, identify with, or disassociate from. Although aristocrats became figures of fun and middle-class characters occupied an unexamined center place in any plot, working-class characters appeared in more stories (and this segment of the population had serials that catered to them), though issues of class hinted at great divides. While there was a continued denial of sexuality, gender stereotypes were changing. As socialization took a decidedly secondary place to entertainment and escapism, the content of twentieth-century serials and pulp fiction portrayed and normalized the increased independence, equality, and agency of girls, women, and working people. Overt indoctrination had given way to a kind of taken-for-granted or unconscious acculturation.

Serials played to the love of adventure within youthful readers. Publishers such as Thompson of Dundee produced the boys' thrillers, the Big Five: *Adventure* (1921), *Rover* (1922), *Wizard* (1922), *Skipper* (1930), and *Hotspur* (1933). These featured sports, adventure, and school—historical and futuristic stories aimed at the subconscious desires of younger boys who wanted to fly, be invisible, create shrink potions, and read fantasies about animals with supernatural powers, such as O'Neill, the Six-Gun Gorilla. [13] After dominating the prewar market, Harmsworth weeklies faced stiff competition, and the firm launched twenty-eight new papers in the 1920s and 1930s, many of them concentrating on schoolgirls. *Britannia's Children* author Kathryn Castle cites a survey of reading habits in the interwar years that show consumption of at least two or three story papers a week by school-age children. [14]

An absolute ban on mention of sexuality in respectable journals would continue until the middle of the twentieth century and linger on in uneasiness about addressing sex in contemporary children's stories. Editors often encouraged violence because it was marketable, but sex was taboo—considered unprofitable and likely to lead to social sanctions. In the 1920s, journalist James Cameron worked on the *Red Star Weekly*, a paper that he described as catering to working-class girls who liked stories filled with gore and violence. It featured shootings, disembowelment, live burials, and various torments but never the slightest hint of sexual impropriety. In *Point of Departure: Experiment in Biography*, Cameron recounts how he commissioned an illustration to accompany the story of a young girl's murder. The enthusiastic artist showed her cut throat in almost clinical detail—a torn tendon, severed blood vessel, and blood that streamed into the rain-swept gutter. When Cameron confidently took it to Mr. McDonald for approval,

> he blenched. He tore it from my hand and studied it aghast and in speechless outrage. Finally he said: "You must be mad!"
>
> Accepting that I might possible on this occasion have overdone it, I murmured: "It is a bit strong, maybe."
>
> "Strong, strong," cried Mr. McDonald. "It's no' a question o' strong; it's no a bad scene. But for God's sake, boy—look at the lassie's skirt; it's awa' above her knees!"
>
> Abashed, I realized what rule I had broken. I took the drawing back and had the hemline lowered a modest inch or two, and in the cover went, slit windpipe and all.[15]

Gender differentiation remained editorial policy, and publishers approached girl readers differently. They labeled magazines as either for boys or girls but rarely both. In the new century, girls were seen as having interests and were allowed a greater presence in their own serials and school stories. In stories that featured all-girl environments, girls were the central actors, and a life outside of the home became possible. Though their domestic roles were upheld, females were slowly allowed to descend from their pedestals, and even in boys' books, girls began to make appearances as useful helpmates and companions.

* * *

By the end of the nineteenth century, the separate spheres theory, which had relegated women to roles of passive domesticity, was under attack, overtly by feminists and covertly as a function of social changes that provided new aspirations of women and acceptance of some level of the irrepressibility in girls. In 1870 and 1882, the Married Woman's Property Act passed, and wives could own property. New schemes of national education allowed women to become literate (by 1900, the literacy rate for women had climbed to 73 percent). Unmarried women outnumbered married women, and females began to desire the careers and higher education they'd been denied. Girls' periodicals were part of a mechanism that eventually encouraged a measure of female independence, though editors fought last-ditch efforts to maintain domestic roles. The needs of respectable girls were addressed in 1880 by the publication of the *Girl's Own Paper*; like other middle-class girls' publications to come, the magazine focused on domestic life. It purveyed Yongeian traditions in which girls were to be inculcated with missions of passivity and serving others, their life limited to the home or charity work. Unlike boys' serials, which put the imagination to work and used adventure and action to instill the masculine code, girls had to be protected from passion and experience. The essence of girlhood lay in passivity and spiritual qualities rather than in actions: "Let our girls aim at being nothing but women."[16] Eventually other magazines (such as the *Girl's Realm*) appeared: these were aimed at younger girls than those of the *Girls Own Paper* and were more progressive. There was a surge of girls' adventure books, such as the 150 titles written by Bessie Marchant ("the girls' Henty").

In the Edwardian era, feminism was a presence (this was when the movement turned militant), and great concern was exercised to protect girls from the siren songs of the New Woman.[17] Girls desperately wanted empowerment and some of the pleasures allotted to boys. They tried to join the scouting movement so that they could wear uniforms, march, and acquire survival skills, but there was immediate pushback. Baden-Powell was appalled at the notion of girls behaving like boys ("One doesn't want women to be soldiers" and "We none of us like women who ape men").[18] Baden-Powell and his sister Agnes set up the Girl Guides, with their official code of practice: *Girl Guides: A Suggestion for Character Training for Girls*. Just as Boy Scouts were to be trained in manliness, Girl Guides were to learn a womanliness that would enable them to become "future matrimonial and maternal helpmates of Scouting Englishmen."[19] They were to learn to be diligent, cheery, and self-controlled, to suffer silently and exercise quiet self-restraint and "uphold the honor and high character of our nation at home."[20] Domestic mandates were sugarcoated by some measure of adventure and excitement.

New forms of girls' school stories and fiction were allowing girls more scope for exuberance and tomboyishness, but authors were still driving with the brakes on. They had to write with a careful eye to propriety and ensure that girls aimed for marriage and domesticity. Nevertheless, school stories provided "the notion of an independent female community within which female adolescence can find scope for redefinition."[21] In school stories such as Angela Brazil's *The Fortunes of Philippa* (1906), girls were allowed a measure of spirit and more independence than allowed at home. Brazil and others took "the boarding school, a place of safety and closure, always ideals of female destiny, and made it into a site of adventure, experience and opportunity."[22] Life did not revolve around boys in a world where girls were the central characters. Games eventually became a force in girls' stories as they had in boys' public school stories, and girls took on other public school values. In Brazil's *A Patriotic School-girl* (1918), female characters were allowed a measure of heroism, and a typical interwar plot would involve a falsely accused schoolgirl who will not betray the real culprit. Girls, as young knights, take on the "distinctively English" values of public school boys: "The English girl is a slim, upright figure, who will stand up against anyone in a just cause, perform acts of bravery (especially in rescuing people from drowning), but modestly refuse public acknowledgement of her actions. She will not countenance the slightest deviation from her code of honor."[23] While often honorable, fictional schoolgirls tended to be of average goodness, which made them easier to relate to. The notions of higher education and access to a wider world were there, underneath the jolly accounts of school life.

It's not that Angela Brazil necessarily thought through women's roles and issues of character. It seems likely that she wrote to entertain herself and portrayed school as a kind of fantasy world that she wished she had inhabited as a child. In *The Heirs of Tom Brown: The English School Story*, Isabel Quigly makes the case that Brazil herself conforms exactly to a type of fictional character, a writer of bad children's books. As revealed in her autobiography (and some would say in her books, though less so), Brazil comes across as coy and in arrested development. The unmarried Brazil thought of herself as a "chronic child" and

> she lived in a world of exciting fantasy in which everything she experienced or remembered was recycled at a girlish level of fun; she believed in—or at least talked about—fairies, pixies, and "little people," seemed genuinely fond of the company, the chatter, the letters of schoolgirls and the memory of her own schooldays, and gave children's parties, with games and rich, sweet food, not just to children but to (sometimes disgruntled) adults. A narcissistic, prosy child who happened to grow up and grow old but never lost the self-admiring attitudes that made her see herself, idealised, in her own heroines.[24]

To Quigly, Brazil is a perennial juvenile who wrote flawed books: "What is limiting and wrong and absurd is not the set-up of the stories but the outlook that produced them, the total lack of irony that can say: 'I still can't quite, quite believe it—it's too absolutely, perfectly, deliciously scrumshus,' bleated Gwen hysterically."[25] The dialogue in girls' school story fiction is often extremely girlish: holidays were "holls"—"jolly" and "absolutely ripping." One could make the case that Brazil's school stories were kitschy imitations of early boys' schools stories and bore the ossified values of a dead world, but fans see them as deserving praise and pose Brazil as a laudable popularizer of a genre that has had significant effects on the consciousness of generations of girls. She helped sweep away Victorian "mawkishness and smothering dialogue"[26] and portrayed lively girls.

Brazil wrote fifty school story books over the course of forty years. She was one of the "Big Four of Girls' Fiction," along with Elsie Oxenham (fifty-two books), Dorita Fairlie Bruce (twenty-eight books), and Elinor Brent-Dyer (fifty-nine books about one school). The Big Four's heyday was during the interwar period, when the girls' school story picked up steam in terms of offering a radicalizing message and widening the horizons of young readers. Judith Humphrey, in *The English Girls' Story: Subversion and Challenge in a Traditional, Conservative Literary Genre,* makes the case that interwar books showed women as active and physically, mentally, and morally strong: "girl as rescuer not rescued, achiever not spectator, woman as autonomous and authoritative, creating her own story." [27]

Girls gave up "their affectionate Brazil-like ways and became more androgynous, even being given boys' names at times or hermaphroditic nicknames": Freddie and Bill, Twerp, and Midge. They cut their hair, eschewed prettiness, and played sports, an activity no longer considered unhealthy for girls and unfeminine. A girl no longer had to be passive and sentimental. Indeed, Brazil even used sports as an antidote to these states.

> Cynthia Greene falls in love with a soldier and languishes until teased out of it by the Games Prefect, who confiscates her Poems of Love and substitutes instead a Manual of Cricket with the comment, "I'm not going to have all those Juniors wandering about the garden reading poetry instead of practicing their cricket—it's not good enough!" [28]

Some stories come across as farces—comedies based on unlikely situations and exaggerated effects; contemporary adults thought of them as pulp fiction, and some girls' schools banned them as a silly waste of time. But there was a lot going on below the surface. While the girl characters were always channeled toward marriage, examples of strong, intelligent, well-educated women (often headmistresses) countered stereotypes of unmarried career women as dried-up failures. A substantive education had been denied to most women throughout the nineteenth century; in place of academics, they were given training in the roles and functions that society had allotted to females. It was hard to maintain prevalent notions of female vacuity and a woman's place as being in the home, when girls were allowed out to leave home and enter an environment where education and learning were valued and intelligence in a woman was acceptable. Author Elinor Brent-Dyer was known for portraying authentic classrooms and was interested in the pupils "acquiring depth of knowledge and active, thinking minds—in becoming intelligent, autonomous people." [29] Her girls' stories helped make that happen.

* * *

While girls' school stories were popular and persisted in both serial and book form until the 1960s, serial school stories for boys were largely discontinued during the Second World War. They had had a great run. By the First World War, Harmsworth's *Magnet* and *Gem* had achieved dominance in the school stories market. The prolific author Charles Hamilton, writing under the pen name of Frank Richards, would ultimately churn out four thousand school stories, mostly notably those about Greyfriars School. This series ran from 1908 to 1940 in *Magnet*; Richards's stories then appeared in book form until his death in 1961. While the Greyfriars stories had many of the conventions of *Tom Brown's Schooldays* (sports, fighting, bullying, and beatings), the emphasis was on amusement rather than religion, character development, and socialization. The stories were aloft from social issues of the day: war, sex, poverty, and class were never mentioned. In fact, Richards did not believe in politics and was blind to his own extreme conservatism. There was very little violence, just some ragging, and games were not compulsive, though sports success did come with recognition. Richards was also anti-intellectual, once writing, "If there is a Tchekov among my readers, I fervently hope that the effects of *The Magnet* will be to turn him into a Bob Cherry!"[30] Cherry was an exuberant and energetic sportsman.

The prominent Greyfriars characters are variations on normal, high-spirited British boys. Form Captain Harry Wharton takes leadership seriously and is a founding member of the Famous Four, later known as the Famous Five. Wharton, Cherry, Frank Nugent (self-effacing and loyal), Johnny Bull, and Hurree Singh (the Nabob of Bhanipur) were great friends. That the first four were considered to be British types was manifest in the character and name of Johnny Bull, a link to John Bull, the personification of Britain and England that is often featured in cartoons. John Bull has been described by Washington Irving as

> [a] plain, downright, matter-of-fact fellow, with much less of poetry about him than rich prose. There is little of romance in his nature, but a vast deal of a strong natural feeling. He excels in humor more than in wit; is jolly rather than gay; melancholy rather than morose; can easily be moved to a sudden tear or surprised into a broad laugh; but he loathes sentiment and has no turn for light pleasantry. He is a boon companion, if you allow him to have his humor and to talk about himself; and he will stand by a friend in a quarrel with life and purse, however soundly he may be cudgelled.[31]

Richards's Johnny Bull is plainspoken, bullheaded, Yorkshire bred, and prone to saying, "I told you so." Irving thought that the English were captivated by their eccentric national caricature because John Bull expressed something particular to their national character: "their love for what is blunt, comic, and familiar. . . . They have taken a singular delight in exhibiting their most private foibles in a laughable point of view."[32] Richards played to this kind of popular humor.

Foreigners, who could be good guys or villains, were stereotyped and cast as comic relief. Hurree Jamset Ram Singh (nicknamed "Inky") was a figure of fun in terms of his amusing way of talking: he once tried to induce his "esteemed and ludicrous chums ceasefully to stop talking slangfully and to use speakfully only the pureful and honoured English language as taught by my learned and preposterous native tutors in Bhanipur."[33] Unlike Singh, who was generally respected, Heracles Ionides, son of a wealthy Greek and much prone to heavy use of hair oil, was not. There were many idiosyncratic characters, such as reckless Herbert Vernon-Smith, a bounder and occasional blackguard; Gerald Loder, a Sixth Form prefect who liked to torment fags; and the avaricious Fisher Tarleton Fish, a brash and obnoxious American. The slim, blue-eyed Lord Maulever, a languid aristocrat who was actually a good judge of character, "would doubtless have become one of those heroic silly asses."[34] Maulever's contemporary adult personifications were aristocratic detectives Albert Campion and Lord Peter Wimsey, whose monocles and seeming idiocy masked razor sharp minds and considerable courage. In boys' school stories, there were weak characters and strong ones, slackers, jokers, and Billy Bunter, who stood alone.

Bunter, an amusing antihero, was in almost every Greyfriars story and eventually appeared in over thirty books and forty-five television shows. He became a household word. A larger-than-life character, Bunter came across as owl-like because he wore spectacles and was fat and bulged out of his clothes; an insatiable glutton, he stole everyone's tuck. To further his shameless and blatant machinations, he feigned afflictions and affection and claimed credit for others' actions. He never had any money and was notorious for claiming that a postal order was coming momentarily. His laziness, cowardliness, greed, snobbishness, and stupidity made him the foil and butt of other characters. Always in trouble, usually as the result of his denseness, Bunter never shut up and was known for exchanges such as this, when he was accused of playing pranks with a pin:

> "No Sir! Nothing of the kind," sputtered the confused fat owl. "I never had a pin, sir. Besides, fellows are allowed to have pins, sir I-I-I was going to pin a page into my Latin grammar, sir. Not that I had a pin!" added Bunter cautiously. "You can ask Skinner, sir. He knows—he gave it to me."

Or this one:

> "Please sir," gasped Bunter, "it wasn't me who ragged your study!" "What?" snapped the Remove master. "You should say, 'It was not I,' Bunter." "Oh, sir," said the Oaf of the Remove, blinking. "I never thought it was you!" "Wh-a-at?" "It stands to reason you wouldn't rag your own study, sir!"

Bunter seemed totally unaffected by the kicks administered by his fellow students or the canings of the masters. Oddly enough, he wasn't unpopular: "In the vast acreage of Frank Richards' never-never land, it was the despised outsider, who never became accepted as part of anyone's cozy study life at Greyfriars who took over."[35]

Interwar boys' school stories featured the remnants of Tom Brown–like manners and rituals, shorn of their spiritual components. Their purpose was entertainment, not socialization. According to author Geoffrey Trease, "a new story in 1920 or 1930 tended to be a fossil in which one could trace the essential characteristics of one written in 1880 or 1890."[36] It was their fossilized nature—or perhaps, more important, the lack of fit with contemporary society—as well as their vulgarization and homogenization—that led boys' school stories to have largely run their course by the Second World War. According to Quigly, the school story was popular and influential because of its "sense of continuity and certainty, the ritual and repetition, and a feeling that it reflected, if only remotely, something real, some ideas that mattered. When the reality behind it was clearly crumbling and the ideas no longer mattered, it seemed empty, ridiculous, almost tasteless."[37] In 1940 George Orwell targeted Amalgamated Press and Frank Richards in an essay called "Boys' Weeklies." Claiming that all fiction is reactionary and geared toward the interests of the ruling class, Orwell said that boys' fiction is above all "sodden" in outmoded prewar ideas about class and race, a fact that is important if one believes that what is read in childhood leaves an impression: "It is probable that many people who would consider themselves extremely sophisticated and 'advanced' are actually carrying through life an imaginative background which they acquired in childhood from (for instance) Sapper and Ian Hay."[38] According to Orwell, the imaginative world that was fed to boys in interwar school stories was snobbish and stagnant:

> The year is 1910 or 1940, but it is all the same. You are at Greyfriars, a rosy-cheeked boy of fourteen in posh, tailor-made clothes, sitting down to tea in your study on the Remove passage after an exciting game of football which was won by an odd goal in the last half-minute. The ivy clusters thickly round the old grey stones. . . . At the outposts of Empire the monocled Englishmen are holding the niggers at bay. . . . Everything is safe, solid and unquestionable. Everything will be the same forever and ever.[39]

In a spirited defense of his school stories, Richards countered with the following plea:

> Let youth be happy, or as happy as possible. . . . Every day of happiness, illusory or otherwise . . . and most happiness is illusory—is so much to the good. It will help to give the boy confidence and hope. Frank Richards tells him that there are some splendid fellows in a

world that is, after all, a decent sort of place. He likes to think himself one of these fellows, and is happy in his day-dreams.[40]

With the Second World War casting shadows, Richards thought that the British child needed "a capacity for laughter and the pursuit of the comic . . . to overcome the gloom—indeed blackout—of the future."[41] And Orwell eventually acknowledged the role of Richards and serials in training his readers in "comedy, courage and comradeship, all of which they would need."[42] If one accepts the argument that the boys' serial school story was based on "certainty and self-confidence, insularity, cheerfulness, and acceptance of the accepted,"[43] then the subgenre's uneasy fit with a gloomy, self-conscious, and uncertain world may explain why boys' serials did not survive the war and were soon transformed into comics. It is interesting to reverse the logic to account for why girls' school stories remained popular for another twenty years. I think it was that they entertained girls, made them happy, and bolstered confidence. Girls could still absorb from them content and values conducive to empowerment. They provided something girls wanted, needed, and accepted in terms of identity.

* * *

The notion of popular interwar fiction as fossilized remains is also an issue in looking at memorable books. Many twentieth-century children's authors continued in the tradition of Beatrix Potter, who advocated a life lived in freedom and in accordance with one's nature, and E. Nesbit, whose escapist vision posed childhood as a playful time, satisfying in itself. Nesbit influenced one of the main strands of contemporary children's literature: stories about small adventures, juxtaposed against a secure domestic background. P. L. Travers, A. A. Milne, and Arthur Ransome followed her lead in writing children's stories grounded in daily life. They sustained her tension between the exciting and the prosaic and her notion of childhood as a series of adventures. While most children's books of the late 1920s and 1930s can be seen as carrying forward Edwardian attitudes and tropes, the books with enduring appeal were original. A. A. Milne held on to the fantasy mode and extended the irony introduced by Potter and Nesbit; his works were far more than the last gasp of the Beautiful Child cult. And while Arthur Ransome owes much to Nesbit and Kenneth Grahame, he provided realism grounded in place and a presence that marks him as something more than the "last Edwardian."

Milne can be regarded as a survivor of the sentimental late Victorian era because he supported the myth of England as a golden rural world, a place where right feeling was still to be found.[44] However, he ushered irony into the world of romanticized childhood. Christopher Robin, the

son who inspired his poems and children's books, is certainly not portrayed as a moral icon or symbol of eternal innocence. The boy is a dear
but very real. In 1923 Milne published a poem, "Vespers," that has been
described as the last major appearance in English literature of the Beautiful Child.[45] In it, the first stanza introduces Christopher Robin at two
years old, bowing his little golden head while kneeling at his prayers. But
the vision of innocence gives way in the next few stanzas. The boy is just
parroting his prayers, his mind instead on more important things—the
bath he just took and his hooded dressing gown. In the end, he remem-
bers to thank God for the lovely day and concludes with "God bless me."
Milne recognized that along with artless beauty and innocent grace, children are possessed of an almost ruthless narcissism.[46] It was hardly a
Wordsworthian view of childhood, but sentimentalists around the world
hung illustrated copies of "Vespers" in nurseries, entirely missing the
irony.

Unlike many of his Victorian predecessors, such as Burnett, Milne
enjoyed a happy childhood. Young Alan was intellectually precocious
and good in sports. He admired his schoolmaster father intensely and
would adore his brother Ken all his life. After Ken's death, Milne quoted
Leigh Hunt's poem:

> Jenny kiss'd me when we met,
> Jumping from the chair she sat in;
> Time, you thief, who love to get
> Sweets into your list, put that in!
> Say I'm weary, say I'm sad,
> Say that health and wealth have missed me,
> Say I'm growing old, but add
> Jenny kiss'd me.

He said that throughout his life he had never lost his brother, that he
remained a "sweet" (a lovely, beneficial element) to Milne.[47] I think the
true "Jenny's kiss" for Milne was a happy childhood. Except for his
World War I service, his adulthood was happy too. He did well at Cambridge University, graduating in 1903, and found success as a writer for
Punch, the British satirical magazine. He married a woman who shared
his sense of humor, and he enjoyed success as a playwright. By all accounts, Milne was content. His happy adulthood and the culture of postwar blitheness help to explain why his vision of the child is more whimsical than stylized and Romantic.

In 1924, the year after "Vespers" appeared, Milne began to sketch out
some light verses about children. About the poems, he wrote to a friend,
"I am writing a book of children's verses. Like Stevenson, only better. No,
not a bit like Stevenson really. More like Milne. But they are a curious
collection; some *for* children, some *about* children, some by, with or from
children."[48] Milne's book, like Stevenson's *A Child's Garden of Verses*, con-

veyed comfortable visions of childhood as a happy, unsullied existence that would hit the mark with children and adults. But Milne was of another era, and his stories were more self-conscious, ironic, and tongue-in-cheek.

Milne's stories revolve around an imaginary, self-contained community of animals (modeled, in part, on toys purchased at Harrods) and a young boy, Christopher Robin. In the Hundred Acre Wood, adults are absent, there are few rules, and boy and animals are independent. There is plenty of food and adventures involving birthdays, explorations, tree-houses, jokes, and a small element of natural danger. The title of the first collection, *When We Were Very Young*, raises the question of who the book is for. It was reviewed as a children's book, but its appeal was such that adults bought it for themselves. It sold like hotcakes despite a nasty review by critic Geoffrey Grigson, who found the Romantic innocence tatty and the poems smug and snobbish. Grigson advised parents that in Milne's book, they could be sure to finding a Little Lord Fauntleroy stripped of frills and velvet and no longer an heir, but still the Beautiful Child. For the most part, however, readers loved the middle-class complacency that Grigson mercilessly decried, perhaps because of the irony that Grigson missed; while he took the books seriously, his adult readers did not.[49] Perhaps the survivors of World War I just wanted to enjoy poems and stories that were fun to quote and easily parodied. Readers in the 1920s had had their innocence tempered by war and wanted to revisit it. But even those who thought that sweetness and goodness could still be real and possible and relevant knew that it couldn't exist without some leavening.

A key difference between Milne and his late Victorian literary predecessors is that his sights were not set on achieving aesthetic perfection and providing icons of absolute goodness. In *When We Were Very Young* (1924), *Winnie the Pooh* (1926), and *The House at Pooh Corner* (1928), he created a self-contained child-oriented world that appealed to his era. The stories had the simplicity and power of animal fables and nursery rhymes and satisfied in much the same way. Milne's language was simple and child friendly. Much of the whimsy came in the way that he played with words. Pooh, "a Bear of Very Little Brain," puzzles over what "Crustimoney Proseedcake" (customary procedure) means but is reassured when told that it is the thing to do. Milne had fun with spelling and introduced new creatures called "Heffalumps." He conveyed portent by using capital letters: "Kanga was Generally Regarded as One of the Fiercer Animals." Reminiscent of an older style of writing, capitals conveyed a sense of wide-eyed and childlike innocence and earnestness. The playfulness of the language and conventions mocked the seriousness of the past.

Unlike perfect Little Lord Fauntleroy, Christopher Robin occasionally bluffs his way along but overall is a kind and supportive friend. He often saves the day, and the animals look up to him the way that children often look to adults, with respect and deference. And he always comes through in some form. Ultimately, Milne's characters—Pooh especially—are lovable despite being occasionally obtuse and selfish. Their mistakes are portrayed as a natural part of being human. When Pooh eats Eeyore's birthday present on his way to deliver it (honey, after all, is his favorite food), it is okay. All is forgiven when Christopher blurts that he loves him. Pooh is benignly self-centered, greedy about food, and occasionally ignorant and boastful but also occasionally brave and loyal. It was a new version of goodness in children's literature that owed more to the Edwardians than the late Victorians.

Just as *A Child's Garden of Verses* reminded of childish pleasures and simple joys, Milne offered readers characters that could be new "favorite things" to improve the post–World War I mood of England. He assembled woods, a lovable child, and endearing and very human animals into an enchanting, deceptively simple world whose ironies are so gentle that a reader can choose to ignore them altogether. The illustrations by E. H. Shepherd captured the safety and charm of this world, in the same way that Crane, Caldecott, and Greenaway did but without evoking the historical past. The pictures were also quirky, endearing, and relaxed images of a boy that were atypical of the late Victorian era.

Milne's nostalgia was pervasive but uncomplicated: he enjoyed being nostalgic. Indeed, the adult Christopher Robin wrote that his father's most deeply felt emotion was nostalgia for his own childhood.[50] Milne's nostalgia was not the elegiac kind of Ruskin or Carroll, Caldecott or Greenaway, and the world that he created was not meant to be an impetus to spirituality, as was that of Yonge, Farrar, or Hughes. He did not worship children, nor did he idealize purity. He handled innocence with tongue in cheek rather than with spiritual reverence. His work is nuanced and celebrates a variety of human expression that contrasts sharply with the flat portrayals of Burnett's early books and Greenaway's stylized images. The Pooh books still offer a Romantic treatment of childhood, but Milne's irony and satire of human nature marked the end of attempts to freeze children in goodness and tout the ideal child as selfless. With Milne's example, the child in children's books has become no less beautiful, endearing, or lovely for being also flawed. Milne's portrait of Christopher Robin, a very young child, expresses new humanistic-Romantic notions of the English character that were emerging in the twentieth century.

* * *

Arthur Ransome's books spoke about and to somewhat older children, ages nine to twelve. In his twelve children's books, published between 1930 and 1948, three sets of siblings have substantive adventures, primarily on boats and in isolated settings in England. Ransome's respect for the competency and potential of children is obvious in every line. He took over from where the Edwardians left off, portraying childhood as a place to play but happiness as a by-product of acquiring skills and experiences and achieving competency. He wrote from the base of a happy childhood and a fulfilled adulthood, as did Milne. When writing his first book for children, at the age of forty-six, his emotional involvement was such that night after night he used to carry the unfinished manuscript of *Swallows and Amazons* to his cottage and place it so that he "could reach out and lay my hand on it in the dark beside my bed."[51] This echoes James Barrie's reaction to the publication of his first magazine article in 1833: "I walked down to Westminster Hall, and turned into it for half an hour, because my eyes were so dimmed with joy and pride, that they could not bear the street, and were not fit to be seen there."[52]

Like Henty and Ballantyne, Ransome had an adventurous and quirky life. He led a Bohemian lifestyle as a hack writer in fin de siècle London and lived dangerously as a correspondent in Russia during the revolution. Like Grahame, Ransome adored nature and the outdoors and messing about in boats. Like Nesbit, he loved to recount the small adventures of bands of children. But his focus was on realism, naturalism, and the child's perspective. He takes the time to create a full picture of daily life. In his books, whole chapters are descriptions of what the children eat and drink; their activities, which include sailing, swimming, fishing, and camping; and the interactions among siblings.

Ransome's young characters were believable, their behavior and achievements consistent with their age and circumstances. The dangers were real and sometimes frightening. In *We Didn't Mean to Go to Sea*, the children must cope when the boat on which they are spending the night drags anchor and drifts out to sea in dense fog. While seasick and scared, they save themselves by remaining coolheaded and practical. In Ransome's books, youthful heroism is un-self-conscious and understated; indeed, the children are possessed of a reserve and self-restraint that can be seen as peculiarly English.[53]

Ransome shared a quiet sort of happiness that mirrored the yearning for peace that preoccupied post –World War I adult society. He gave a whole new twist to the holidays by focusing on the vacation adventures (over a period of five years) of three different sets of children. Championing leisure came naturally to a man who spent most of his life "looking forward to, enjoying or looking nostalgically back" at his own vacations.[54] A countryman by nature, Ransome had always lived for holidays, which from youth were spent in the Lake District and later in East Anglia. In his autobiography, he recounts a ritual performed throughout his life: every time Ransome arrived at Conistan Water, he would run down and dip his hand in the water, "as a greeting to the beloved lake or as proof to myself that I had indeed come home."[55] Ransome would set his stories in locations where he had grown up and flourished.

He identified himself with literary adventures and writers from an early age. His mother read aloud to him, and his grandmother took him to tea in a garden where, "silently worshipping," he shook hands with Ballantyne. At the age of four, Ransome began reading and rereading *Robinson Crusoe* and, at eight, wrote a story about a desert island. He clung to his ambition to be a writer in the face of parental disapproval. Young Arthur loved *Treasure Island* and would later have his characters dream of desert islands and channel Defoe and Stevenson in real life and fantastic adventures. In Ransome's *Swallows and Amazons* (1930), four Walker siblings children set up camp, all by themselves, on an island in the English Lake District. Their small library includes *Robinson Crusoe* because, as Titty says, "it tells you just what to do on an island." The children often acted out the plots and characters they had read about: for example, in *The Big Six* (1940), they mimicked the Big Five, Scotland Yard detectives, whose adventures were a feature of contemporary serials.[56] Readers would in turn act out scenes from Ransome's books and the worlds he created. The roles of Master, Mate, Able-seaman, and Ship's Boy assumed by the Walker children were reprised endlessly by thousands of readers, including Princess Elizabeth and her sister Margaret.

The adult Ransome was considered "child-like" in that he was an enthusiast who sailed, fished, and wrote with passion. What made Ransome's books so unique was his ability to engage children in ordinary and age-appropriate activities of an absorbing nature. Characters were vested in his passion for outdoor life, fascination with how things worked, and the survival skills he valued—such as the ability to make maps, navigate with a compass, devise a signaling system, run homing pigeons, skin a rabbit, make a broom, and light fires with sticks. Ransome's emphasis on the acquisition of skills was mirrored in the career books of contemporary Noel Streatfeild, especially in her first book, *Ballet Shoes* (1936). She was an actress, and her books show children struggling to achieve careers in the arts.

Like his early heroes, Henty and Ballantyne, Ransome found detail absorbing and carried on the Victorian preoccupation with useful knowledge. In *Coot Club*, a seaman initiates the children into the mysteries of ropes and knots: "Bowlines and Fisherman's and Carrick bends, Rolling, Blackwall, Timber and Handspike hitches, Cat's Paws and Sheepshanks, Eye splices and Long splices, Grommets and a Selvagee strop." The technical skills and lore acquired through reading Ransome's books stayed with readers for life: as one adult commented, "when I finally had a chance to sit at the tiller of a dinghy, I knew the heft, the feel and the arcane language as though I were a secret inhabitant of a nautical world. As, indeed, I was."[57] Ransome also provided principles of conduct and influenced those with something to prove. Commander Walker's dictum—"Grab a chance and you won't be sorry for a might-have-been"—was adopted by noted mariner and author Eric Hiscock. In preparation for circumnavigating the world, Hiscock had the motto carved on the beam above the companionway of *Wanderer III*.[58]

Ransome doesn't seek to control or sentimentalize children. The children act out of a code of values that is based on family solidarity and self-reliance, and the parents trust the children enough to let them have real adventures. The parental style is set immediately in *Swallows and Amazons* when Mother receives a telegram from her husband, an active duty naval officer. Commander Walker advises her to let the four children take a dinghy out to Wild Cat Island and camp all by themselves: "Better drowned than duffers if not duffers won't drown." For the most part, adults (called "natives" by the children) are good-natured and willing to support the children's adventures and games. The rural folk are "never mere ciphers; they have definite character, unlike the background yokels of so many children's books."[59]

According to biographer Peter Hunt, Ransome offered a vision of a democracy of childhood—"not so much an ideal world in which children can play, but a world of ideals to which his readers can aspire: a world of equality and respect."[60] Boys and girls worked together and were supported by friendly adults who respected their capabilities and fostered independence. The situations were credible and the characters memorable. Readers could identify with at least one of the different types—domestically inclined Susan; Titty, the dreamer; the tomboy, Nancy; Roger, who is obsessed with chocolate and engines; the studious Dick (a "swot"), who is interested in science; and the Romantic Dorothea, who yearns to be a writer. Ransome validated the various personalities by demonstrating each child's contribution to the group and adventures. His young characters have integrity and live by a code of ethics and principled behavior, which is demonstrated through actions and responses. Loyalty, solidarity, and familial bonds are taken for granted. There were direct lines to late Victorian moral codes, and self-sufficiency and a stiff upper lip were obligatory, but right conduct was illustrated rather than articulated or preached. The children were kind, game, and loyal, and it has been suggested that Ransome thought being nice was essential to being happy.[61]

Milne's and Ransome's interwar children's books had understated cultural heft and promoted an Englishness that was gentle and intrinsic. While their visions were conservative in many ways, the Englishness they wove into their books was no longer the exclusive prerogative of the upper middle class. Becoming a gentleman or a lady involved something more than mastery of a code and moral superiority; it wasn't the exclusive property of boys and girls and men and women who remained rigidly in role. Males were increasingly domesticated and females hardier; the quieter virtues were celebrated. There was a selection process under way in which certain values previously lumped into a conservative middle-class vision and coded as English came up against new values and post–World War I mentalities. The pulse of Englishness stabilized around a love of place and country (with less militarist overtones), and a realism that became a taken-for-granted element within children's literature, much like religion and utilitarian rationalism had transmuted into every-day morality in the nineteenth century. Here we see a down-to-earth Englishness in books that support group solidarity and an identity with potential for rooting children in what was increasingly a troubled, complex world. It would help sustain the British in the Second World War.

Swallows and Amazons was not an immediate best-seller. For a while, it was submerged in "an ocean of terrible trash . . . unreal school stories, impossible adventure, half-witted fairy tales."[62] Ransome helped turn the tide and create a market for quality books. The new aspects that Ransome brought to the genre have led him to be known as the father of modern British children's literature.[63] Ultimately, new sources of reviews (such as the *Times Supplement*) and incentives for higher literary standards (such as the annual Carnegie Medal begun in 1936) were put in place. The sixth book in the Swallows and Amazons series, *Pigeon Post*, won the first Carnegie Medal. The medal is awarded annually in Britain for an out-standing children's book, and a glance at the criteria reveals a close fit with what Ransome had to offer in terms of literary quality: a well-constructed plot, rounded characters interacting convincingly, and effective use of setting. The award's sponsors judged books on their literary criteria and, as well, believed that "the whole work should provide pleasure, not merely from the surface enjoyment of a good read, but also the deeper subconscious satisfaction of having gone through a vicarious, but at the time of reading, a real experience that is retained afterwards."[64] *Pigeon Post* (and the whole series) met this profile to an extraordinary degree. Ransome's many imitators would now be policed by professionals who took it upon themselves to judge literary quality and disseminate standards. Librarians began speaking out about what children should or should not be reading. In the 1950s, experts and reviewers in the field of children's literature led a backlash against pulp books and an adult revolt against the most popular British children's writer of the era, Enid Blyton.

* * *

In a time of the professionalization of children's literature, Enid Blyton wrote against conventions by eliminating the development of character and discomfort and tension altogether. She offered a watered-down realism. Her exploitation of the commercial potential of small adventures and her almost manic production of series books for various ages made Blyton the children's publishing phenomenon of the mid-twentieth century. While wildly popular with children, her retro perspectives on childhood and the trivialized Victorian and Edwardian middle-class values that she served up were a poor fit with post–World War II tastes. She rubbed adults the wrong way and became a lightning rod for criticism. In light of contemporary iterations of national consciousness that had been affected once again by global war, Blyton and others were accused of being un-English or, worse, expressing an Englishness that was unappealing and tawdry; her children came under fire as inappropriate models for a modern multicultural Britain.

Blyton was heir to Nesbit's tradition of middle-class siblings engaged in small, safe adventures, embroidered upon by Milne, who wrote about an enchanted forest and a band of small friends free of nursery rules, and Ransome, who rooted adventure in reality and a strong sense of place. Blyton wrote family stories, animal stories, moral tales, and adventure tales about treasure, caves, islands, circuses, and holiday fun; two well-known series involved groups of children called the "Famous Five" (1942) and the "Sacred Seven" (1947). Her high-quality pioneering work in the 1940s has been overshadowed by what has been called a "triumphant [publishing] machine": her success in merchandising the series concept in the 1950s was such that the shelves of Britain's libraries were host to hundreds of thousands of her books.[65] Children found them addicting. They were in some sense a replacement for the children's magazines, many of which did not survive the Second World War. Blyton's books carried on the tradition of serial stories but were highly sanitized and geared mainly for preadolescents.

With Blyton, we have an author who turned the serial sensibility into book form. The stories were easy to read and well written, the characters accessible and stereotypical, the worlds they inhabited protected, and the focus on action. Blyton was determined to give children what they liked—undemanding enjoyment—and they responded with adoration.[66] But unlike Potter's, Nesbit's, Milne's, and Ransome's stories, which could be read and reread with pleasure by all ages, Blyton's books tended to be rather flavorless and to appeal to the young child. It was a taste children grew out of rather quickly.

Blyton's books came to represent the standardization and stagnation of the dynamic of small holiday adventures and were dismissed from literary discussions for their lack of nuance, retreat into trite notions of goodness, and political incorrectness. In the 1950s, educators, librarians, and reviewers began to turn against them for perceived undercurrents of racism (black wolligogs that served as villains in a Toyland tale), elitism ("All four boys admired Bob and liked him, and because he was better dressed than they were and came from a better home they were proud to have him share their cellar," in *The Six Bad Boys*), superficiality, and overall literary mediocrity. Blyton had teamed up with a clever artist and savvy editor to develop her Noddy books, and they sold millions of copies and turned the doll Noddy into a household name. Adored by children, the character became a favorite target for unenchanted adults. While Blyton thought of Noddy as charming and childlike, critics characterized him as a numbskull who sucked up to authority. Blyton seemed to have deteriorated after the war: her better characters dwindling into comparative insignificance before the all-conquering grotesque Noddy: as one critic quipped, "heroes declined and boobies advanced. It was a fair comment on the Britain of the 1950s."[67] Needless to say, Noddy was considered an undesirable model for British children, and Blyton herself engendered a level of distaste. In parallels drawn between Angela Brazil and Enid Blyton, Brazil has been posed as slightly more likable: each was snobbish, self-regarding, fey, self-centered, and strong willed, "at once wildly romantic and a tough businesswoman with a touch of meanness."[68]

Blyton was an uncomfortable mixture of cloying sentimentality and post-Victorian didacticism. Unlike Nesbit, Potter, Milne, and Grahame, her voice was complacently "aunt-like" and imbued with "teacherliness."[69] A conformist, she wanted to protect her readers from reality and provide them with a world that was predictable and undemanding. In a letter printed in the *Library Association Record* in September 1940, Blyton described her books as giving "children a feeling of security as well as pleasure—they know they will never find anything wrong, hideous, horrible, murderous or vulgar in my books, although there is plenty of excitement, mystery and fun. . . . I'm not out only to tell stories, much as I love this—I am out to inculcate decent thinking, loyalty, honesty, kindliness, and the things that children *should* be taught."[70] Conspicuous in its absence were the social criticism, subversiveness, irony, creativity, and realism that one would expect in contemporary works (and previous authors had set readers up to expect). Absent were elements of character development and inner growth that were becoming important factors in children's literature.

The Edwardian legacy placed the imagination and play at the forefront of notions about childhood. Romantic notions of the child as spontaneous and natural (i.e., living according to their innate proclivities rather than social templates) were firmly established at this time and carried to their extreme when Barrie confronted his audience with the implications of childish freedom as a static state. This paved the way for a divergence within notions of childhood that would come to characterize twentieth-century children's books. In serials and popular series like Blyton's, younger children were invited to "be" and play rather than to perform for adult expectations or engage with the hard work of self-development. In more substantive literary works, like those of Ransome, development within the genre was converging on older children, who would be asked to reject the allure of Peter Pan–like irresponsibility and grow up. Play helped them to do this. Side by side with literature of small adventures and happy escapism were stories with the mandate of self-development and psychological growth. There was a normalization of childhood and realistic approaches (even in fantasy works), and though happiness was the ultimate goal, it was to be found in achievement and inner growth rather than in escapism.

NOTES

1. Turner, *Boys Will Be Boys*, 10.
2. Turner, *Boys Will Be Boys*, 59.
3. Turner, *Boys Will Be Boys*, 118–19.
4. Castle, *Britannia's Children*, 4.
5. Orwell, "Boys' Weeklies and Frank Richards's Reply."
6. Castle, *Britannia's Children*, 173.
7. Trease, "The Revolution in Children's Literature," 14.
8. Bristow, *Empire Boys*, 100, 129.
9. Ashley, *George Alfred Henty*, 52.
10. Turner, *Boys Will Be Boys*, 123.
11. Turner, *Boys Will Be Boys*, 207.
12. Jacobs, *The Narnian*, 207.
13. Turner, *Boys Will Be Boys*, 231.
14. Castle, *Britannia's Children*, 167.
15. Cameron, *Point of Departure*, 32.
16. Mackay and Thane, "The Englishwoman," 199.
17. Reynolds and Humble, *Victorian Heroines*, 32.
18. Featherstone, *Englishness*, 35.
19. Featherstone, *Englishness*, 34.
20. Mackay and Thane, "The Englishwoman," 216.
21. Foster and Simmons, *What Katy Read*, 18.
22. Humphrey, *The English Girls' Story*, 26.
23. Mackay and Thane, "The Englishwoman," 221.
24. Quigly, *The Heirs of Tom Brown*, 215.
25. Quigly, *The Heirs of Tom Brown*, 218.
26. Cadogan and Craig, *You're a Brick, Angela!*, 53.
27. Humphrey, *The English Girls' Story*, 6.
28. Humphrey, *The English Girls' Story*, 153.
29. Humphrey, *The English Girls' Story*, 85.
30. Musgrave, *From Brown to Bunter*, 225.
31. Irving, *The Sketchbook*, 318.
32. Irving, *The Sketchbook*, 316.
33. Turner, *Boys Will Be Boys*, 206–7.
34. Turner, *Boys Will Be Boys*, 208.
35. Quigly, *The Heirs of Tom Brown*, 259.
36. Trease, "The Revolution in Children's Literature," 14.
37. Quigly, *The Heirs of Tom Brown*, 274.
38. Orwell, "Boys' Weeklies and Frank Richards's Reply."
39. Orwell, "Boys' Weeklies and Frank Richards's Reply."
40. Tucker, *The Child and the Book*, 124.
41. Edwards, *British Children's Fiction*, 11.
42. Edwards, *British Children's Fiction*, 68.
43. Quigly, *The Heirs of Tom Brown*, 276.
44. Carpenter, *Secret Gardens*, 210.
45. Carpenter, *Secret Gardens*, 196.
46. Milne, *It's Too Late Now*, 240.

47. Thwaite, *A. A. Milne: His Life*, 95.
48. Thwaite, *A. A. Milne: His Life*, 250.
49. Thwaite, *A. A. Milne: His Life*, 265.
50. Milne, *The Enchanted Places*, 160.
51. Ransome, *The Autobiography of Arthur Ransome*, 331.
52. Smiley, *Charles Dickens: A Penguin Life*, 1.
53. Giles and Middleton, "Introduction," 7.
54. Shelley, *Arthur Ransome*, 9.
55. Ransome, *The Autobiography of Arthur Ransome*, 26.
56. Hunt, *Arthur Ransome*, 59.
57. Hunt, *Arthur Ransome*, 142.
58. Shelley, *Arthur Ransome*, 48–49.
59. Shelley, *Arthur Ransome*, 40.
60. Hunt, *Arthur Ransome*, 143–44.
61. Shelley, *Arthur Ransome*, 60.
62. Hunt, *Arthur Ransome*, 140.
63. Hunt, *Arthur Ransome*, xii.
64. Chartered Institute of Library and Information Professionals, "The Carnegie Award Criteria."
65. Edwards, *British Children's Fiction*, 253.
66. Rudd, "From Froebel Teacher to English Disney," 257.
67. Edwards, *British Children's Fiction*, 67.
68. Quigly, *The Heirs of Tom Brown*, 215.
69. Hollindale, "'And Children Swarmed to Him Like Settlers,'" 275.
70. Stoney, *Enid Blyton: The Biography*, 212.

EIGHT

Autonomy and Affirmation

Narnia is a spiritual address, a world imbued with ultimate destinies deter-mined by profound personal choices. — Bruce Edwards

Edwardians often defined being good as retaining the heart and sensibil-ities of a child. While Kenneth Grahame encouraged this notion and of-fered escapism, beneath the hedonism of the carefree life on the river-bank, the notion of Arcadia, and the thrills of the Wild Wood lurked a subtext that the challenges of life must finally be faced. And many twen-tieth-century books took on this responsibility. A body of literature, no less entertaining than mass-market works, began encouraging children to grow up and struggle with moral questions and their own humanity. After all, with *Peter Pan* had come something of a warning of the fruitless-ness of staying a child forever, and authors began responding to a cultu-ral shift that posed maturing as inevitable and desirable. After Barrie's convincing demonstration of the pitfalls of eternal childishness, the en-thrallment with childhood was broken. The imagination was pressed into use to help young people, especially adolescents, make growing up a momentous quest.

Young people were given an important role in shaping their own choices and lives and saving the world. Authors offered youthful minds and souls more to work with in terms of the serious business of develop-ing a sense of self, autonomy, moral imagination, and a philosophy of life. There was a shift away from idealizing childhood (or freezing chil-dren in that state) and, instead, a growing inclination toward realism (even in fantasy literature) and appreciation of the child as possessing flaws and potential. Characters began to show an openness to negative and positive experiences, and they began to make high-stakes choices. In short, a lot more was expected of protagonists and child readers alike.

Recognition of a new audience—the older child—brought subtler age distinctions to the categorization of children's books. Twentieth-century children's literature is often characterized as having split into popular fiction for five- to eleven-year-olds, which usually provided a modicum of learning and celebrated small and safe adventures and fun, and books for twelve- to eighteen-year-olds (the latter referred to as "young adult" or "adolescent" literature), which often carried the mandate of self-development, dealing with harsh realities, and growing up. However, as the century wore on, there was so much blending and overlap between these categories that it is important to remember that modern children's literature is nevertheless one genre. The major achievement of twentieth-century children's authors was the development of the genre to encompass a fully fleshed out literature for children that incorporated compelling models of virtue based on autonomy and internal development.

The roots of this accomplishment lie in an early-twentieth-century shift in social attitudes: older children were now thought to be in a different stage of development from younger children and possessed of the necessary mental resources to deal with complexity. The field of psychology was rapidly providing new insight into human development and, by World War I, had established that while younger children concentrate on learning basic moral values and are particularly concerned with fairness, the older child has (or should have) different concerns. At this point in the evolution of children's literature, authors became increasingly interested in late childhood and then adolescence, periods when young people could think more abstractly and were ready for themes and plots that invited them to question dominant values.[1] This shift was encouraged by sociologist and educational reformer G. Stanley Hall's identification of adolescence as a discrete stage of development that allowed for more complex exploration of self and the development of "higher" and "more completely human" traits.[2] While Hall favored an authoritarian approach, he understood the importance of inspiring youth through a curriculum that was rich in myths, folk and fairy stories, classics (including *Robinson Crusoe*), Bible stories, and historical accounts of the deeds of great men.

The shift toward the humanistic exploration of self as a viable theme in children's literature built on the late-nineteenth-century adult fascination with self-expression, self-fulfillment, and discovering authenticity within and, then, the new spiritual and psychological understandings that came to the fore in the twentieth century. According to philosopher Charles Taylor, nineteenth-century Romantics believed in the epiphanies of the creative imagination.[3] These deep, soul-stirring experiences of truth provided access to some greater spiritual reality or significance that is the key to fullness, intensity of life, and wholeness. Previous chapters discuss how children's books and their images of childhood elicited intense emotional responses from children and adults. This played out when religious piety as well as rationalism gave way to the cult of the Beautiful Child and Romantic notions of innate innocence, spontaneity, and goodness within the child. Taylor believes that as late Victorian–era responses to beauty challenged the primacy of morality and forced its redefinition, epiphany increasingly took the place of religion.

In the twentieth century, children's fiction continued to provide the opportunity for epiphanies as well as refinement of the notion. Modern children's authors would return over and over to the conundrum of growing up and the importance of imagination and emotional engagement in the process. Readers experienced the transformation of Frances Hodgson Burnett's Colin and Mary as they discovered themselves in a secret garden. They learned about the rawness of human nature and the existence of evil from George Orwell and William Golding; the importance of taking a stand (and the possibility of redemption) from C. S. Lewis; and from J. R. R. Tolkien—the corruption of power, the necessity of personal choice, and the joys of fellowship. In the sometimes fine line between opposing elements, the center that held in children's literature was hope. The subtext was Englishness in its latest form.

We can make sense of the influence of such books (and new thoughts on the imagination and epiphany) through an after-the-fact recourse to the pop literature that has informed contemporary adult readers. Late in the twentieth century, lapsed priest Thomas Moore articulated the trend toward fascination with the imagination as an instrument of a new non-religious "soul."[4] Moore poses the imagination as allowing transcendent or spiritual experiences, such as laughter, play, and glimpses of truth. His work can help us to understand the role of children's fiction in allowing readers to tap into their souls via the imagination and feel wonder at the everydayness of our world while feeling awe at what is eternal and mysterious. Twentieth-century stories for older children are concerned with the foundations of identity—laid through the imagination working soulfully with the imagery of story. In engaging imaginatively with a story, readers navigate the psychic underworld, experience vicarious pain and pleasure, experience epiphany, and arrive at self-knowledge and self-acceptance. Imagination invests us in humanness and infuses life with significance.

Iconic twentieth-century children's authors put the idea of imagination to work in helping young people gain insight into why it was important to commit themselves to living honorably and authentically in a richly human environment. Authors offered older children numinous works that allowed them to channel epiphanies about human nature into self-awareness and a social conscience. Being good was a product of self-reflection, inward striving, and outward agency—you had to act on your beliefs. But you didn't have to be perfect.

* * *

In the literature emerging in the new century, children were portrayed with personal imperfections that made their plights moving and their accomplishments real. Frances Hodgson Burnett's *The Secret Garden* (1909) introduced to children's literature a new kind of child character, one proving that children were capable of transforming their own lives while inspiring others. The main characters—the orphaned Mary and her crippled cousin Colin—are quite unlike the beautiful and naturally good children in Burnett's previous books *Little Lord Fauntleroy* (1886) and *A Little Princess* (1905) and in much of the earlier children's literature. Instead, Mary and Colin are unattractive, obnoxious children. Raised in isolation by servants, Mary has no idea how to relate to others, and her alienation and unhappiness are apparent. The first sentences of the book introduce a truly unbeautiful child:

> When Mary Lennox was sent to Misselthwaite Manor to live with her uncle everybody said she was the most disagreeable-looking child ever seen. It was true, too. She had a little thin face and a little thin body, thin light hair and a sour expression.

Mary's cousin Colin is a tyrannical recluse who has shut out the world in an angry attempt to deal with loneliness and a physical handicap. After Mary shares the secret of a mysterious abandoned garden with Colin, he takes a new interest in life and begins to go outside regularly and exercise his body. As winter gives way to spring and then summer, the children bring the garden to life and are themselves regenerated into attractive, healthy beings. They learn to care for each other, experience themselves as likable, take control of their minds, and celebrate life.

Transformation—which the garden and characters both undergo— was a prominent theme in Burnett's life and her children's books. Her early books presented stories of lives changed by dramatic shifts in fortune. In a twist of events that seem merited by his innate goodness, Cedric, the protagonist in *Little Lord Fauntleroy*, becomes heir to an earldom. In *A Little Princess*, the good-hearted Sara swings from riches to poverty and back again. For both, it is the circumstances that change their lives, not the changes in character or the choices of their own volition. The children are loving and good from the first to last page, and there is no inner shift, no sense that the children grow and mature. In *The Secret Garden*, Burnett's third book for children, she handles transformation differently.

This book was written late in the Edwardian era, when there was a tremendous interest in physical and mental self-development. Adults were throwing off lingering remnants of ultrarationalism (with its emphasis on reason and consequences), Evangelicalism (with its intense piety and focus on sin and salvation), and rigid Victorian values of duty and respectability. They found meaning in the outdoors and linked the healing powers of nature with internal spiritual revival. The end of childhood now signaled a desirable evolutionary passage rather than a tragic exile from a perfect world.

Burnett's work reflects a shift that was occurring throughout English society: toward a new understanding of children as evolving human beings, chockful of potential. But Burnett was also portraying her own discovery that regeneration was a lifelong process. When chronic illness and overwork left her in despair, she turned to her own wild and neglected garden, where she found renewed vitality and purpose as well as the central image for her third book. English society had a newfound appreciation for unfettered rather than idealized happiness and a fascination with human potential. Instead of rejecting maturity, adults became fascinated with the notion of growing up and adulthood as multifaceted. Childhood gained importance as a time of transformation rather than a merely blissful experience of Eden; as well, earlier notions of the period as an adult-administered laboratory for mastering lessons and morality were downplayed. The child was seen as a participant in his or her own learning; the development of character was a meaning-making, internal activity. The old, authoritarian mode of early reformers and Victorian authors, as well as the indoctrination of the Romantic-nationalist approach, was giving way as children were granted some degree of control over their own development. Self-actualization emerged as a new goal for children (and adults as well). In moving toward a meaningful future, it was essential for the child to think independently and develop a personal value system by which to live.

Burnett cared deeply about these ideas, and *The Secret Garden* gave children new spiritual and secular perspectives with which to undertake the task of self-actualization. Her notion of what gave the universe purpose incorporated Christian Science and Buddhism but seemed most influenced by New Thought, a movement that was gaining popularity in America in the new century. It was a belief system that posed the human mind as the most potent force on earth.[5] Burnett believed that the mind could bring love, optimism, hope, and goodness together into "beautiful" thoughts that yielded positive results. When the mixed-up, tantrum-prone Colin chooses health over narcissistic self-pity, he opens himself up to friendship and the healing influence of nature, and in the end he realizes that happiness is attainable through his own attitude and effort. With this realization dawns a belief that everyone has inner resources and can learn things by repeatedly saying and thinking about them. Colin ultimately concludes, "The flowers are growing—the roots are stirring. That is the Magic. Being alive is the Magic—being strong is the Magic. The Magic is in me. . . . It's in every one of us." The magic is positive thought and, of course, the power of agency.

Mary and Colin demonstrated to readers of the early twentieth century that everything one needs to live fully is already inside them. Other twentieth-century children's authors would follow Burnett's lead and move from concentrating on the child as "a kind of purity, an absence, an inability to do" to writing stories that helped children evolve through their own agency.[6] As the characters in stories took on the same challenges that society was beginning to assign to children, readers acquired more resources for dealing with reality.

* * *

That reality could be harsh indeed. In a century that saw horrific world wars and revolutions that led to the deaths of millions and new media coverage that brought these events into the home, adults were worried about the influence that violence, abuse of power, and corruption would have on children. The shift toward exposing the older child to complex themes and the dark side of human nature was evident when teachers in the 1960s began to assign two novels as standard reading texts for adolescents. Assigning these works seems to have reflected a broad-based societal concern with the state of the world.

George Orwell's *Animal Farm* (1945) introduced young people to the processes by which utopian ideals can provide a path to autocracy for corrupt individuals with a will to power, such as Stalin and Hitler. *Lord of the Flies* (1954), by William Golding, had child protagonists, and this aided in making its portrayal of the breakdown of civilization and the propensity for evil within all of us accessible to youth. Orwell and Golding were both disillusioned by socialism and horrified by Stalinism. Both authors were consciously protesting against the modern world and the regression toward primitive instincts that had resulted in devastating wars and oppressive rogue states.

Animal Farm is a fable, a genre associated with children that invokes the basic principle of "unfairness," the basis by which children judge right and wrong.[7] A response to a perceived need for revolutionary literature for young people, the story satirizes authoritarianism and human stupidity by recounting the failure of the Russian Revolution and the abuses of absolute power. The characters are farm animals that reprise the role of Bolshevik revolutionaries and plan to overthrow the human owners of the farm. Once free, the animals set up a utopian commune based on commandments, the central one being *All animals are equal*. But power is soon seized by a group of avaricious pigs led by Napoleon, a boar whose character is based on Stalin. Soon the commune's commandments are reduced to just one: *All animals are equal but some animals are more equal than others*. Unbounded power and the contradictory skewing of the idea of equality had corrupted Napoleon-boar absolutely.

Orwell had some trouble getting the book published because in 1944 Russia was an ally and the British Ministry of Information warned off the publisher Jonathan Cape. Also, T. S. Eliot, "a right-wing pillar of (recent)

Englishness thought it fundamentally anti-establishment and hence no choice for Faber & Faber."[8] During the war, Eliot was involved in cultural exchanges and, three months after vetoing *Animal Farm*, gave a speech in which he discussed the issue of whether any more children's books needed to be published since there were so many established children's classics. While Eliot ultimately dismissed the idea, such notions of cultural control and government involvement in controlling publication (and from the right not the left!) were problematic to say the least. Orwell was finally able to publish *Animal Farm* but not in the category of a children's book.

Golding's novel came out nine years after *Animal Farm*, in 1954, when the threat posed by the atomic bomb had become evident and the Cold War was heating up. *Lord of the Flies* is a realistic allegory that explores innate destructive inclinations within humankind and the propensity for human communities to begin savaging one another. It centers on the fate of a group of British schoolboys (aged thirteen and under) who are stranded on an isolated island, the only survivors of an airplane crash. At first they find a "strange glamour" in the island and their situation and attempt to build their own society, but they soon divide into factions. One group becomes tribal and animalistic and begins to hunt and murder the other group. The war that ensues is brought up short when a British naval ship arrives and the boys are rescued from themselves. An officer looks them over and says, "I should have thought that a pack of British boys—you're all British aren't you?—would have been able to put up a better show." Golding does not accord children exemption from the human condition based on innate innocence or national identity, and he doesn't expect more from them than from adults.

Both Orwell and Golding were part of a trend toward teaching young people about the evil in human nature, the inevitability of social conflict, and the corrupting potential of power. While the two authors provided the hard knowledge that society felt adolescents should possess, they provided no specific purpose to learning about the dark things in life, except as a warning or perhaps in introducing the notion that knowledge is power. Their stories lacked the leavening and optimism that tend to characterize classic modern children's and young adult literature. What Orwell and Golding did have in common with Burnett and other twentieth-century authors, however, was a focus on moral development and a realization of how much this could be influenced by the imagination.

* * *

Fantasy emerged, arguably, as the dominant literary mode and stimulant to internal development in children. The roots of modern children's fantasy lie in traditional tales, which served as a precursor for the focus on sociopsychological development that has come to characterize so much of modern writing for children. Encoded in traditional folk and fairy tales is matter that has the potential to shape character by allowing one to see consequences and make choices—albeit vicarious—thereby satisfying basic needs for justice. Before stories were written down at all and long before children's literature developed as a genre, fairy and folk tales had served as warnings and moral inspiration for all ages. Eighteenth- and early-nineteenth-century chapbooks preserved these early tales of good and evil, although in a sensationalized form, and respectable children's authors railed against their influence. Nineteenth-century authors such as Lewis Carroll and Edward Lear experimented with traditional stories and rhymes to liberate and indulge children. John Ruskin and George MacDonald created original fairy tales that allowed the imagination to soar in a fashion akin to folk tales of past eras, while late Victorians loved fairy tales that were idealized, whimsical, and charming. Nesbit introduced safe magic that intersected with daily life. Authors such as Nesbit invited children to enjoy being young and to possess an unconfined imagination, while others, such as Kenneth Grahame, demonstrated that escapism could exist side by side with probing explorations of human character. With the new century, children's books acquired more purpose, as modern writers used fantasy to help young people understand themselves, the dark side of human nature, and the world around them.

The iconic figure in contemporary fantasy is J. R. R. Tolkien, whose scholarly work on Beowulf and the fourteenth-century legend of Gawain provides complex models of courage and selflessness. In 1938 this Oxford professor delivered a lecture (later published in 1947 as "On Fairy-Stories") that signaled a turn back to early stories. Tolkien introduced and articulated the concept of Faerie, which he defined as a wide and deep domain where magic was taken seriously.[9] In Faerie were simple archetypal accounts of good and bad fairies, evil stepmothers, and charming princesses as well as complex portrayals of monsters and heroes. His schema accommodated sensational chapbook tales and the sanitized, sentimental, and literary tales of the last century. Tolkien retained the notion of emotional catharsis: like the triumph that follows in the story of Hansel and Gretel after their abandonment and the trials they endured, Tolkien also acknowledged the primal desire of readers to stand outside their own time, commune with others, and feel imagined wonder. In his theory and writing, he plugged into a rich heritage bequeathed forward orally for centuries: age-old motifs (fairies, dwarfs, and trolls) and the more complex legacy of forms (rhyme, riddle, tale, legend, and myth) that carry truths about what gives life purpose and meaning. Tolkien was preparing the way for using Faerie-based fantasy to help young people make sense out of chaos, express a full range of emotions, and—often unconsciously—figure out what to identify with and, from a sea of values, what is beautiful, genuine, and good.

In his fictional works, the element of fantasy allowed him to deal with entire civilizations, wide sweeps of time, and themes and events of mythical proportions. Tolkien was ambitiously seeking to make (in his own self-deprecating words)

> a body of more or less connected legend, ranging from the large and cosmogonic to the level of romantic fairy-story . . . which I could dedicate simply: to England; to my country. . . . I would draw some of the great tales in fullness, and leave many only placed in the scheme, and sketched. The cycles should be linked to a majestic whole, and yet leave scope for other minds and hands, wielding paint and music and drama. Absurd.[10]

His mythology, "The Silmarillion," was set in Middle-earth. Existing in an ancient time somewhere between the age of Faerie and the age of man, it's a recognizable but alien world. Tolkien saw himself as re-creating what he felt was a lost civilization and recording, not inventing, glimpses of underlying reality or truth.[11] In *The Hobbit* and *The Lord of the Rings*, Tolkien reworked traditional elements in such a way that they retained their universal dynamism but had a revolutionary effect on children's literature. His theory of Faerie and the complex models of good and evil in his works helped young people come to terms with the violent modern world.

* * *

In a world darkened by global war, fascism, and totalitarianism, older children, including adolescents, were expected, in their literary pursuits, to engage imaginatively with harsh reality, even evil. Many writers had learned through bitter personal experience that young people needed to acquire knowledge about human nature if they were to make sense of the bloody century they were living in — and thrive. Both J. R. R. Tolkien and C. S. Lewis, for example, served in the trenches of World War I at a very young age and were forced to come to terms with ugliness and violence. In their fantasy books, adolescent heroes learn hard lessons while still carrying the hope and purpose of the young child forward into mature life. As if in compensation for the conflict and threat that their works contained, these authors portrayed life as meaningful and gave their characters friends to travel with, mentors to guide them, and a home to come back to.

Tolkien's and Lewis's books depict an imperfect world in which young characters face difficult choices and acquire knowledge of good and evil, with some mentorship but little adult mediation or protection. Personal growth is portrayed as a significant, often heroic, process, and the consolation for loss of innocence is empowerment and a feeling that individual lives matter and some things are worth fighting for. In the

Narnia series, most notably *The Lion, the Witch, and the Wardrobe* (1950), C. S. Lewis offers children a path to these kinds of epiphanies: the path he himself had taken—reading. Throughout his life, Lewis had had exhilarating experiences in finding meaning through reading and the imagination. Transcendent experiences that he labeled "Joy" sustained Lewis through traumatic childhood experiences and the losses of war,[12] and this was his offering to children.

The Lion, the Witch, and the Wardrobe emerged from Lewis's concern about the lack of imagination in English children, likely resulting from his contact with a family of evacuee children during World War II.[13] The story presents four children (Lucy, Edmund, Peter, and Susan) who are temporarily lodged with an old professor to escape World War II bombing raids on their city. Lucy begins the adventure when she hides in a wardrobe and finds a snowy world beyond the coats. When she introduces her siblings to the strange, wintery world of Narnia, they must quickly decide whether to align themselves with the forces of good (led by the lion, Aslan) or the forces of evil (under the White Witch). When Edmund succumbs to vanity and greed and throws his lot in with the White Witch, Aslan sacrifices himself to save him. To fulfill their destiny as Kings and Queens of Narnia, all four children must wrestle with betrayal, discouragement, and fear, and in the process they discover faith and hope to be their greatest tools. They confront the dark side, make courageous choices, and are in charge of their own destiny and that of Narnia.

Though Lewis didn't start *The Lion, the Witch, and the Wardrobe* as a Christian story, it emerged with the purpose of preparing children for accepting Christianity later in life. In his words, he was "aiming at a sort of pre-baptism of the child's imagination"[14] at telling stories involving choice and moral freedom but in such a way as to strip morality of its "Sunday school associations" and make religious truths appear in their real potency.[15] With religious and moral motives almost out of sight, Lewis wove together strands of influence and a dominant theme within children's literature (the encouragement of goodness) into a book that wooed children by appealing to their emotions and imagination rather than hitting them over the head in a didactic manner.

"Narnia is a spiritual address," argues Bruce Edwards, "a world imbued with ultimate destinies determined by profound personal choices driven by individual allegiances either to eternal truth or to temporal falsehood."[16] The book presents the Gospel story, recast as a fantasy that young readers could understand and relate to. Lewis believed in children's moral discernment enough to leave them free to interpret his book however they pleased. He could step back: lessons were not spelled out (in the style of Maria Edgeworth), and religious doctrine was not driven home (as it was in Hannah More's and Mrs. Sherwood's work). It was now possible to have great faith in the child and imagination. Lewis was a writer who was comfortable enough with faith to embed religious allusions deeply and tell a great story.

The temptations that drove Edmund to betray his brother and sisters would be familiar to any child: envy, sibling rivalry, and a desire for candy. In a story that resonates with quasi-mythological truth, Lewis shows readers that it is possible for children to recast their lives physically and spiritually and to live fully, even heroically. Goodness was a choice; transformation a very real possibility. This was not about the perfect child but the real child: Edmund made mistakes, as any child does, but he learned from them and then recovered his honor and a place on the side of the good guys. In ensuring that Edmund, who betrayed his family, was not eternally damned, Lewis offers the consoling possibility of redemption and recognition of the child as an evolving being full of potential. Edmund too could grow into a King of Narnia and help save the kingdom.

During the 1950s, when Lewis wrote the Narnia series, growth and expansion were important themes in children's literature. It has been suggested that he was not interested in the growth of personality for its own sake but for "God's sake" —freedom and expansion was in terms of relating to Aslan, not betterment of a human state or society.[17] Whatever his ultimate agenda, Lewis seemed to understand instinctively that stimulating the imagination of children was a powerful means of helping them engage deeply with their soul. Ready access to their imaginations and openness to new experiences and feelings greatly enhance their capacity for growth. Like other twentieth-century children's authors, Lewis recognized in fantasy the potential to move beyond the urge to protect children from the darkness and complexity of life and the realities of human nature in the raw. He thought they needed beheadings, battles and dungeons, giants and dragons, and villains that were soundly killed at the end of the book: "Nothing will persuade me that this causes an ordinary child any kind or degree of fear beyond what it wants, and needs, to feel."[18] He added, however, that evil should frighten but not overwhelm the child reader. This was a far cry from the zealous indoctrination of the earlier periods of children's literature and the escapism and Romantic idealism of the immediately preceding period. Lewis recognized that fear and violence, mediated by imagination, can lead to catharsis: through stories, children can move beyond fear and find happiness. The Narnia books give young readers a model of how to live well, by caring about others, summoning courage that is grounded in virtue, and standing up for what is right. In addition, Lewis validates the potential of all children when he poses four siblings as heroic and key to saving a whole world.

* * *

Lewis was stepping through a door that had been opened by his friend, Oxford professor J. R. R. Tolkien, with the publication of *The Hobbit* in 1937. *The Hobbit* shook up the world of children's books with its invitation to older children to ponder the human condition. It is ironic that some critics panned it at first, as lamentably mass-market, unmodern, unrealistic, and unlikely to improve children. But at the time, fantasy was not taken seriously, nor was it associated with literature that assists children with growing up.

Tolkien's scholarly interest in oral tradition and heroism may have encouraged him to write a popular book with folk and storytelling elements. A personal habit of telling stories to his own children influenced his decision to write it as a children's book. Certainly *The Hobbit* has many elements that children like in a story: simple pleasures, such as food and jokes, strange beings, adventure, and a likable hero. Tolkien's prose is matter of fact; the language is simple; and the tone fluctuates between lighthearted Romanticism and somber dramatics. It has songs, small tales within tales, and the arc of an epic quest. Imaginative odysseys and journeys, large and small, are the very stuff of childhood, the mode through which children enact, over and over, the material of life and forge identity. It has been said that *the* essential human story is that of the hero's quest.[19] A hero begins in one state of being, embarks on a journey full of trials, and finally returns transformed. The story line parallels the process by which children grow up.

In *The Hobbit*, Tolkien explored the human condition in much the same way as Lewis did later in *The Lion, the Witch, and the Wardrobe* (1950) but without a religious agenda and with a more-nuanced portrayal of heroism. Tolkien's character, Bilbo, walks the path laid out in *Treasure Island* (1883) when Robert Louis Stevenson gave us (ahead of its time) the adventure novel for adolescents—the hero's journey in which a protagonist breaks away from normal, everyday life, endures tribulations, learns from them, and returns seasoned. Tolkien developed the adventure story into a new form, the modern quest fantasy. Like Stevenson, he made leaving home a perilous choice; the danger in small and large adventures is a catalyst in transforming experience into self-knowledge.

The Hobbit is a classic story of a young adult (who seems even younger because he is small and rather simpleminded) who is shaken out of a rut by his decision to embark on adventure. Bilbo is a type—a middle-class Englishman, wedded to his pipe and cozy chair.[20] However, once stirred to action, he becomes ever more independent and heroic as he meets elves, trolls, and goblins; confronts a dragon; and, in a violent climax, participates in the battle of Five Armies. The end is a compromised victory, as is evident in Bilbo's comment: "Victory after all, I suppose! Well, it seems a very gloomy business." But he does make it home—a great victory indeed. Realizing that "winning" or prevailing may entail psychological damage is an important part of maturing and involves a non-Romantic coming to terms with the conditional nature of existence.

As a result of Tolkien's contribution, the hero's quest is now a staple of young adult literature. From the vicarious experience of a hodgepodge of feelings and desires, evoked through confrontation with the valleys of the soul, maturity can emerge. The quest fantasy that Tolkien pioneered provides journeys upon which the child is asked to proceed hopefully. The recognition of hard realities on the way is offset by the consoling knowledge that life can be joyous as well as harsh. The ultimate destination, the happily ever after, involves losses as well as victories. Ultimately, what counts are the lessons learned along the way and the personal decision to stand against evil. In both Lewis's and Tolkien's works, the child characters become warriors.

After *The Hobbit*, Tolkien was besieged by requests for a sequel. The book's main ideas struck the right notes—subtly influencing adult thinking about children and the way that children thought about themselves. Response in turn influenced the author, as did the turbulent social context, wartime and postwar Britain, in which he lived. It took him ten years to write *The Lord of the Rings* and several more years to revise it. He wrote for an older audience, in fits and starts, throughout the dark days of World War II. *The Lord of the Rings* can be read as an exploration of war, and Frodo's return, as that of a battle-scarred and disillusioned veteran.[21] But it is not an antiwar novel, and the character Faramir may have expressed Tolkien's feelings about war in this comment to Frodo in the third book in the trilogy, *The Two Towers*: "War must be, while we defend our lives against a destroyer who would devour us all; but I do not love the bright sword for its sharpness, not the arrow for its swiftness, not the warrior for his glory. I love only that which they defend: the city of the Men of Numenor." For Tolkien, what had to be defended was England.

World War II was a time of great anxiety for a man who was a veteran and had two sons on active duty. In a wartime letter, Tolkien gave his son Christopher a way of thinking about his service, the approach of considering himself within a story.[22] He told his son that all stories feel chaotic when you are in them and that he was "inside a very great story." Implicit in this notion is the idea that the war will have an ending like all stories do: the hero usually learns things and comes through the experience; and good can prevail. Through *The Lord of the Rings*, Tolkien gave readers a vicarious experience of war and its horrors, with the message of survival.

The Lord of the Rings was finally published in three volumes in 1954 and 1955, when Tolkien was over sixty years of age. The books intricately told the same story that was simply told in *The Hobbit*: both works have the same theme (a quest on which a most unheroic being becomes a hero), the same structure (the "there and back again" of the quest romance), and the same time frame—a year.[23] Both stories are set in Middle-earth, with The *Lord of the Rings* taking place less than a century after

The Hobbit. But *The Hobbit* is a children's story, and readers who approach *The Lord of the Rings* as a mere continuation of the first book are likely to become disoriented. It is the same story reworked for adolescents and adults.

The Lord of the Rings is complex and darker, less fairy tale, and more epic high fantasy. It is an extended exploration of heroism that picks up on themes introduced in *The Hobbit*. The basic plot involves a magic ring of invisibility that Bilbo Baggins, the original hobbit, has bequeathed to his kinsman Frodo. In a council of the major races (Elves, Dwarves, and Men), it is decided that saving Middle-earth requires destruction of the Ring, which must be cast into the fires of Mount Doom in Sauron's land of Mordor. Frodo volunteers to take on this task, and he and his companions travel to faraway lands and endure battles and tests in which they encounter the enemy within and without. Frodo learns that a real hero is one who can make choices, exercise self-control, and deal with physical threats or those of a really dangerous nature—spiritual ones.[24]

Frodo, the modern hero, is lonely, lost, and frightened yet willing to keep on even when confronted with the full horror of Sauron's power: "wall upon wall, battlement upon battlement, black, immeasurably strong, mountain of iron, gate of steel, tower of adamant, he saw it: Barad-dur, Fortress of Sauron." It is a Beowulf image of courage, fighting bravely on in the face of sure defeat, but modern in that the goal is less willed achievement or personal glorification, more a personal code predicated on the idea that the human spirit can prevail, even in the face of annihilation.[25] Bilbo and Frodo are not the Romanticized heroes of the boys' stories and historical novels of the nineteenth century. They have flaws and doubts and must overcome these failings. Frodo in particular must reach deep within himself to resist corruption, sacrifice himself for an important cause, and achieve something of great importance.

Tolkien once told an interviewer, Humphrey Carpenter, that hobbits were "just rustic English people"; Carpenter suggests that the hobbits represented, for their creator, a particular combination of small imagination with great courage that characterized the quintessentially English soldiers with whom he fought with in World War I.[26] From his scholarly work on northern myths and legends, Tolkien had learned to value courage in the face of impossible odds. His war experiences in turn contributed to shaping him into a man to whom obstinate bravery, individual action, self-sacrifice, and personal honor always meant something.[27] To him, these were characteristically English qualities.

Tolkien was conservative in many ways. His Shire evokes images of England between the two world wars. After the First World War, people were sick of what came to be known as "Big England," with its imperialistic, hyperpatriotic mind-sets. The English turned inward toward antiheroic, cozy domesticity. Author J. B. Priestley hit the right note when he spoke affectionately of the little England that he loved. He wanted to have been born one of the "Little Englanders," those who lived in stark contrast to the "Big Englanders," whom he saw as "red-faced, staring, loud-voiced fellows, wanting to go and boss everybody about all over the world, and being surprised and pained and saying, 'Bad show!' if some blighters refused to fag for them."[28] Being a "Little Englander" sounded good to others beside Priestley. It was a period of political and social tranquility (despite a depression) in which an inward-looking form of Englishness prevailed: the English saw themselves as a peaceful, commonsensical people. Social conflict was alleviated by stressing the common interests shared by the people (desiring decency) and the property owners (fearing disorder); they combined into a more inclusive social organism, the nation.[29] Pastoral and prewar images of England, a country rooted in the past, had transmuted into a model of society: "an organic and natural society of the ranks, and of inequality in an economic and social sense, but one based on trust, obligation and even love—the relationship between the 'good Squire' and the 'honest peasant.'"[30]

Interwar prime minister Stanley Baldwin presented himself as "the quintessential country-loving Englishman," a kind of English country squire: "To the public he seemed to embody the English spirit and his speeches to sound the authentic note of that English character which they so much admired and so seldom resembled. Pipe-smoking, phlegmatic, honest, kind, commonsensical. Fond of pigs, the classics and the country, he seemed to represent to Englishmen an idealized and enlarged version of themselves."[31] Baldwin argued that one could rely on the proven decency and integrity, courage, and faith of the common men and women of the country.[32] These interwar notions of Englishness became a basis for mobilizing the population in World War II. It was to be a "people's war" fought by ordinary English civilians and military personnel. Their stoic courage and refusal to be beaten deployed a different kind of patriotism, an Englishness in which little Jacks faced down the giants—fascist bullies.[33]

Tolkien's Shire mirrors interwar imagery of an idealized England. Bilbo (a squire-like, home-loving countryman) and his faithful companions were traditional English countryfolk: little men who put their lives on the line to preserve a way of life and their home. The idea of England as a rural retreat that must be protected has roots back to the nineteenth century. In the wake of the Second World War, this became a dominant motif in children's fantasy: in Tolkien's and Lewis's books, we have the idea of "little pastoral-idyllic Britain up against the big battalions."[34]

Tolkien was extraordinary in that he captured the values and images so close to the soul of the nation during this time and yet wrote works that provided a culturally resonant yet universal mythology for future generations. On the surface, Tolkien was an unlikely person to write a revolutionary work that would be adopted by the counterculture movement of the sixties and then retain its numinous appeal into the twenty-first century. Conservative and religious, he was rather repulsed by the indulgence and extravagance of hippies and probably would have felt the same about hard-core "Ringers," modern fans of *The Lord of the Rings*. And yet he spoke to modern youth at a deep level and seemed to anticipate the issues that preoccupy them: injustice, addiction, ecological destruction, and war. Tolkien had an uncanny grasp on the dangers to modern youth of ideological extremism, the great pitfalls of grasping for identity in the twentieth century.

Tolkien's books took young people further along the path to developing a moral compass. Tom Shippey's *J. R .R. Tolkien: Author of the Century* makes the case that Tolkien's contribution to mapping the moral dimensions of the modern world has been profound. Tolkien, he writes, investigated power, evil, and psychological enslavement and demonstrated how easy it is to turn into a wraith, like Sauron: the will is paralyzed and resistance disarmed when people

> accept the gifts of Sauron, quite likely with the intention of using them for some purpose which they identify as good. But then they start to cut corners, to eliminate opponents, to believe in some "cause" which justifies everything they do. In the end the "cause," or the habits they have acquired while working for the "cause," destroys any moral sense and even any remaining humanity.[35]

In the twentieth century, the spectacle of a person eaten up inside by devotion to some abstraction has become horribly familiar, and we have seen multiple cases in which desire for possession at any price has produced corruption of unparalleled magnitude.[36] The possession of absolute power (acquired through a fictional ring that gives people the power to enforce their will upon others or through, in real life, unlimited political power or technology) is conducive to absolute corruption. Tolkien was giving youth the tools by which to comprehend the use of power by modern monsters and concrete examples of the dangers of slipping into their patterns and becoming monstrous as well.

Tolkien acquired cult status as a writer for adolescents in part because he refused to shield them from complex social and political problems. He spoke to their concerns about the dehumanized destructiveness of modern life: the relentless progression of technology, mechanized warfare, pollution, and exploitation of the environment.[37] He probed the cruelties of ideological single-mindedness, the corruption of absolute power, and the allure of addiction but unflinchingly presented the importance of heroism, honesty, loyalty, and the need for good to dominate evil. Modern young people, alienated by social and environmental conditions, needed a concrete way to confront toxic forces, and Tolkien helped them to forge a sustaining, steadying worldview.

Many works of fantasy since his time bear Tolkien's mark. He established the heroic fantasy "trilogy" as a literary form and set a precedent for fantasy series, such as those of Ursula K. Le Guin, David Eddings, and others. In their works, young people, posed as adventurers, embark on quests to save the world from the armies of evil, dark forces. There is moral purpose in quest and war. For adolescents coming of age in the 1960s and later, the patriotism and nationalism that had served their parents and grandparents no longer seemed adequate for comprehending a world in which power was too often abused. Tolkien and his successors provided young readers with a way of understanding the moral undercurrents of a world fraught with bloodshed, broken dreams, and the horrific consequences of attempting to realize utopian ideals, like those of the Communists and Nazis.

Fantasy for children came into its own in Britain in the 1970s in a "second golden age" of children's literature. In *Four British Fantasists: Place and Culture in the Children's Fantasies of Penelope Lively, Alan Garner, Diana Wynne Jones, and Susan Cooper*, Charles Butler makes the case that these authors were shaped by their backgrounds. They all experienced the trauma of a childhood lived in the shadow of World War II, which gave them unique perspectives on evil and the forces of darkness. The four authors attended Oxford in the 1950s, when Lewis and Tolkien were lecturing and reinventing fantasy. According to Cooper,

> Tolkien's Middle-earth, like his prose, was full of echoes of the Anglo-Saxon, Norse, and Icelandic literature we were studying, and its firm delineation of good against evil had a more personal appeal. Whether or not we had any religious beliefs, we had all spent a noisy childhood under the bombings of World War II, and our imaginative growth had been rooted in the reality of Allies versus Nazis, Us versus Them, Light versus Dark. We were familiar with Mordor; when we were children, it had been ruled by Adolf Hitler.[38]

All four used fantasy to take readers to places impossible in ordinary modes.

The fantasists whose works dominated the 1970s had a fascination with the past, and Britain's mythology, history, and landscapes became a powerful force in their fiction. The five books in Susan Cooper's *The Dark Is Rising* series are based on Arthurian myths and Norse and Celtic legend. Will Stanton, the boy hero, is an Old One who serves The Light in battles with The Dark. Cooper uses magic, old speech, and rhyming prophecies. The center of the universe for children's fantasy at this time was undeniably England. Indeed, the action in the four authors' books took place in an England, which was rooted and in some cases ingrown. It was not unusual to find hostility to strangers—a sense that there were those who are English and those who weren't. The Us—and the Them whom they defined themselves against—might be determined on a village-to-village basis. Butler observes, "The form of Englishness to which fantasy writing typically aspires—or to which it harks back—is quite specific: rural, homogenous, unpolluted, and politically docile."[39] It is the vaguely medieval imaginary England that had such imaginative appeal in the fin de siècle, Edwardian, and interwar years. Butler embraced and updated this type of Englishness and made this version of England "the site of the decisive events in a cosmic moral struggle."[40] However, she was inclusive and took a stand against racism, associating it with evil. In *The Dark Is Rising*, a gathering of the good guys, the Old Ones, reveals "an endless variety of faces—gay, somber, old, young, paper-white, jet-black, and every shade and gradation of pink and brown in between." What fascinated Butler about England's past was its mongrelism, the country's distinctive combination of many different cultures and races that, "in magical terms, made Britain a spell-ridden island thickly encrusted with deep sentiments of enchantment."[41] The past is a constant presence in contemporary fantasy. In Penelope Lively's award-winning children's books, deeply rooted in rural surroundings (Oxfordshire and Somerset), the past is present in the future, and children "are forced to confront some force from the historical past, either to exorcise it or, more typically, to achieve some kind of negotiation and accommodation with it and, by extension or analogy, with themselves and the world at large."[42]

* * *

Burnett gave young readers the vicarious experience of hope and autonomy, of having some measure of control over the quality of their life by embracing life and their own capacity for growth. Orwell and Golding provided harsh realities in the form of allegory or realistic fiction—demanding forms that offered little consolation and inspiration. They also provided models of how not to be: Golding showed what it was like to be un-British and put up a poor show. Orwell demonstrated how easily revolutionaries can slide into new forms of tyranny. Fantasists such as Lewis and Tolkien gave their young readers hard lessons but, in addition, a way of living, a philosophy and code of honor that was fleshed out and given concrete form. Contemporary fantasy in general has allowed young people to grow and develop a sense of self; it helps them seek epiphanies and live fully with eyes wide open and moral purpose.

But fantasy authors walked a fine line between promoting the necessity of ideals and mission and warning of the corrupting power of utopian extremism. They urged adolescents to feel powerful, yet they demonstrated the potential corrosiveness of power. In requiring youth to find a worldview instead of training them into one, twentieth-century English society turned over so much responsibility to its youth that it risked the ultimate ruin of youth: the danger of seeing life as ugly and believing in nothing at all. English children's authors, fantasists in particular, created imaginary worlds in which young people had agency and an important role to play in making the world a decent place to live. The worldview they fostered linked knowledge with hope.

As to Englishness, in Bilbo we have a rendition of the countryman (this time half peasant, half squire) completely representative of the spirit of rural England. Bilbo is like Lob, the folk hero of a poem written in 1915: "One of the lords of No Man's Land, good Lob, / Although he was seen dying at Waterloo, / Hastings, Agincourt and Sedgemoor too / Lives yet." Lob is "the ubiquitous, irrepressible spirit of the people and their culture," which, according to Brooker and Widdowson, recalls the tradition of the freeborn Englishman who survives as an anachronistic myth in the face of modern war.[43] The myth owes something to late-nineteenth-century Romantic Englishness, with its reverence of home and countryside and celebration of rural Anglo-Saxon values. Respectable Bilbo loves his pipe and home yet is willing to go "There" and put himself on the line to save all that he holds dear. It is a much more sacrificial vision than that of a Henty character, more about real danger and perils from within and without, less about conquering and more about defense. Bilbo is not the mere embodiment of a masculine code, an un-self-examined figure embarked on adventure as a game. In his ordinariness and decency, Bilbo is the sane and merry "bearer of the essence of English culture."[44] He is English in the mid-twentieth-century sense—his patriotism and courage expressed through stoic commitment and persistence in the face of all odds. In Tolkien's books, we have the model of an organic and natural society of all ranks, bound by obligation and love, which is reminiscent of the relationship of men and officers in the trenches of World War I.[45] And we have the tenacity of the stoic British population in the face of World War II bombings. Tolkien provided models of the kind of rooted courage necessary for the little man (the Little Englander) to survive in war and the modern world.

NOTES

1. Tucker, *The Child and the Book*, 144.
2. Mackay and Thane, "The Englishwoman," 200.
3. Taylor, *Sources of the Self*, 424–25.
4. Moore, *Care of the Soul*, xiii.
5. Gerzina, *Frances Hodgson Burnett*, 241.
6. Kincaid, *Child-Loving*, 69.
7. Edwards, *British Children's Fiction*, 84–85.
8. Edwards, *British Children's Fiction*, 224.
9. Tolkien, "On Fairy-Stories," 3.
10. Tolkien, *The Letters of J. R. R. Tolkien*, 144–45.
11. Carpenter, *J. R. R. Tolkien*, 99–100.
12. Lewis, *Surprised by Joy*.
13. Sayer, *Jack*, 311.
14. Sayer, *Jack*, 318.
15. Sibley, *Through the Shadowlands*, 73.

16. Edwards, *Not a Tame Lion*, xv.
17. Manlove, *From Alice to Harry Potter*, 84.
18. Lewis, "On Three Ways of Writing for Children," 40.
19. Campbell, *The Power of Myth*.
20. White, *Tolkien: A Biography*, 150.
21. Croft, *War and the Works of J. R. R. Tolkien*, 47.
22. Tolkien, *The Letters of J. R. R. Tolkien*, 78.
23. Helms, *Tolkien's World*, 21.
24. Chance, *Tolkien's Art*, 161.
25. Sale, *Modern Heroism*, 11.
26. Carpenter, *J. R. R. Tolkien*, 180.
27. Croft, *War and the Works of J. R. R. Tolkien*, 8.
28. Priestley, "Little Englanders," 126.
29. Smith, "Englishness and the Liberal Inheritance," 260.
30. Lunn, "Reconsidering 'Britishness,'" 98.
31. Kumar, *The Making of English National Identity*, 229.
32. Smith, "Englishness and the Liberal Inheritance," 264.
33. Giles and Middleton, "War and National Identity," 112.
34. Manlove, *From Alice to Harry Potter*, 75.
35. Shippey, *J. R .R. Tolkien*, 125.
36. Shippey, *J. R. R. Tolkien*, 260–61.
37. Shippey, *J. R. R. Tolkien*, 120.
38. Cooper, "There and Back Again," 143.
39. Butler, *Four British Fantasists*, 135.
40. Butler, *Four British Fantasists*, 143.
41. Butler, *Four British Fantasists*, 145.
42. Butler, *Four British Fantasists*, 4.
43. Brooker and Widdowson, "A Literature for England," 133.
44. Howkins, "The Discovery of Rural England," 72.
45. Howkins, "The Discovery of Rural England," 80.

NINE

Into the Story-Pot: Harry and Heroism

There is a sense of threat, "a feeling of being up against forces that can really be defeated only with fantasy." —Colin Manlove

Throughout the development of print culture, authors have recombined literary elements and given them fresh form. Tolkien pictured the literary heritage they created as a huge pot of soup flavored by all of the stories that had ever been told: he called this always-boiling metaphorical pot the "Cauldron of Story."[1] Traditional forms (nursery rhymes, fairy tales) and folk and fantasy elements such as talking beasts have added substance to the mixture, as have the bones of history, great figures of myth and legend, and quirky original characters. Into the broth went stories supporting the development of character and decency. For example, for hundreds of years, authors have explored the potential of Arthurian romances, drawing from the pot and shaping new texts that expose the reader to poignant portrayals of human nature at work. The story of King Arthur and his knights has been retold many times; yet, its chivalric ideals of beauty and goodness never lose their relevance, and new versions testify to the legend's centrality in British culture.

Tolkien's notion of the story-pot helps explain the contributions that traditional materials and modern children's works have made to lives and culture. The cauldron metaphor also provides a way to think about the contribution of individual authors and storytellers to the genre of children's literature. Like all books, those for children are created by experimenting with forms and elements—like recipes and ingredients—handed down by predecessors who themselves were drawing from a collective cultural reservoir. Memorable authors are master cooks who, in their turn, have added original elements. Tolkien himself took from the pot the bones of myth and legend and fantastical beings. To it he returned the imagery of Middle-earth, an entire mythology, and the scaffolding of the modern heroic quest. Children's authors brewed up new dishes, augmenting them with fantastical details and new notions of honor, courage, loyalty, and autonomous thinking as a foundation for character.

If we suppose a separate cauldron of English children's literature, we might imagine books that have moved young readers for the last two hundred years steeping in a broth rich with ageless lore and Faerie. Children's stories have always been preoccupied with human nature, instruction in necessary values, and the provision of basic models of goodness. The cauldron of children's literature holds a hearty brew that is instrumental in building character and shaping identity. Over time, through social and cultural changes, what these values and models look like change and evolve, as do the stories. In the pot are oral tales with their lessons in ethics and common sense; there are fables and folk tales with their rudimentary values; and there is story after story about the importance of generosity, charity, and humility. Then there are myths, infusing the mixture with heroes and stirring ideals. Modern children's stories have added new flavors and substance, further stimulating the imagination and offering lessons and role models delivered in fantasy, realistic and historical fiction, and adventure stories. The mandate of amusing readers while improving them has been given a steady increase in influence.

A debt is owed to eighteenth- and nineteenth-century Romantics, such as William Wordsworth, who believed in the power of story and the ability of the imagination to foster goodness. Romantics experienced tales and ballads as delightful in themselves but also productive to the heart and character. Author Samuel Coleridge felt that legends and tales of old had tutored him in morality and sympathy for others, ultimately increasing his awareness of the power in his own nature.[2] The Romantics' defense of old tales was tied in with robust notions of humanity; as well, they advocated new stories that were vested in imagination and passion and supported their vision of living well in a world where emotions had a place. The Romantics saw human nature as something that developed organically, not something with frightening potential that had to be denied or rigorously controlled.

Throughout the history of English children's literature, there has been a clear progression from heavy-handed didacticism to more thoughtful and tolerant ways of engaging the child's mind and imagination and stimulating healthy development. The shift mirrors the evolution of English social culture and its understanding of children. During early periods, in the late eighteenth and early nineteenth centuries, when the economy, social order, and national security were under threat, the kind of control that adult culture sought to exercise over children intensified. The content and tone of children's stories mirrored an increased didacticism and commitment to preserving the status quo and controlling behavior.

But when the social environment stabilized, individualism rose in value, and children were approached with more optimism: they were deemed capable of reflection and autonomous growth, and writers reflected the shift by leavening "correctness" agendas in their stories. While still concerned with writing notions of goodness into their stories, writers set out to woo the child through engaging narratives. The notion that children can develop their moral sense through imaginative responses to stories gradually became an accepted principle of children's literature. Its importance persists to this day, though debates continue over what is best for children and their social development—simplicity and explicit moralizing or complexity of theme and resonant imagery.

A decisive shift occurred in the latter half of the nineteenth century when a diverse range of recast traditional materials and original fantasy became available (and popular). Fears of revolution had abated; imperialism made the English feel powerful and purposeful; and literacy and education were extended to more people. The increased confidence made a return to the more didactic forms unnecessary and unlikely. There was a broader reading public, and children's stories of this era often covered Romantic and educational purposes by invoking the imagination. Vicariously living the larger ideals presented in fiction, children could gain a sense of life's significance and purpose and role models and heroes, too. Indoctrination and socialization were more subtle, incorporated in domestic fiction, through which girls absorbed their roles as angels of the home and community. Through school stories, historical fiction, and adventure stories, boys were validated for displaying the self-sacrifice and courage necessary to defending the nation in times of war and preserving the empire. Development was fostered along collective lines as children's literature continued, iteratively, to promote personal qualities that the nation needed and contemporary society admired.

Ideological purposes were supplemented by liberal Romantic impulses in which reworked oral tales and exciting new ones taught age-old lessons in an entertaining, imaginative way and encouraged empathy. Cultural diffusion came into play with tales from France written in the eighteenth century for the amusement of the court. They were moral but not dogmatic: Cinderella was rewarded for her niceness, Red Riding Hood for resisting seduction. When the Grimm brothers' tales appeared in English, children were exposed to evil in many forms and a rich cast of villains, such as Snow White's wicked stepmother. Empathy, a critical element in character, was fostered through resonant images like those of Denmark's Hans Christian Andersen (1805–1875): his portrayal of a little match seller who burns her last matches for momentary light is an image that few readers can forget.

Fantasy came into its own in the golden age of children's literature, which is generally thought to begin mid-nineteenth century with Edward Lear and Lewis Carroll and end with A. A. Milne in the 1930s. Authors used the mode to convey insight into human nature. Beatrix Potter and Kenneth Grahame used fantasy as a means of supporting species-specific naturalness and exploring personality types: they demonstrated the outcome of doing what comes naturally. Peter Rabbit's adventure reinforced the importance of common sense and the temptation of the locked door: he is warned not to go into Mr. MacGregor's garden and has to accept the consequences of choosing to do so. In Grahame's *The Wind in the Willows*, Toad demonstrates the dangers of excessiveness and running wild. Milne followed Potter's and Grahame's lead. In the Hundred Acre Wood, a child encounters figures whose names thereafter instantly evoke a specific character type that can be associated with a particular kind of selfishness: Pooh's appetite for honey, Piglet's interest in saving his own skin, Eeyore's self-pity, Tigger's exuberance and aggressive bonhomie, Rabbit's bossiness, and Owl's overinvestment in his own cleverness.[3] Each character represents a way of reacting to the world as Milne demonstrates the effect of personality on character and models options for relating to other people and being in the world.

Fantasy (and sometimes adventure stories as well) demonstrated that life was more complicated than the simple mastery of doctrine or behavioral templates. Characters were taken to new frontiers where the rules in human experience didn't always hold and certainly could not be transmitted dogmatically. Success required imagination, spontaneity, and initiative. When real characters were placed in a fantasy world or sent off on imaginative adventures, they could try various personalities on for size. Books such as *Treasure Island* (1873) introduced young readers to violence and greed, villains and role models, and over the course of the adventure they could discover for themselves what was admirable and what was not. Even when the geographical boundaries of an adventure were narrow, there was the sheer divergence of human nature to study and learn from. When taken to exotic places—either quasi-realistic (as in the case of Stevenson's island) or, later, absolutely fantastical (in the case of Middle-earth and Narnia)—readers can escape day-to-day existence and vicariously experience a full range of human experience. Rowling mixed fantasy and reality by creating worlds (a real one and a wizard one) that exist side by side and occasionally overlap, thereby exponentially increasing exposure to personalities and predicaments.

Of course, children experience trials and tribulations in real life, and English children's authors often combined entertainment and hard truths with emotional support and something akin to consolation for some of the deepest wounds that a child can imagine. Authors who have been scarred by their own experiences often use words and images to project an empathy that helps and heals their readers. Lear, Carroll, Burnett, Tolkien, and Lewis all lost their mothers at a young age, and in each case the event marked the end of childhood. Lewis wrote of his mother's death that it was the end of all settled happiness and security: "It was sea and islands now; the great continent had sunk like Atlantis."[4] Lewis and other well-loved authors tried to write comfort and security into their works, not by skirting fearsome events, but by confronting them—in imaginary worlds. They provided child readers with a powerful array of weapons to fight the shadows: tolerance, consolation, validation, affection, laughter, and hope.

Novels and stories also offered escapism. It's true that reading is enjoyable, and some books are designed primarily for pleasure, but modern fantasy is not mere escapism, although of course there is a component of distraction in the exotica of strange worlds. As Tolkien pointed out, escapism can be practical, as long as those who use the word *escape* do not confuse "the Escape of the Prisoner with the Flight of the Deserter."[5] In contemporary terms, it is a question of whether the reader is "checking in" or "checking out," whether the drive is toward meaningful engagement or easy obliviousness. In the former case, paradoxically, even while escaping the bonds of reality with one's book of fantasy, the reader is doing quite a bit of heavy lifting, emotionally and psychologically. Vicarious experiences can elicit painful responses and be transformational.

Through reading, children can explore who they are and what they believe in. Children's imaginations, while stimulated on a hedonistic level, are also engaged at a deeper realm, a preconscious level where the child may experience truth and profound joy. Along with enjoying the plot, children respond to the emotive elements in the story—they feel the story, each in his or her own way, and their emotional response may carry a lasting charge. Some of our most well-known children's writers know firsthand the experience of joy in childhood reading. Engagement with books often fired up their imaginations for life and allowed them to experience truth passionately and personally. For the young book-starved Frances Hodgson Burnett, discovering a cache of books in her mother's cabinet was one of the peak experiences of her young life.[6] The young C. S. Lewis read voraciously as solace, after the loss of his mother. Lewis described experiencing certain passages like thunderbolts; as a young reader, he was uplifted "into huge regions of northern sky" by a passage from Longfellow's *Saga of King Olaf*.[7] In his autobiography, Lewis writes about this and other transcendent experiences when, during reading, he felt shock at recognizing something absolutely real in human nature. Stories often elicited a stabbing pang and a sense of inconsolable longing and mental ferment that Lewis later identified as "joy" in his autobiography.

For many authors, it was their own profoundly emotional experience of story as a child that inspired their efforts to pass on stories. James Barrie, for example, set out to give children the same sense of imaginative transport to a different dimension that he had experienced in his childhood reading and play. His success is evident in actress Eva le Gallienne's comments on her American performances as Peter Pan in the 1920s:

> None of us will ever forget the first of those matinees. The children did not know the ordinary applause and they simply *yelled* their approval. . . . When Tink is dying and Peter goes to the footlights crying out, "Don't let Tink die: if you believe in fairies, clap your hands," etc. Hand clapping was not enough for them. They screamed, "Yes! Yes! We believe! We believe!" in a frenzy of anxious excitement. Never has Tink been saved as she was that day. In the Ship scene where Peter yelled, "Down boys and at 'em!" It was pandemonium! The children hopped up and down on their seats, some of them jumped up and ran down the aisles in a wild effort to help us conquer the pirates, and when Peter finally jumped on the barrel and with a mighty blow felled Hook to the ground, the cheers that went up stopped the show for three minutes. I have never heard such a noise inside a theater. We were all complete wrecks after the performance! It was so hard not to break down and cry, the response was so touchingly genuine.[8]

The children had given in to the abandonment of childhood that Peter personified when he exclaimed, "I'm youth. I'm joy." Immersed in the action, their emotions engaged and disbelief suspended, they were transported by the power of their own imaginations. They were in touch with something beyond themselves—not social notions of goodness but a collective spirit of full engagement and aliveness. Fantasy was a powerful mode for stimulating modern readers to believe. It was an antidote to emotional deadness and signaled a heightened commitment to emotional vitality in works by and for children and as an element of personality.

Twentieth-century writers enlisted along with those of the golden age in what the author of *Fantasy and Reason*, Geoffrey Summerfield, calls "Jack's party"—those with a particular sympathy for the weak in their struggle against the strong.[9] While some readers, of course, read just for the narrative ride, others enlist emotionally and are thrilled when oh-so-ordinary child characters square off against the world of evil. Empathy is stimulated when Lewis has the Pevensie siblings—mere children and with everything against them—take on the awesome White Witch in the battle for Narnia; Tolkien has Bilbo and Frodo, small and peaceful hobbits, battle against powerful and evil coalitions with the fate of Middle-earth hanging in the balance. Readers often appreciate characters who stick up for themselves and humanity, against authority figures and internal and external threats and temptations. The reader is happy to enlist in the battle for Narnia, against the White Witch and on the side of good. The process of identification and conscious choice clicks into place over and over again when the reader finds a book that plugs into his or her deepest aspirations and ideals.

Along with affiliation and purpose, readers want emotional support and reassurance about their (and childhood's) essential okayness. Some authors may have sensed the gallantry of children and reached out to them through books that project tolerance, as A. A. Milne did in standing up for the acceptability of being small and acting foolish when Pooh says that everyone is all right and Christopher Robin agrees. Readers of any age can find affirmation in such passages, particularly when feeling most beleaguered. In English mythology and fiction, the hero is often an outcast who is only temporarily dispossessed. In the end, his society will recognize him and save him from his plight, or he will save himself, as in the case of Harry Potter.[10]

Authors model empathy. Lewis Carroll was passionately moved by the innocence and natural beauty of children. Likely in reaction to the rigid Victorian world of *should* and *must*, he kept his Alice books free of morals. Instead, his nonsensical tales were hopeful and carried the themes of emotional survival in an arbitrary world. The stories led readers to the realization that they, like Alice, can face down craziness and survive. Carroll's deep sense of the child's subjection to the unpredictable, undependable world of adult society is complete: "'Only it is *very* lonely here!' Alice said in a melancholy voice; and, at the thought of her loneliness, two large tears came rolling down her cheeks." There is no mistaking the author's empathy for loneliness in these lines from *Through the Looking-Glass*.[11] Feeling vulnerable is not a mandate for quitting, just part of being human.

Laughter and humor provide another kind of consolation and sustenance—medicine for the ailing child soul. Carroll and Lear both borrowed from the weirdness of nursery rhymes to score off against a repressive, alienating society—Victorian England. Lear's *Book of Nonsense* (1846) is a joyous testimony to freedom and irresponsibility. The spoofing and spontaneity were laced with sincerity. For despite being an odd, eccentric misfit himself, Lear adored children and wanted to cheer them with a gift of silliness:

> The Owl and the Pussy-cat went to sea
> In a beautiful pea-green boat:
> They took some honey, and plenty of money
> Wrapped up in a five-pound note.
> The owl looked up to the stars above,
> And sang to a small guitar,
> "Oh lovely Pussy, O Pussy, my love,
> What a beautiful Pussy you are,
> You are,
> You are!
> What a beautiful Pussy you are!"

Lear and Carroll desperately wanted children to be happy. Laughter was their device to ease troubled feelings and banish seriousness. Both tried to take away the sting of having one's high spirits and idiosyncrasies extinguished in the process of growing up. They accepted children as they were and even celebrated oddness. Their offering was joy.

A century later, Roald Dahl (1916–1990) made children laugh too, but his blend of romance and humanism also offered defiance and improvisation as antidotes to despair. Alice survived a crazy world; Dahl's characters took it on. He plugged into the childlike preoccupation with fairness and offered wild revenge scenarios in which nasty people got their comeuppance and children triumphed over their oppressive circumstances. In *James and the Giant Peach* (1961), the orphaned James is launched on a heroic journey when the grossly tyrannical Aunt Sponge and Aunt Spiker are squashed by a giant peach. In *Charlie and the Chocolate Factory* (1964), greedy children suffer for their selfishness, and Charlie, a good kid, is rewarded. In *Matilda* (1988), a small but clever child bests a truly horrific headmistress.

Dahl fused fantasy and reality in such a way that children can face down their worst fears in the externalized forms of barbaric giants, scheming witches, and other nasty, sadistic characters.[12] Dahl's child characters survive in an arbitrary world by actively engaging in beating the system—more like the folklore figure Jack than Carroll's passive but resilient Alice. Dahl is part of a group of authors (including Carroll and Nesbit) who criticize society and take the child's side. They are antiauthoritarian in some measure, and reading their books can build confidence—something we all need but children most especially. A child, after all, lives in a constraining and judgmental world in which one has little power and standing.

In the spectrum of children's literature, the works that have enduring value and appeal are often those in which authors address their own vulnerabilities and in their stories offer children creative ways to face up to life and find consolation and meaning. Dahl, for example, blended fiction and biography and disseminated a model for living through his books and a carefully constructed personality cult. In interviews and his written-for-children autobiographies, *Boy* (1984) and *Going Solo* (1986), Dahl portrayed himself as a schoolboy who ruthlessly faced down villains and, later, an adult who responded to life's crises with energy and initiative. Dahl shared about the traumatic deaths of his sister and father, his service as a pilot in World War II, a brief fling with spying, and his role in rehabilitating his son after a brain trauma and his wife from a stroke—it was the stuff of legend. Dahl has been characterized as a hero: his positive, imaginative, and defiant responses to pain and suffering provided a model to children of how they can respond heroically to the absurdities and cruelties they encounter.[13]

Dahl's books are popular with children because they are fun and outrageous and somehow relevant to modern kids. There is a resonance with modern tastes in his irony and flouting of convention and his latitude on issues such as the sanctity of authority figures. And yet his stories are for younger kids, and there are no serious challenges to the universe—there is no pretense of reality. In Dahl's books, childhood is never a safe haven, but it is a time when improvisation and determination can save the day. It is a kind of wish fulfillment for a world in which so much negativity is beamed out by the media that it is possible to feel chronically put upon and alienated.

Early in the twentieth century, Hodgson Burnett had introduced realism and the notion of change as coming from within. Fantasy then proved the perfect medium for larger-than-life struggles against evil, and Lewis's and Tolkien's young heroes paved the way for folkloric and fairy tale motifs and complex mythic-scale quests. Dahl whetted the appetite for humor, over-the-top villains, and child heroes who responded to injustice with defiance and wild improvisation. The stage was set for a new kind of hero, Harry Potter.

* * *

In the late 1990s J. K. Rowling burst on the scene through her multivolume *bildungsroman*, a story of survival and character formation in which a child meets challenges and, over time, discovers his true self and his place in the world. Like Dickens, Edgeworth, Hodgson Burnett, Lewis, and Tolkien, Rowling took childhood seriously for the contribution that young people can make to moral consciousness. Harry Potter stands out from previous characters in children's literature because he has the childlike joie de vivre of a Nesbit character and values fellowship like a hobbit and sports like Tom Brown but is called on, like the Arthur of English legend, to take a stand and do great things. He doesn't have a home to sally forth from and retreat to—he must create one. The story is a classic hero's journey, with a multitude of genres, themes, and literary devices.

Rowling's updated mélange of message, playfulness, personality types, values, empathy, and myth was a culmination of children's literature to date. The Harry Potter books invoke Nesbit with their small band of adventurous children; however, the intersection of magic and the everyday is not safe. Rowling's story is Lewis-like in that children champion good and save the world; it has portals, the same plethora of beasts and magical elements, and the story is presented in a series of seven books. It is Tolkienesque in that the hero must fight inner as well as external corruption and courage is paramount. Harry responds to challenges with all the spunk and creativity of a Dahl character, but he ages and faces more complex challenges. As in other twentieth-century fantasies, there is a sense of threat, "a feeling of being up against forces that can be defeated only within fantasy."[14] *Harry Potter*, like the works of Carroll and Lear (and Dahl), is laced with silliness and eccentricity, but there is great elaboration as Rowling uses irony and satire as way to face down darkness. The child is offered story and lightness of being along with hard knowledge, a mission, and empowerment. Harry the individual matters very much. He is an every child called to heroism. In Harry, the genre's emphasis on self-development culminates, yet the child's desire for amusement, companionship, and adventure are met as well.

Through the Potter books, with their juxtaposition of fantasy and everyday realism, a key turning point in children's literature was effected. Rowling's comprehensive view of one child's development provided a vehicle for exploring ideas about growing up that fully recognized the younger child and the older child and the hero's quest as a path between childhood and adulthood. With Harry, we have the relevant and unidealized child, full of imperfections. He struggles and makes choices, fully engaged in trials that involve triumph and loss. Pain and harsh conditions are offset by the consolations of companionship, small pleasures (such as humor and food), the empowerment of magic, the thrill of living life intensely, and the satisfactions of rising to a challenge. Young readers are encouraged to believe that commitment can be morally important and humanity is worth investing in. A child's potential for growth and contribution and heroism is fully recognized.

Though written in a fantasy mode like its predecessors, with *Harry Potter*, there is borrowing from other genres. Rowling revived the notion that a school can instill in its students an ethos by which to live, but she added to the old school story formula by including the thrills and wish fulfillment elements normally found in serials and pulp fiction.[15] Within *Harry Potter* are horror, sports, and detective stories that incorporate meaningful challenges, survival itself, and the possibility of real achievement. A grounding effect is provided by the school story elements. According to Colin Manlove, an expert on children's fantasy, from 1950 to 2000, a gradual loss of fixed values and the moorings of social identity have produced frightened, insecure children. He thinks that may explain why "children have turned with one voice to a writer whose fantasies of school life are founded on a social structure and values no longer to be found in the outside world."[16]

The school story formula plays out against a new backdrop for growing up, the Hogwarts School of Witchcraft and Wizardry, a setting that has stirred the imagination of children and adults alike. Harry's fate as an ordinary boy who is chosen to fight evil is charted throughout the series, with each book occurring over the course of one school year. School rituals frame the action, which centers on the challenges of classes, exams, peer and teacher relationships, and sports—and the compensations found in fun and friends. Instead of studying standard academic subjects, Hogwarts students take such classes as the History of Magic and Defense Against the Dark Arts. They study the technology of magic and learn how to use their wands and cast spells, while examining the ethics involved in wielding such power. To thwart the enemy's designs, Harry must apply his new knowledge and skills and master himself socially and emotionally, and over the course of the series, he grows from an ignorant boy to a tested young man.

Important themes emerge in the first books, as readers learn that Hogwarts divides students into "houses" (social units), following a hallowed convention of English boarding schools. At Hogwarts, students internalize a particular character type after being sorted into one of four houses: they must live by house ideals for their entire time at school as they eat, sleep, compete, and study with other members of their house. A sorting cap, influenced by the wishes of the child, determines whether a child becomes a Huffenpuff (who is characteristically just, loyal, patient, and hardworking), a Ravenclaw (quick witted and intelligent), a Slytherin (cunning, unscrupulous, and ambitious), or a Gryffindor (brave, daring, and chivalrous). Harry's choice to become a Gryffindor sets the trajectory of his social and moral development—a theme that is central to the series.

Free will and the importance of one's choice of worldview and peer group are explored with ever-increasing depth as the series progresses. When Dumbledore points out that choices, not ability, make people what they are, Harry learns that his sense of self doesn't depend on whether he is innately a Slytherin or a Gryffindor (good or evil) but what he wills himself to be, with whom and what he allies himself, and what values he embraces. In other words, character is not fixed, and it certainly doesn't lie in a code that can be mastered and lived by thereafter. In *Harry Potter and the Chamber of Secrets*, a very young Ginny Weasley, in Gryffindor House, is taken over by Voldemort and betrays Harry. But like Lewis's Edmund, her choices do not place her beyond redemption. Appearances can be deceiving: the angelic-looking Slytherin, Draco Malfoy, is extremely nasty but still chooses not to kill when pressured to do so. The slimy and cruel Professor Snape, head of Slytherin House, delights in tormenting Harry but in the end turns out to be heroic and courageous. In the last volume, *Harry Potter and the Deathly Hallows*, Harry finally achieves his heart's desire: a fully developed moral compass (and a country that is aligned with this worldview), a loving family (and extended community), and a safe, decent world where he can safely send his children off to learn the lessons of Hogwarts and life.

There was almost an audible *click* as the books locked into late-twentieth-century notions of what is good and what defines a hero. There are many scenes in which Harry is willing to sacrifice himself to defeat malign forces of the worst kind: an antagonist whose ambition is to control humanity and devastate the world. His victories (though sometimes exacting a terrible price) often elicit a rush of cathartic emotion and vicarious empowerment. Like other children's authors, J. K. (Joanne) Rowling conveys in full measure the playful, blissful aspects of being young, but as Harry ages in each successive volume, she delves deeper and deeper into the human psyche and the hard business of growing up. In *Harry Potter* we see the full extension of contemporary children's literature:

recognition of the older child (twelve to seventeen or eighteen years of age) and a comprehensive view of one child's development as a vehicle for readers to explore ideas about growing up. Now, part of growing up is to develop a social conscience, independent judgment, and a critical approach to authority figures. Rowling invests Harry in traditional virtues, such as courage and loyalty, and something new—autonomy in facing the temptations of power and cruel impulses, including the racism and economic and social elitism that modern Western societies struggle to reject. This makes him a truly modern hero as well as a classic one.

As if it were a mirror, the books show what is frightening and disturbing in Rowling's own universe and questioning of authority. The series can be seen as a response to challenges in her own life. She was born in 1965, in a time when English children's literature was past its prime, post-Tolkien and pre-Dahl. Rowling grew up in a Britain that was divided by social and economic differences and seeking to redefine itself as a tolerant and multicultural society. As a single mother, she was forced to go on welfare for a time.[17] A failed marriage and her mother's death were devastating events: she wrote loss into Harry's life with great poignancy. Rowling had to fight a bureaucracy that she both benefited from and was victimized by. She had to take control of her life as a single mother, deal with poverty, and achieve her dream of being a writer despite negative conditions.

The development of Harry's self plays out in a harsh world as well. There is abuse, unfairness and meanness in many forms, loss, and a constant struggle for identity and a sense of personal power. But like Rowling, Harry finds a support system, wrestles with himself and his predicament, and finds his way out of the situation. Each circumstance plays an important role in the development of Harry's mature social consciousness. Harry is given the chance to act on a social concern that preoccupies many contemporary adolescents: the evils of elitism (and here Rowling looked to the class system in Britain as well as to fascism). Racism is at the core of the Dark Side, but issues of prejudice and class appear again and again. Harry takes an ethical stance early on when Draco Malfoy invites him to be part of his circle. He's from an elite wizarding family and tells Harry that he doesn't want to go making friends with the wrong sort. Harry resists Malfoy. He soon learns that the two friends he holds most dear fall into Malfoy's unacceptable category. Ron is from a wizarding family that is poor. Hermione has nonwizard parents—Muggles— and Draco calls her "a filthy little Mudblood." Pure-blood wizards such as the Malfoys want to exterminate Muggles and assume control of a purified world, and they look to Voldemort for empowerment to carry out this vision.

Prejudice is not just a characteristic of Slytherins and Death Eaters. Harry is frequently confronted with taken-for-granted attitudes that justify cruelty. Ron tells Harry that giants are naturally vicious and just like killing. The giants have been banished and are dying out. Only Hermione, who, like Harry, is new to the wizard world, questions the exploitation of house elves; their servitude is so much a part of the natural order that Hermione, who advocates freeing them, is dismissed as a crackpot. Her resistance causes Harry (along with the reader) to question his beliefs and take a stand for what is right. This is the latest extension of the shift within children's literature, from representing children as passive and subject to adult authority to conceiving of the child as an autonomous individual capable of making choices and standing against social wrongs.

Rowling has Tolkienesque concerns about the corruption of power. The epitome of evil, which Harry must fight against (and the primary person he defines himself against), is Voldemort, a dark wizard who possesses his followers and offers them, in turn, absolute domination over others and the opportunity to act on racial and class prejudices. Voldemort is a demonic rendition of Hitler, Stalin, and Orwell's bovine Napoleon. Unlike previous characters, Harry proves capable of withstanding an absolutely corrupt and power-hungry cult leader. But as well as external threats, there is misconduct within the system, including authority figures who don blindfolds to deny harsh realities and resist taking action against powerful enemies. Bureaucrats in the Potter books often use any excuse to extend their power and put authoritarian beliefs into practice. Rowling looks within the system as well as at outsiders: she gives evil new faces, the banal ones of modern authoritarianism.

Rowling's books were entertaining in all the different ways that children's stories have pleased children across the centuries (including through nonsense, adventurous escapism, and catharsis). They brought zest to literary explorations of what it means to live richly and decently. Modern young readers had access to levity and good cheer for their own sake; antidotes to various real-life problems; hope, pleasure, escape, consolation, and epiphany. But Rowling reached new heights in the way that she addressed the contemporary drive to expose children to corruption and the need for heroic resolve. At the same time, she urged young people to strive for happiness and live with energy and creativity as they learn how to survive, mature, and contribute in an imperfect world.

The story of Harry, a flawed human being who nevertheless finds himself and lives heroically, invokes the Jack myth and, as well, the humanistic myth of self-actualization, which is a subtext of contemporary Western life. Harry Potter is a modern Arthur, a child hero within whom all the trends and patterns in English notions of goodness and childhood converged. He's a twentieth-century Tom Brown, a Little Englander, a Colin, and a Bilbo. Rowling writes with a synthesis of Romanticism and humanism that has formed specifically modern expectations of children's literature: she offers culturally consonant models of how to live at more than a survival level. Rowling suggests that our confusing, alienating world is best approached with resolution, stoic courage, and hard knowledge, as well as empathy, tolerance, and joie de vivre. Harry models what it currently means to be vulnerable and live consciously, and his story counters contemporary experiences of meaningless drift through life and, alternately, an excessively rational and pragmatic world, as experienced by both children and adults.

Harry Potter added to the depth and range that now characterize the genre of children's literature, once again demonstrating that through reading, children have access to reconstructed ancient lore and, in addition, a new lore—modern stories that accomplish many of the same purposes as traditional tales. The entirety of children's literature now includes serious, earnest works, such as Maria Edgeworth's moral tales, which drive the message home through reason, and *Black Beauty*, which encourages empathy. Wistful, playful, numinous works live on: *The Secret Garden*, *The Wind in the Willows*, and *Winnie the Pooh* each offer varying models of personality and ways of living. Readers have enjoyed a plethora of heroes and villains and the complex mythological qualities in *Peter Pan*, *The Lion, the Witch, and the Wardrobe*, and the *Lord of the Rings* trilogy. And they have Harry Potter, a contemporary hero, and new stories that provide the latest dishes—ones that draw generously from the cauldron of children's literature and will in turn augment the broth.

* * *

Over the course of two centuries, English literature has evolved to support the child's ability to live with joy and an enhanced understanding of self. Since the late twentieth century, children's stories have evolved further into a genre that supports wholeness and helps to define what a good life is: one enriched by giddy sensory pleasure and revelations of truth through epiphany. Children's books now can present the human condition to children through exciting stories that freely activate the imagination, as opposed to the simple story lines, lofty moral agendas, and behavioral templates favored by early didacts or the flat Romantic portrayals of the Beautiful Child that shut out the possibility of growth and change in character. Identifying with a hero or character helps children conceive of their own life as something that unfolds like the plot of a story. Grasping one's life as a narrative makes it possible to be deliberate about the progression of aspirations (concerning the attainment of evolving notions of goodness) and choices that make a life. Stories that encourage reflection can supplement religion or even take its place: the moral and spiritual significance of the stories helps the reader to find meaning and purpose in life.[18]

We know now that children's books have the power to shape and change the growing child, to assist in the growing of character. To help children learn to be good is the same agenda as the early moralists, but what goodness is, as well as its reflection in the content of children's stories, has undergone constant revision. Since its earliest beginnings, children's literature in England has presented notions of goodness more or less in line with the prevailing worldview of adults, who are the dominant consumers and producers of children's books. The ideals expressed in books written for children reflect the general security levels of adult society and sometimes the influence of self-appointed cultural arbiters. The challenge of childhood—as construed by adults—was to learn behavior and thinking that would maintain or improve the social order and serve the nation. But the rub, of course, comes in defining right thinking and behavior.

Nineteenth-century writers such as Henty portrayed boys and young men as "all of a pattern," possessing the identical characteristics of a manly Englishman. Later English children's authors often rejected conformist expectations and unthinking deference to authority and chafed at the narrowness and hypocrisy considered fit fare for children. Contemporary heroes such as Harry are not painted as ideals: they are both heroic and ordinary and do not conform.[19] Children's literature is a mode for social criticism, and combating injustice is now a primary theme. Authors know that children must learn to live in a constantly changing world and in the midst of struggles for power; thus, authors often portray the world as disillusioning while encouraging children to have hope and question the social universe. They stop short of advocating revolution because it is almost universally accepted that social stability is essential: authors know that children need an ordered universe from which to journey outward, so even subversive authors write home and comfort into their stories. The order and structure that are found in the work of even the most anarchic and antiauthoritarian authors are an acknowledgment of the human need for change to be incremental and thoughtful. This does not take away from the sharpness of their observations about humanity, about goodness and evil. The trajectory of children's literature has arrived at a focus on the individual's development and acquisition of a worldview that accommodates autonomy and honor, a healthy skepticism about authority, and a well-calibrated social conscience.

In the twentieth century, liberal and humanistic ideals reinforced Romantic notions about the importance of the individual and freedom. Like the Romantics, modern writers were concerned with what makes us human, but they were a little closer in outlook to the early didacts and religious writers in their determination to find purpose and to stand on certain moral/ethical principles. Their emphasis was on human dignity and a sense of obligation to live up to one's potential. Children's authors of the twentieth century increasingly fused Romanticism, with its emphasis on feeling, with liberal expectations that the world would be a better place if individuals determined truth and morality for themselves, through self-exploration rather than by merely following social mores and behavioral codes. Burnett offered readers hope and inspiration through Colin and Mary's story of personal transformation. Tolkien's hobbits had to make hard choices and fight against internal as well as external evil. In the Narnia series, Edmund's betrayal of his brother and sisters demonstrates the corrupting power of selfishness and vanity. The White Witch shows that "there is but one way to be evil: to 'be oneself' to the nth degree without regard for how self-exaltation affects or corrodes the lives around us."[20] Through *The Lord of the Rings* Tolkien invited young people to ponder whether power corrupts or simply allows preexisting corruption within to emerge. Borrowing from Beowulf notions of wrestling with evil, moral scales, and doing right as a victory in itself, he shaped a genre in which protagonists such as Frodo engage in high-stakes battles between good and evil. As they make choices, they struggle with themselves as well as their enemies, and out of this emerges humility as well as moral clarity. Tolkien's hobbits and Lewis's siblings (and later Rowling's Harry) demonstrated the importance of confronting the dark underbelly of life with courage and commitment.

Burnett's garden, Lewis's Narnia, Tolkien's Middle-earth, and Rowling's Hogwarts school are secondary worlds where the reader's imagination can range free and where passionate responses are invited. An antidote to dreary everyday reality, the fantasy worlds in children's books are often experienced as more "real" than real life, in the sense that they evoked a sense of emotional truth and elevated ideals.[21] The numinousness of child characters is heightened when they find their way to a wonderful alternate world and then fulfill an important mission there. The stakes are high. Colin and Mary are shown to be capable of changing their whole life, giving birth to a new reality, and finding meaning and joy in life—ugliness transformed to beauty. The Pevensie children find high spiritual purpose in fighting evil and saving Narnia from eternal winter. They are validated as kings and queens in an alternate universe. The hobbits, Bilbo and Frodo, are harshly tested—physically, emotionally, and spiritually—on battlegrounds that are mythic in scope. Their reward is fellowship, honor, and survival. Harry Potter is the "chosen one" who must vanquish evil and save the world for future generations—and he succeeds. In each battle, greatness is shown to be possible; fear and weakness are surmountable; and the exercising of moral choice has unparalleled effects.

As Rowling led the reader through seven years of Harry's life, she encouraged social convergence around Romantic and humanistic notions that all humans are sentient beings with an unlimited potential for growth and contribution. Tolkien, Rowling, and other writers made the hero's passage familiar and supported the idea that individuals of any age are capable of heroism. Modern English authors have contributed not only to the cauldron of children's literature but to the entire cauldron of story, offering the notion of childhood as a relevant (not artificial) stage of life, important for its own sake but also for the character formation that it can host. The child's path is everyone's path, and the universe of imaginative possibilities once thought to be uniquely accessible to the very young is now open to all. The imagination and storytelling have come into their own as vehicles for soulful living and personal development for all ages. Through entertaining and thoughtful works, English children's authors have illustrated the values important in their culture and nation—what it is important to take from childhood—and how to be a good person. Their works feed a common, evolving consciousness that defines what is good.

NOTES

1. Tolkien, "On Fairy-Stories," 52.
2. Coleridge, *Coleridge's Shakespearean Criticism*, 110.
3. Carpenter, *Secret Gardens*, 202–3.
4. Lewis, *Surprised by Joy*, 21.
5. Tolkien, "On Fairy-Stories," 60.
6. Thwaite, *Waiting for the Party*, 10.
7. Lewis, *Surprised by Joy*, 17.
8. Green, *Fifty Years of Peter Pan*, 162–3.
9. Summerfield, *Fantasy and Reason*, 32.
10. Parrinder, *Nation and Novel*, 30.
11. Wullschläger, *Inventing Wonderland*, 48.
12. Manlove, *From Alice to Harry Potter*, 106.
13. Hollindale, "'And Children Swarmed,'" 278.
14. Manlove, *From Alice to Harry Potter*, 121.
15. Alton, "Generic Fusion," 142.
16. Manlove, *From Alice to Harry Potter*, 201.
17. Shapiro, *J. K. Rowling*, 61.
18. Taylor, *Sources of the Self*, 47, 422.
19. Arnold, *Held Fast for England*, 41.
20. Edwards, *Not a Tame Lion*, 124.
21. Kornfeld and Prothro, "Comedy, Conflict, and Community," 192.

TEN

A Modern English Folklore

Englishness is part cultural literacy, part idealized expression of national temperament, and part nostalgic evocation of Eden. The Englishness in children's literature aids in sustaining emotional ties to place, community, and nation. — Rebecca Knuth

Little Goody Two-Shoes, The Tale of Peter Rabbit, The Secret Garden, The Hobbit, Harry Potter — in this book, I've surveyed two and a half centuries of children's literature in England, from 1750 to 2000, and found that this rich body of mores, metaphors, and popular culture has fostered group cohesion and helped individual children to mature. Britain's children's books have transmitted values from one generation to the next and helped to translate changing cultural expectations. They have encouraged character development, as notions of what constitutes an honorable self were constantly changing, in a dance with social, historical, literary, and cultural forces. The desired character as refracted through stories often served the nation or empire and maintained the status quo. However, these stories, while generally "little c" conservative, were often, like other forms of literature, subversive; they increasingly empowered the individual. The history of children's literature reflects larger social and political trends and what adults hoped to effect in the content and tone of the books they offered children. Social agendas existed side by side with the desire to entertain, and children's literature ultimately played a part in the imagining or inventing of modern Britain. Children's books became vehicles for the dissemination of national character and identity and children's literature an "invented tradition" that supported communal identification with the nation, one foot in conservatism and another in a liberal ethos of humanism.

British children's literature in its entirety constitutes a cultural legacy; it's heritage, with hints of innateness and historical and ancestral roots.

177

Just as a voyage down the Thames can be seen "to be passing all England in review," this survey of children's literature similarly offers a panoramic view of national history and social development.[1] In retrospect, we can see that the genre's narratives and images, replete with geographical and cultural details, are examples of social history. Authors expressed contemporary social concerns as well as their hopes and expectations for children. In children's books, microhistories of English society in a particular time, we can trace the transformation of national values from John Newbery onward. For example, *The History of Little Goody Two-Shoes* is a serious picture of eighteenth-century rural England, and Margery and her circle are "the vehicle of small, intense, and at the time very real social ideas," including the possibility of upward mobility and class-based abuse of power.[2] Newbery blended mercantile values and a pulse of Puritanism in a way that has persisted in children's literature.

Soon turbulent times, a radical atmosphere, and threats from France played into the hands of those who believed that society and children should be locked down and their aspirations fine-tuned to support maintenance of the status quo rather than upward mobility or autonomous personal growth. Little girls couldn't be Primrose Prettyfaces and marry above their station. If you were born into poverty, God (and British society) expected you to accept that state with good grace. From 1780 to 1830 authors sought to indoctrinate children and turn the nation toward piety or rationalism and utilitarianism. Driven by authoritarian and conservative visions, the Evangelicals wanted children monitored, saved, and set on a seamless path of piety from birth to death. The ultimate goal was a society and nation driven by religious principles. The rationalists (notably the Edgeworthians) filled children's tales with consequences and sought to instill morality (rather than religious orthodoxy) and choices and useful facts (rather than dogma). They wanted children and society to accept reason as the supreme authority, although, of course, they had a serious moral agenda. To make their messages palatable to child readers, both groups had to open the door to the imagination and package their messages in tales with at least a modicum of narrative. Their lasting effect on the genre was a legacy of earnestness and the didactic promotion of personal responsibility, morality, and duty as an obligation; leeriness about the imagination and passion; and a penchant for useful knowledge that dominated the next half century.

Victorians believed in the power of print: what one read would powerfully affect what one thought and, in fact, the whole process of becoming and being. Their children's books were designed to advance social institutions and strengthen society's hold over the individual.[3] Authors did this by illustrating the right principles and showing them in action. In the second half of the nineteenth century, in a secular displacement of the Bible and scriptures as a source of inspiration, authors enlisted the novel as a tool of socialization. The longer format allowed them to illustrate fully fleshed-out codes of behavior in the form of role models for young people. Young women were taught, via novels, to be angels of the house, whose worth stemmed from their influence in the home and the support they provided to the family. This role was directly linked to the preservation of the health and prosperity of the nation. Women and young children were sentimentalized, and by the end of the century, the cult of the beautiful, innocent child was in full effect. Girls were locked down in ignorance, dependence, and domesticity. Victorian boys, however, were taught to be leaders: the laboratory for their development was the public school, and the code they assimilated was further disseminated by books and serials. Middle- and upper-class boys, such as Tom Brown, were shaped to lead the nation at home and represent the empire abroad. In the case of Victorian boys' and girls' books, the roles and visions were compelling, and fiction really came into its own as a venue for giving meaning to life and setting aspirations.

The momentum of socialization continued as authors provided imaginative formulas that enticed boys into leaving home and serving the empire. It was an era of romantic nationalism, given form globally as imperialism and imparted through adventure stories. Boys' imaginations were given free rein, and the emphasis was on powerfulness, not piety. Victorian society as a whole was in the grip of hero worship, and Ballantyne's and Henty's boy heroes fought Britain's enemies, subdued natives, killed wild animals, and ended up validated and prosperous. With history and geography, readers imbibed a masculine code that celebrated manliness, honesty, clean living, initiative, and courage. This code would linger for generations.

At home, Victorians were in the grip of a domestic form of romantic nationalism called Englishness. It permeated literature at all levels, including children's books. Englishness was rooted in the superiority of rural life over urban, and it was a rejection of industrialization, urbanization, and, ultimately, empire. The past and historical and legendary figures were invoked in fiction for social purposes—to legitimize the class structure and authority, provide moral examples, enliven cultural processes, and invest both the individual and the nation in a sense of destiny. According to J. H. Plumb, "who could have expected a revival of King Arthur and his knights among the solid middle-class merchants of Victorian Kensington, or that England's widowed Queen would have listened with rapt attention to the mournful voice of her Laureate as he recounted the deeds of Sir Lancelot and Queen Guinevere?"[4] But the nation's literary traditions, mythologies, and history were constantly called on to support social continuity and the moral superiority of the Anglo-Saxon race and Britain. The past was also vulgarized, democratized, and made a part of collective experience[5] by the popular literature of the time, including works for children.

Englishness involved codes and social prototypes that were transmitted by authors who called on good children to be, think, and feel English. That the selfhood that children's books fostered was geared to a specific cultural context is not surprising, for an individual's identity is in fact defined by the geography of social roles, relationships, and moral and spiritual orientations surrounding the person. Books offer a unique place for young people to accumulate vicarious experiences and use their imaginations to walk in the shoes of a multitude of characters. In the late Victorian era, the geographical and imaginative context for readers of children's books became, explicitly, England.

It has been said of humorist P. G. Wodehouse (1881–1975)—best known for creating Wooster and Jeeves—that he was "a world-creator," of "a very English world at that,"[6] and the same can be said of many writers of children's stories. They found England appealing, and they wrote works that conveyed this appeal to readers. They entertained. But beyond this goal, a love for the country and its landscapes, history, and ideals inspired these authors to cumulatively create a common vision—a system of rooted images, qualities, and meanings encapsulated in the term *Englishness*. Englishness is part cultural literacy, part idealized expression of national temperament, and part nostalgic evocation of Eden. The Englishness in children's literature aids in sustaining emotional ties to place, community, and nation.

It is such a potent force that it reaches out to readers worldwide. They experience a kind of secondary Englishness. Iconic tales and images, saturated with English imagery and values, have long evoked an emotional response and nostalgia for a lost paradise in readers from within Britain and abroad. Repeated exposure to such images only tightens their grip on the imagination and allows readers to replenish and expand their identification with England. Expatriate Noel Coward reread E. Nesbit throughout his life. In 1956 he wrote a letter home from Jamaica explaining that he still found her books riveting and completely satisfying, even more so than when he was small because the sensory descriptions matched his memories: he enjoyed Nesbit's "extraordinary power of describing hot summer days in England in the beginning years of the century."[7]

From exposure to English children's stories, readers born elsewhere acquired a craving for things English and a drive to identify themselves with England. American author Phyllis McGinley has testified to the power of English literature in wooing an American into desiring English landscapes and atmospheres. As a child living on a ranch in Colorado, she had discovered,

> I could live in two worlds at once. One was my everyday world of the
> western prairies. . . . But nothing I saw about me was so exciting as the
> other world I lived in at the same time. It was a world called England. I

don't suppose it was much like the real England, even then. *My* country was all primroses and skylarks and water meadows and London
fogs and streets and winds over the moors and children from the vicarage and elms full of cawing rooks. It was an England I got out of books,
out of *Puck of Pook's Hill* and *Peter and Wendy* and *The Wind in the
Willows*.[8]

McGinley's acknowledgment that the England she discovered through
children's books isn't a real world does not take away from the power
and influence of this imagined world.

P. L. Travers succumbed to the charm of England early. Australian by
birth, Travers spent her childhood yearning for England as a result of her
father's tales and her reading; she eventually moved there. In her compelling portrayals of middle-class English childhood, the Mary Poppins series, the world of Number 17 Cherry Tree Lane is one of sensible shoes
and nannies, teatime and nursery food—gingerbread, raspberry jam, thin
bread-and-butter slices, and crumpets.[9] Its sensory preoccupation with
traditional foods and an ordered existence punctuated with magical adventures was English to its core. Travers believed that by grounding her
stories in everyday life, she could give children wings—access to their
imaginations.[10] The mildly anachronistic English way of living and the
nursery childhood that Travers portrayed are entrancing and comforting
(it feels right) to those raised very differently. Indeed, the detail with
which she portrayed everyday life in London had as much appeal as her
flights of fancy for many readers (British and non-British alike).

The Englishness that persists in children's books is rooted in a strong
sense of England as place in children's stories and the literary worlds that
children occupy when reading. The meadows are lush, the cottages cozy,
the heroes heroic, and "home" a very English place to return to. Characters such as Mary and Colin, the Pevensie siblings, Ransome's Amazons
and Swallows, and Harry Potter grow and develop against a world of
gardens, lakes, woods, villages, suburban and city homes, and private
boarding schools—a backdrop of landscapes with details that are unmistakably English (if sometimes anachronistically so). Some books are
grounded in actual locations: Frances Hodgson Burnett's love song to a
walled rose garden expresses everything she adored about English village life and her home, Maytham Hall. The landscape and conventions of
Victorian Oxford form the backdrop for *Alice in Wonderland*: there are
references to the Sheep Shop on St. Aldate's, the deer in Magdalen Grove,
and the coat of arms on Christ Church.[11] Even the fantasy settings of
children's books bear striking resemblances to England. Tolkien's books
locate Rivendell on the same latitude as Oxford, and the Shire is Worces-
tershire.[12] Grahame's river world is that of the Thames as it meanders
near Oxford, an area he explored intimately in his youth.[13] As G. K.
Chesterton explained it, what was central about books such as *The Wind*

in the Willows was the magical portrayal of an ideal England and English-man.[14]

In the authors' idealization of place, love of England is palpable, and their stories support notions of Englishness and the continuity between past and present. Even the prettified and idealized images of Caldecott, Greenaway, and Crane, which memorialized a vanishing English coun-tryside and village life,[15] fostered the genre's ability to convey place and time and induce a sense of history and roots. English children's books are often grounded in a sense of period and ancient habits. Charles King-sley's *The Water-Babies* was an honest account of social life by an "essen-tial Englishman . . . who loved the very soil of England and all its folk . . . and the old ancient habits."[16] Preserved in ballad form and then fictional-ized for all ages, the legends of King Arthur and Robin Hood were vested in moral truths. In Arthur, we have unselfish chivalrous devotion and "a high disdain for all things churlish"; in Robin Hood, we have a "true and hearty English taste and spirit" as well as high moral standards.[17]

From the Late Victorian era onward, children's books celebrated the country's distinctiveness in portraits of England past and rituals, life-styles, and mind-sets that may be perceived as timeless. They encouraged an anachronistic response where the readers' bodies exist in the modern world, yet their literary predilections are Arthurian, Victorian, or Ed-wardian. Imaginary visits to a long-lost English era may satisfy some-thing in the soul in a way that living in real time and place does not. Childhood reading may function like a type of heritage tourism, a way of carrying forward the past—keeping the past (even though it is from afar) alive in the present.[18] Or reading about the past may serve escapist func-tions, as a retreat from the toxic present to an enjoyably exotic yet com-fortable destination. Reading about the past may allow children to work out issues and come to terms with the present.

A penchant for the past may have influenced a new idea that "the past constitutes a fundamental foundation for collective identities in the present."[19] From stories, children learned how to live, what to value, and the preoccupations that fed late-nineteenth-century romantic national-ism. Children's books and serials of the times often fused lore and histo-ry, and boys thrilled to stories of chivalrous knights and manly boy he-roes who participated in stirring historical events and upheld Saxon ideals. The heroic tales acted on child readers and encouraged chivalric desires to sacrifice oneself for something greater. From history and tradi-tional tales comes a sense of destiny, and children's stories of the nine-teenth and early twentieth century often conveyed the notion that the destiny of young people involved serving the time-hallowed nation.

Englishness—with its chivalric notion of England as hallowed ground and as a cultural cosmos worth dying for, part place and part attitude—reached apogee in the years leading up to World War I. An entire genera-tion succumbed to the charm of the timeless rhythms of English life and rituals that celebrated home, security, and abundance—images as recorded in childhood reading and immediately conjured up in Rupert Brooke's invocation of honey for tea and certainty and deep meadows in "The Old Vicarage, Grantchester." Brooke, of course, died in the trenches. But he felt, as did many of his contemporaries, that his death had meaning: he died for England. Untold thousands of young soldiers saw themselves as English knights sacrificing themselves for the home country. And even after Romantic nationalism had proven deadly, romanticized notions of England continued to influence young people, although there was a shift away from rampant militarism and imperialism.

After World War I, the Englishness conveyed in children's literature was either kitschy, as seen in boys' and girls' serials and school stories, or democratized and domestic. The ideal English person of the interwar period was decent, commonsensical, and steady. Now we have Arthur Ransome's sturdy, self-sufficient children. Seemingly on permanent holiday, they live a healthy outdoor life, master boat craft and other skills, and learn many of the lessons of life through sailing. Place was absolutely central. Ransome's books are "pieces of social history"—his depictions of the English Lake District and Norfolk Downs in the 1930s were fully fleshed portraits of Lost Worlds.[20] Much like Christianity, which was toned down to a matter-of-fact morality during the nineteenth century, Englishness became less an ideology and more an atmosphere or geographical and imaginative context in which children were portrayed as living according to certain values and social mores.

The postwar tone of Englishness was gentler, less stirring and demanding, and more suspect than in the previous century. Milne's *Winnie the Pooh* (1926) is shot through with an Englishness—beautiful woods, quirky eccentricity, tongue-in-cheek humor, wordplay, and gentleness—whose power was lost on a few contemporary critics who saw it as a trite portrait of a privileged and complacent upper middle class. New voices, concerned with class and privilege, had begun to express a more skeptical view of the influence of Englishness. And yet Milne's values, on display in his books, continued to have a powerful influence on evolving notions of an Englishman as diffident, kindly, bumbling, and lovable. Christopher Robin was a young prototype for this new kind of person, "the transformation of the Englishman from a stolid, self-reliant, rather aggressive and rugged individualist into something kindlier, gentler, more relaxed, more cooperative, more domesticated, if anything a rather shy and timid sort."[21] During World War II bombing attacks, *Winnie the Pooh* was broadcast on the BBC as a steadying factor, and the people identified with this "little man" who was imaginative and quirky and muddled his way through difficulties with help from his friends. As well, Brits retained Ransome-like images of themselves as courageous, solid, self-sufficient, pragmatic, loyal, and grounded. Ransome's children would have sailed to Dunkirk to pluck soldiers from the beaches. Britain's population drew on childhood reading for sustaining images of themselves as tenacious, courageous, and stoic—beleaguered but unbeatable—defenders of their home and culture.

In the post–World War II world, with the excesses of German ethnocentrism haunting Europe, the issue of national character and the desirability of fostering Englishness became more problematic. Boys' serials with their school stories had run their course. Critics flagged Enid Blyton's books, which flooded the market in the 1950s and were adored by children. She trivialized types and manners in books with a serial sensibility gone stagnant. While Blyton thought her creations possessed a typically English character, they struck many as retrogressive, and she was harshly criticized for portraying an English society that was insular and discriminatory. Though attractive to children, her child characters were too sniveling and snobbish for the tastes of librarians, teachers, and social analysts. Blyton's books contributed to a perception that traditional English virtues enshrined exclusivity and contributed to a climate of political incorrectness that was beginning to surround the subject of Englishness.

Twentieth-century children's authors often contented themselves with writing at a popular culture level and within existing national stereotypes. Englishness became an unconscious legacy, well grounded as an integral part of a fictional child's identity and, as well, a geographical and cultural context and local tone: here we have Ransome, Travers, Milne, and (though lamented as un-English) Blyton. Romantic nationalism became less a matter of patriotism, more a matter of a "living force of sentiment in common."[22] As conveyed in contemporary children's books, Englishness is not to be confused with nationalism, defined as a conscious political ideology with an innate feeling of national solidarity or belonging. Instead, it is national consciousness that serves spiritual ends and plays its part in making the complete person.[23]

In the twentieth century, in the exploration of humanity that we call children's literature, emphasis shifted from focus on the nation to focus on the individual, the complete person. It was a major twist in the development of the genre of children's literature, one more expression of social changes in successive eras. Authoritarianism and conservatism diminished in influence as a remarkable current of liberal humanism surfaced, and children's authors focused on individual autonomy and the potential for growth within children. Contemporary humanism as it permeates children's books is about children living up to their potential and finding their own philosophy of life rather than being inculcated with one or merely mastering behavioral codes. In Tolkien, Lewis, and Rowling, Englishness receded into the background but still remained an important subliminal force. A society needs some sort of unifying self-concept and a common psychological ground, and Englishness (increasingly called *Brit-*

ishness), blended with new liberal and humanistic perspectives and delivered by children's authors, may be filling this need.

Children's literature has evolved as a vehicle for providing the shared metaphors that any society requires.[24] The genre carries a living force of common sentiments and metaphors, which feeds British national consciousness.[25] National character, the notion of values held in common by a people, is a construct that undergoes periodic reconstruction: the attributes associated with Britishness and Englishness have been selected, sifted, and suppressed, in the search for what is taken to be representative.[26] Conservatives had a lock on Englishness in the nineteenth century, but in the twentieth century, it was liberalized and democratized to such an extent that both parties promoted interwar Englishness. Then, after the Second World War, Englishness was caught up in the politics of race. Enoch Powell believed that "the life of nations no less than that of men is lived largely in the imagination."[27] He invoked the imagination and traditional notions of Englishness to justify antipathy to immigration. This kind of exclusiveness led to widespread self-consciousness about the use of "English" over "British." It was politically incorrect to self-identify as English. Yet, for many, "British" didn't have the warmth and cultural resonance of the outlawed term: being English involved an emotional attachment to an ethos. Being British, however, was "a limited utilitarian allegiance simply to the political and legal institutions which still hold this multi-national state together."[28] Yet, using the term *British* made one feel correct and inclusive, as it acknowledged the multicultural nature of modern Britain.

In contemporary Britain, Englishness has sometimes been invoked by individuals and by groups with an ax to grind: wistful conservatives and budding nationalists bent on gaining political traction. Englishness, like other myths, involves a certain set of values and metaphors that can either inspire or revolt. In recent years, images of Englishness have been perceived negatively, as when, in 1993, Prime Minister John Major located the essence of Englishness in the "seemingly exclusively white, quasi-rural middle England of village cricket, bicycling spinsters and warm beer."[29] Major was sneered at, his evocation seen as politically motivated. The "softly rustic and nostalgic cast" it gave to middle- and upper-class culture seemed at best irrelevant and at worst exclusionary and an inappropriate way to portray a multicultural nation.[30] Emotional attachment to such imagery is looked on as socially suspect, and that may be somewhat harsh. In a further development disturbing to some, English symbols such as the cross of St. George have become associated with soccer hooliganism and a right-wing form of English nationalism.

But there has been a growing awareness that it is not necessary to eschew all aspects of English cultural background out of political correctness. A nation needs some sort of jointly experienced cultural heritage[31] and a national self-image that transcends politics.[32] "If a plural society is to hold together, it clearly needs a shared self-understanding, a conception of what it is and stands for, a national identity."[33] And that, according to Krishan Kumar, may lie in cultural ties, "preexisting inheritances of a cultural kind": memories and traditions, symbols, myths and values.[34] Perhaps a depoliticized Englishness crossed with Britishness and laced with liberalism and humanism, as delivered in children's books, has a place in contemporary Britain.

* * *

In Britain, children's literature evolved from a dying oral tradition to become a folk tradition in its own right, teaching and sustaining people in much the same way that oral traditions have for eons. It's not all about Englishness. Englishness is a simple natural fact of the culture within which this literature evolved and a framing point for the ultimate arrival point for this book: the conclusion that the genre of children's literature, as it developed in England, has forged a new storytelling tradition. The oeuvre of British children's literature forms a nouveau folklore, a vehicle for a compelling essence that celebrates national uniqueness while making contributions to the literary world that may be universal and have meaning to people and literatures of other places.

British children's books make up a genre that is socially and culturally powerful. Authors provide direct access to truth, insight, and spiritual dimensions; they strive to make sense of the universe, address society as it exists, meet perceived social needs, and sometimes question distorted social premises. They offer children guidance in meeting the challenges of daily life and food for the soul. According to Joseph Campbell's schema, their works, children's books, meet all the requirements of myth in that they serve mystical, cosmological, sociological, and pedagogical purposes.[35]

But children's books have served other purposes as well. They have helped to build the nation—to shape the British people's worldview and national character and to mold children according to these views. They have aided in religious, moral, and ethical upbringing, though they have increasingly evolved in a secular (though not necessarily nonspiritual) manner, and specific doctrines have given way to an appreciation of the basic goodness, individuality, and potential of children. Traditional folklore and modern children's literature have an outlier quality and occasionally thumb their nose at authority and celebrate individual wit and enterprise. The forms of fantasy and then quest that have come to dominate the genre have empowered children to see their natural selves as autonomous, even heroic. Along the way, various contributions have added nuance to the identity and role of children in modern societies. The characters' antiauthoritarianism and questioning of authority and power have resulted in readers becoming more socially critical and thus perhaps more tolerant.

As in traditional tales, there has been a focus on basic human needs and pleasures, as well as the mandate of providing ethical guidance and an empowering framework for approaching life. In the King Arthur legend "The Quest of the Sangrel," each knight had to enter the forest at a point of his choosing, "where it was darkest and there was no way or path."[36] Choice and challenge were the crux around which traditional tales revolved, and they remain key elements in children's stories. Throughout the genre there is a consciousness of the need to brave the forest and find one's moral compass to live well. Classic heroes struggle with issues of honor, self-sacrifice, loyalty, and bravery. Bilbo and Harry face trials, seek their destiny, and become heroes in much the same way that characters such as King Arthur and Robin Hood did. There is an ongoing emphasis on fighting for good and against evil, but in contemporary stories, the evil is as often internal as external. Modern heroes wrestle with the issue of power and its influence for good and evil. They are fallible and prone to missteps. This makes identification with them and the heroic ideals they eventually embrace easier for modern readers, especially the young, who are all too aware of their own imperfections. Traditional tales and legends and contemporary children's stories hunt the same game—the instillation of ideals that give life meaning, direction, and, at times, grandeur.

In British children's literature, there is the direct application of myths to life and folklore's usual mixture of the nonsensical and mundane with the grand and the transcendent. At times, the boundary between child and adult has been broad and clear, but as childhood was extended to encompass adolescence and as a weakening of distinction between child and adult audiences occurred, British children's literature came to include complex and sophisticated original myths and quest stories. It lived up to its full potential as folklore and came full circle to again appeal to all ages, as folklore did for centuries. In effect, children's books have subsumed and supplanted traditional materials: they teach, entertain, inspire, transmit cultural values, confront social wrongs, and provide for the vicarious catharsis that eases stress. The genre in its vitality displays the same kinds of patterns and purposes that folk literature once did and then subliminally serves to achieve the same effect: an affirmation of common values and continuity.

* * *

The full spectrum of children's literature—which includes Newbery's romps, moral tales, domestic novels, historical and adventure stories, and fantasy and quest stories—has kept the genre in touch with its early oral roots and provided us with archetypes. Children's stories express concerns normally associated with folklore, and like folklore in general, the cosmology of English children's literature grounds the nation's consciousness and, as well, has many elements with universal appeal. As C. S. Lewis contended, the child who has once met Kenneth Grahame's Mr. Badger has thereafter a concrete knowledge not only of English social history but of humanity as well.[37]

English children's authors have always concerned themselves with age-old speculations about human aspiration, character building, and right living. While fleshing out these traditional preoccupations, twentieth-century children's authors have moved away from romantic nationalism and into the fold of an emerging ethic of humanism. Contemporary humanism is concerned with a general love of humanity and the ultimate goal of human flourishing. Human beings are responsible for finding meaning and shaping their own lives and for leaving the world a better place. Liberal humanism has been encouraged by English children's literature and has ultimately served as a force in sustaining the genre's commitment to serving children. Contemporary Englishness and Britishness coexist with liberal humanism very well.

A child brought up on popular classics of children's literature—such as those written by Barrie, Grahame, Travers, and Milne (and "new classics," such as Dahl's and Rowling's)—will often acquire a sense of England as a special place. Of course, it is the nature of fiction that "unreal" imaginary literary experiences can arouse stronger feelings than things that one has actually experienced. For those born in England and in the case of those like McGinley and Travers, who were imbued through childhood reading with a secondary Englishness that persisted all their lives, this may result in nostalgia and regret, a feeling for things as we should like them to have been, rather than what they had been. A book that is distinctly rooted in one place can still speak to readers from another place and give them feelings of great identification: that is the nature of good literature. But an attachment to Englishness for non-British readers, as well as an identification in the form of secondary Englishness, is something different from the appeal of regional literature beyond its geographical origins. People may fall in love with England's "otherness"—its exotic magic—but just as often, the hook is the way in which the exotic is mixed, paradoxically, with cozy details (we see this clearly in *Mary Poppins* and *The Hobbit*). The young reader feels at home in the nursery world, schools, and natural settings of fictional England: the lifestyle seems enchanted and grounded. Such backgrounds and compelling ideals (Englishness tempered by humanism and liberalism) engender a sense of cultural rightness and identification within the reader.

In my reading, I came across John Ruskin's phrase "birthrights and bookrights."[38] I use the words in a different sense, to refer to the humanistic notion that children have a right to use their imaginations to learn who they are as individuals and to absorb culturally significant material that helps them to find common ground with others, as well as an individual sense of purpose. English children's literature imparts an ethos of importance to the British, but, as well, the distinctive ethos of Englishness has jumped its own confines (of elitism and nationalism) in the same way that authors such as Tolkien and Rowling have bridged cultural divides with their mythical modern tales of heroism and battles against evil. Modern works, replete with ancient truths yet updated with contemporary issues and values, have often had an appeal that crosses boundaries of time and place. How else can we explain why American publishers and librarians named an annual award for the most distinguished children's book published in the United States after Londoner John Newbery? Or why the award for the best U.S. children's picture book, the Randolph Caldecott Medal, is inscribed with one of his typically English images—a squire galloping with his hunting dogs? And why books such as those of Carroll, Milne, Burnett, Tolkien, and Rowling are translated into over a hundred languages and sell millions of copies?

Englishness underwent many changes in the twentieth century, and the values it expresses have become more democratic and inclusive. The concept continues to express values and metaphors that are key to identity and, like religious values in a secular society, are not easily willed away on the basis of political correctness. So public dialogue continues on whether Englishness exists, perhaps as a useful shorthand term for national character, and whether it should be asserted as such. English is an emotive word and public notions of Englishness are often expressed with recourse to feelings: Englishness has long been perceived as difficult to define, as something felt rather than constructed.[39] Commentator Christopher Hitchens approaches the concept warily: its association with sentimentality is drawn out, and it is sometimes imposed on others and put to dubious purposes. But even Hitchens (2003) acknowledges, "And yet, and yet, I know Englishness does exist, and I know it not when I see it but when I feel it."[40] He discusses it as, among other things, a general temperament that encompasses being a gentleman, a predisposition to eccentricity and sentimentality, an urge toward victory against overpowering odds, and ironic stoicism.

This basic notion of Englishness as a type of character refuses to die, perhaps because it is fed to new generations through printed materials and cultural institutions. It suggests a national consciousness that functions along with language, culture, history, and ancestry to provide a common cultural base and reinforce the will to remain together as a nation.[41] (Of course, English nationalism brings up the question of whether "the nation" will be Britain or England). Even recently, in a speech at a literary festival in 2009, Dr. John Sentamu, archbishop of York, suggested that Englishness, defined most of all as a value for fair play, kindness, and tolerance, could be a unifying force in multicultural Britain.[42] In a 2000 Internet magazine article, folklorist Mike Sutton makes a distinction between Britishness (a matter of civic rights and obligations), and Englishness, which is a matter of cultural identity. Sutton suggests that with its deep indigenous roots, Englishness has a lot to offer to a nation that increasingly celebrates group identities of all kinds, as well as some particularly resonant overarching human values.[43]

Like folklore, literary explorations of humanness by any one country inevitably serve national purposes and, as well, comprise the common heritage of all people. As Peter Mandler concludes in 2006 in his book on the English national character, there is an investment in the notion of national identity: "People continue to display a commitment to certain values—individuality, diversity, tolerance, fair play, the rule of law—that have in the past been coded as 'English' or 'British.' But the same values have in the past also been coded as universal human values, and may now be re-emerging in that form."[44] The notion that British children's books have proven international appeal and may express broad human values offsets the association of contemporary Englishness with elitism and exclusivity and the well-meaning red ink of critics who justify consigning the concept to the dustbins on the basis of political incorrectness. It may be a leap from the material in this book, but a case can be made that mid- and late-twentieth-century Englishness has a role as an animating force in a modern folklore that, because it is permeated with a concern with tolerance and fair play, has the potential to support a multicultural and egalitarian Britain that is in community with the rest of the world.

NOTES

1. Parrinder, *Nation and Novel*, 304.
2. Darton, *Children's Books in England*, 128, 134.
3. Ashley, *George Alfred Henty*, 329.
4. Plumb, *The Death of the Past*, 51.
5. Hunter, "The Preconditions of Preservation," 25.
6. Lobdell, *England and Always*, 13.
7. Lesley, *Remembered Laughter*, 370–71.
8. McGinley, "Foreword," 5–6.
9. Lawson, *Mary Poppins, She Wrote*, 150.
10. Lawson, *Mary Poppins, She Wrote*, 161.
11. Cohen, *Lewis Carroll*, 136.
12. Day, *The World of Tolkien*, 18.
13. Green, *Kenneth Grahame*, 43.
14. Lobdell, *England and Always*, xii.
15. Lundin, *Victorian Horizons*, 3.
16. Darton, *Children's Books in England*, 255.
17. Barczewski, *Myth and National Identity*, 91.
18. Hubbard and Lilley, "Selling the Past," 221–32.
19. Olsen, "The End of History?," 42.
20. Hunt, *Arthur Ransome*, 97–98.
21. Mandler, *The English National Character*, 164.

22. Parrinder, *Nation and Novel*, 237.
23. Parrinder, *Nation and Novel*, 237.
24. Parrinder, *Nation and Novel*, 44.
25. Parrinder, *Nation and Novel*, 237.
26. Langford, *Englishness Identified*, 14.
27. Wiener, *English Culture*, ix.
28. Kumar, *The Making of English National Identity*, 6.
29. Giles and Middleton, "Introduction," 5.
30. Wiener, *English Culture*, ix.
31. Kumar, *The Making of English National Identity*, 21.
32. Pears, "The Hero Gentleman and the Hero," 232.
33. Kumar, *The Making of English National Identity*, 261.
34. Kumar, *The Making of English National Identity*, 21–24.
35. Campbell, "Mythic Reflections."
36. Campbell, "Mythic Reflections."
37. Carpenter, *Secret Gardens*, 168.
38. Batchelor, *John Ruskin: A Life*, 259.
39. Lunn, "Reconsidering 'Britishness,'" 85.
40. Hitchens, "That Blessed Plot."
41. Seymour, Couture, and Nielsen, "Introduction," 15.
42. Sentamu, "Archbishop's Speech on 'Englishness.'"
43. Sutton, "England, Whose England?"
44. Mandler, *The English National Character*, 242.

Bibliography

Ackroyd, Peter. *The Life and Times of Charles Dickens*. Irvington, NY: Hydra, 2003.

Adrian, Arthur A. "Dickens's Crusade for Children." In *Charles Dickens*, edited by Clarice Swisher, 50–58. San Diego, CA: Greenhaven Press, 1998.

Altick, Richard. *The English Common Reader: A Social History of the Mass Reading Public 1800–1900*. Chicago: University of Chicago Press, 1957.

———. *Lives and Letters: A History of Literary Biography in England and America*. New York: Knopf, 1966.

Alton, Anne Hiebert. "Generic Fusion and the Mosaic of Harry Potter" In *Harry Potter's World: Multidisciplinary Critical Perspectives*, edited by Elizabeth E. Heilman, 141–62. London: RoutledgeFalmer, 2003.

Anderson, Benedict. *Imagined Communities: Reflections on the Origin and Spread of Nationalism*. Revised ed. New York: Verso, 1991.

Armstrong, Nancy. *Desire and Domestic Fiction: A Political History of the Novel*. Oxford: Oxford University Press, 1987.

Arnold, Guy. *Held Fast for England: G. A. Henty Imperialist Boys' Writer*. London: Hamish Hamilton, 1980.

Ashley, Leonard. *George Alfred Henty and the Victorian Mind*. Bethesda, MD: International Scholars, 1998.

Backscheider, Paula R. *Reflections on Biography*. Oxford: Oxford University Press, 1999.

Baden-Powell, Robert. *Scouting for Boys: A Handbook for Instruction in Good Citizenship*. London: Horace Cox, 1908.

Barczewski, Stephanie. *Myth and National Identity in Nineteenth-Century Britain: The Legends of King Arthur and Robin Hood*. Oxford: Oxford University Press, 2000.

Barrie, James. *My Lady Nicotine* and *Margaret Ogilvy*. New York: Charles Scribner's Sons, 1928.

Batchelor, John. *John Ruskin: A Life*. New York: Carroll & Graf, 2000.

Bayly, Mary. *The Life and Letters of Mrs. Sewell*. London: Nisbet, 1989.

Beer, Gillian. *The Romance*. London: Methuen, 1970.

Birkin, Andrew. *J. M. Barrie and the Lost Boys: The Real Story behind Peter Pan*. New Haven, CT: Yale University Press, 2003.

Bradley, Ian. *The Call to Seriousness: The Evangelical Impact on the Victorians*. New York: Macmillan, 1976.

Briggs, Julia. *A Woman of Passion: The Life of E. Nesbit 1858–1924*. New York: New Amsterdam Books, 1987.

Bristow, Joseph. *Empire Boys: Adventures in a Man's World*. London: HarperCollins, 1991.

Brooker, Peter, and Peter Widdowson. "A Literature for England." In *Englishness: Politics and Culture 1880–1920*, edited by Robert Colls and Philip Dodd, 116–63. London: Croom Helm, 1986.

Brooker, Will. *Alice's Adventures: Lewis Carroll in Popular Culture*. London: Continuum, 2004.

Brown, Penny. *The Captured World: The Child and Childhood in Nineteenth-Century Women's Writing in England*. New York: St. Martin's Press, 1993.

Brownell, David. "The Two Worlds of Charlotte Yonge." In *The Worlds of Victorian Fiction*, edited by Jerome H. Buckley, 165–78. Cambridge, MA: Harvard University Press, 1975.

Butler, Charles. *Four British Fantasists: Place and Culture in the Children's Fantasies of Penelope Lively, Alan Garner, Diana Wynne Jones, and Susan Cooper*. Lanham, MD: Scarecrow Press, 2006.

Cadogan, Mary, and Patricia Craig. *You're a Brick, Angela! A New Look at Girls' Fiction from 1839 to 1975*. London: Gollanz, 1976.

Cameron, James. *Point of Departure: Experiment in Biography*. London: Barker, 1967.

Campbell, Joseph. "Mythic Reflections: Thoughts on Myth, Spirit and Our Times." An interview with Joseph Campbell, by Tom Collins. *The New Story* 1985/1986 (Winter): 52. Available in *In Context: A Quarterly of Humane Sustainable Culture*, http://www.context.org/ICLIB/IC12/Campbell.htm.

Campbell, Joseph, with Bill Moyers. *The Power of Myth*. New York: Doubleday, 1988.

Carpenter, Humphrey. *The Inklings: C. S. Lewis, J. R. R. Tolkien, Charles Williams, and Their Friends*. Boston: Houghton Mifflin, 1979.

———. *J. R. R. Tolkien: A Biography*. New York: Houghton Mifflin, 2000.

———. *Secret Gardens: A Study of the Golden Age of Children's Literature*. Boston: Houghton Mifflin, 1985.

Castle, Kathryn. *Britannia's Children: Reading Colonialism through Children's Books and Magazines*. Manchester: Manchester University Press, 1996.

Chalmers, Patrick R. *Kenneth Grahame: Life, Letters and Unpublished Work*. London: Methuen, 1933.

Chance, Jane. *Tolkien's Art: A Mythology for England*. Lexington, KY: University Press of Kentucky, 2001.

Chaney, Lisa. *Hide-and-Seek with Angels: A Life of J. M. Barrie*. New York: St. Martin's Press, 2005.

Chartered Institute of Library and Information Professionals. "The Carnegie Award Criteria." http://www.carnegiegreenaway.org.uk/carnegie/.

Chesterton, G. K. "Harsh Truth in *Hard Times*." In *Charles Dickens*, edited by Clarice Swisher, 133–40. San Diego, CA: Greenhaven Press, 1998.

Chitty, Susan. *The Beast and the Monk: A Life of Charles Kingsley*. New York: Mason/Charter, 1975.

———. *The Woman Who Wrote "Black Beauty": Anna Sewell*. London: Hodder and Stoughton, 1971.

Cockshut, A. O. J. *Truth to Life: The Art of Biography in the Nineteenth Century*. New York: Harcourt Brace Jovanovich, 1974.

Coe, Richard N. *When the Grass Was Taller*. New Haven, CT: Yale University Press, 1984.

Cohen, Morton N. *Lewis Carroll: A Biography*. New York: Vintage Books, 1995.

———. *Rider Haggard: His Life and Works*. London: Hutchinson, 1960.

Coleridge, Christobel. *Charlotte Mary Yonge: Her Life and Letters*. New York: Macmillan, 1903.

Coleridge, Samuel. *Coleridge's Shakespearean Criticism*. Vol. 2. Edited by Thomas Middleton Raysor. Cambridge, MA: Harvard University Press, 1930.

Conway, Jill Kerr. *When Memory Speaks: Reflections on Autobiography*. New York: Knopf, 1998.

Cooper, Susan. "There and Back Again Tolkien Reconsidered." *The Horn Book* 78, no. 2 (2002): 143–50.

Croft, Janet Brennan. *War and the Works of J. R. R. Tolkien*. Westport, CT: Praeger, 2004.

Cutt, Nancy. *Mrs. Sherwood and Her Books for Children*. Oxford: Oxford University Press, 1974.

Darton, F. J. Harvey. *Children's Books in England: Five Centuries of Social Life*. Revised by Brian Alderson. 3rd ed. Cambridge: Cambridge University Press, 1982.

Dartt, Robert L. *G. A. Henty: A Bibliography*. Cedar Grove, N.J.: DAR-WEB, 1971.

Davidoff, Leonore, and Catherine Hall. *Family Fortunes: Men and Women of the English Middle Class, 1780–1850*. London: Hutchinson, 1987.

Day, David. *The World of Tolkien: Mythological Sources of "The Lord of the Rings."* New York: Gramercy Books, 2003.

Day-Lewis, Cecil. *The Buried Day*. New York: Harper, 1960.

Dennis, Barbara. *Charlotte Yonge (1823–1901), Novelist of the Oxford Movement: A Literature of Victorian Culture and Society*. Lampeter, UK: Edwin Mellen Press, 1992.

Dickerson, Matthew, and David O'Hara. *From Homer to Harry Potter: A Handbook on Myth and Fantasy*. Grand Rapids, MI: Brazos Press, 2006.

Doyle, Brian. "The Invention of English." In *Englishness: Politics and Culture 1880–1920*, edited by Robert Colls and Philip Dodd, 89–115. London: Croom Helm, 1986.

Edwards, Bruce L. *Not a Tame Lion: Unveil Narnia through the Eyes of Lucy, Peter, and Other Characters Created by C. S. Lewis*. Wheaton, IL: Tyndale House.

Edwards, Owen Dudley. *British Children's Fiction and the Second World War*. Edinburgh: Edinburgh University Press, 2009.

Engen, Rodney. *Kate Greenaway: A Biography*. London: MacDonald, 1981.

Featherstone, Simon. *Englishness: Twentieth-Century Popular Culture and the Forming of English Identity*. Edinburgh: Edinburgh University Press, 2009.

Ferguson, Moira. "Breaking in Englishness: Black Beauty and the Politics of Gender, Race and Class." *Women: A Cultural Review* 5, no. 3 (1994): 34–52.

Foster, Shirley, and Judy Simmons. *What Katy Read: Feminist Re-readings of "Classic" Stories for Girls*. Iowa City: University of Iowa Press, 1995.

Gannon, Susan. "Robert Louis Stevenson's *Treasure Island*: The Ideal Fable." In *Touchstones: Reflections on the Best in Children's Literature*, edited by Perry Nodelman, 1:242–52. West Lafayette, IN: ChLA, 1985.

Gavin, Adrienne E. *Dark Horse: A Life of Anna Sewell*. Phoenix Mill, UK: Sutton, 2004.

Geertz, Clifford. *The Interpretation of Cultures: Selected Essays*. New York: Basic Books, 1973.

Gerzina, Gretchen Holbrook. *Frances Hodgson Burnett: The Unexpected Life of the Author of "The Secret Garden."* New Brunswick, NJ: Rutgers University Press, 2004.

Giles, Judy, and Tim Middleton. "Introduction." In *Writing Englishness 1900–1950: An Introductory Sourcebook on National Identity*, edited by Judy Giles and Tim Middleton, 1–12. London: Routledge, 1995.

———. "War and National Identity: Introduction." In *Writing Englishness 1900–1950: An Introductory Sourcebook on National Identity*, edited by Judy Giles and Tim Middleton, 110–14. London: Routledge, 1995.

Gillis, John. *A World of Their Own Making: Myth, Ritual, and the Quest for Family Values*. New York: Basic, 1996.

Grahame, Kenneth. *The Golden Age*. London: John Lane, 1905.

Green, Martin. *Dreams of Adventure, Deeds of Empire*. New York: Basic Books, 1979.

Green, Peter. *Kenneth Grahame: A Biography*. New York: World, 1959.

Green, Roger Lancelyn. *Fifty Years of Peter Pan*. London: Peter Davies, 1954.

———. *Kipling and the Children*. London: Elek Books, 1965.

Haining, Peter, ed. *The Penny Dreadful; or, Strange, Horrid and Sensational Tales!* London: Gollancz, 1976.

Harman, Claire. *Myself and the Other Fellow: A Life of Robert Louis Stevenson*. New York: Harper Perennial, 2006.

Hayter, Alethea. *Charlotte Yonge*. Plymouth, UK: Northcote House, 1996.

Helms, Randel. *Tolkien's World*. Boston: Houghton Mifflin, 1974.

Herrera, Andrea O'Reilly. "Introduction." In *Family Matters in the British and American Novel*, edited by Andrea O'Reilly Herrera, Elizabeth Mahn Nollen, and Sheila Reitzel Foor, 1–13. Bowling Green, OH: Bowling Green State University Popular Press, 1997.

Heywood, Colin. *A History of Childhood: Children and Childhood in the West from Medieval to Modern Times*. Cambridge: Polity, 2001.

Hibbert, Christopher. *Queen Victoria: A Personal History*. London: HarperCollins, 2000.

Hilton, Tim. *John Ruskin*. New Haven, CT: Yale University Press, 2002.

Hitchens, Christopher. "That Blessed Plot, That Enigmatic Isle." *Atlantic Monthly* 292, no. 3 (2003): 126–33.

Hollindale, Peter. "'And Children Swarmed to Him Like Settlers. He Became a Land.' The Outrageous Success of Roald Dahl." In *Popular Children's Literature in Britain*, edited by Julia Briggs, Dennis Butts, and M. O. Grenby, 271–86. Burlington, VT: Ashgate, 2008.

Hopkins, Chris. "Tolkien and Englishness." In *Proceedings of the J. R. R. Tolkien Centenary Conference at Keble College, Oxford, 17th–24th August 1992*, edited by Patricia Reynolds and Glen Goodknight, 278–79. Milton Keynes: Tolkien Society, 1995.

Houghton, Walter E. *The Victorian Frame of Mind 1830–1870*. New Haven, CT: Yale University Press, 1957.

Howarth, Patrick. *Play Up and Play the Game: The Heroes of Popular Fiction*. London: Eyre Methuen, 1973.

Howkins, Alun. "The Discovery of Rural England." In *Englishness: Politics and Culture 1880–1920*, edited by Robert Colls and Philip Dodd, 62–88. London: Croom Helm, 1986.

Hubbard, P. J., and K. D. Lilley. "Selling the Past: Heritage-Tourism and Place Identity in Stratford-upon-Avon." *Geography* 85 (2000): 221–32.

Humphrey, Judith. *The English Girls' Story: Subversion and Challenge in a Traditional, Conservative Literary Genre*. Bethesda, MD: Academica Press, 2009.

Hunt, Peter. *Arthur Ransome*. Boston: G. K. Hall, 1991.

Hunter, Michael. "The Preconditions of Preservation: A Historical Perspective." In *Our Past Before Us: Why Do We Save It?* edited by David Lowenthal and Marcus Binney, 22–32. London: Temple Smith, 1981.

Irving, Washington. *The Sketchbook*. New York: Dodd, Mead, 1954.

Jackson, Mary V. *Engines of Instruction, Mischief, and Magic: Children's Literature in England from Its Beginning to 1839*. Lincoln: University of Nebraska Press, 1989.

Jacobs, Alan. *The Narnian: The Life and Imagination of C. S. Lewis*. San Francisco: Harper, 2005.

James, Henry. "Robert Louis Stevenson." In *Henry James and Robert Louis Stevenson: A Record of Friendship and Criticism*, edited by Janet Adam Smith, 123–60. London: Rupert Hart-Davis, 1948.

Jeal, Tim. *The Boy-Man: The Life of Lord Baden-Powell*. New York: William Morrow, 1990.

Kincaid, James R. *Child-Loving: The Erotic Child and Victorian Culture*. New York: Routledge, 1992.

Kinnell, Margaret. "Discretion, Sobriety and Wisdom: The Teacher in Children's Books." In *Myths of the English*, edited by Roy Porter, 168–91. Cambridge: Polity Press, 1992.

Kipling, Rudyard. *Rudyard Kipling: Something of Myself and Other Autobiographical Writings*, edited by Thomas Pinney. Cambridge: Cambridge University Press, 1990.

Kornfeld, Jack, and Laurie Prothro. "Comedy, Conflict, and Community: Home and Family in *Harry Potter*." In *Harry Potter's World: Multidisciplinary Critical Perspectives*, edited by Elizabeth E. Heilman, 187–202. London: RoutledgeFalmer, 2003.

Kowaleski-Wallace, Elizabeth. *Their Fathers' Daughters: Hannah More, Maria Edgeworth, and Patriarchal Complicity*. Oxford: Oxford University Press, 1991.

Kumar, Krishan. *The Making of English National Identity*. Cambridge: Cambridge University Press, 2003.

Kuznets, Lois R. *Kenneth Grahame*. Boston: Twayne, 1987.

Lane, Margaret. *The Magic Years of Beatrix Potter*. London: Frederick Warne, 1978.

Langford, Paul. *Englishness Identified: Manners and Character 1650–1850*. Oxford: Oxford University Press, 2000.

Lansbury, Coral. *The Old Brown Dog: Women, Workers, and Vivisection in Edwardian England*. Madison: University of Wisconsin Press, 1985.

Lawson, Valerie. *Mary Poppins, She Wrote: The Life of P. L. Travers*. New York: Simon & Schuster, 2006.

Lesley, Cole. *Remembered Laughter: The Life of Noel Coward*. New York: Knopf, 1976.

Lewis, C. S. "On Three Ways of Writing for Children." In *On Stories and Other Essays on Literature*, edited by Walter Hooper, 31–43. New York: Harcourt Brace Jovanovich, 1982.

———. *Surprised by Joy: The Shape of My Early Life*. New York: Harcourt, Brace & World, 1955.

Lobdell, Jared. *England and Always: Tolkien's World of the Rings*. Grand Rapids, MI: William B. Eerdmans, 1981.

Lord, John. *Duty, Honor, Empire: The Life and Times of Colonel Richard Meinertzhagen*. New York: Random House, 1970.

Lundin, Anne. *Victorian Horizons: The Reception of the Picture Books of Walter Crane, Randolph Caldecott, and Kate Greenaway*. Lanham, MD: Scarecrow, 2001.

Lunn, Kenneth. "Reconsidering 'Britishness': The Construction and Significance of National Identity in Twentieth-Century Britain." In *National and Identity in Contemporary Europe*, edited by Brian Jenkins and Spyros A. Sofos, 83–100. London: Routledge, 1996.

Lurie, Alison. *Don't Tell the Grown-Ups: Subversive Children's Literature*. New York: Little, Brown, 1990.

MacDonald, Ruth K. *Beatrix Potter*. Boston: Twayne, 1986.

Mackay, Jane, and Pat Thane. "The Englishwoman." In *Englishness: Politics and Culture 1880–1920*, edited by Robert Colls and Philip Dodd, 191–229. London: Croom Helm, 1986.

Mandler, Peter. *The English National Character: The History of an Idea from Edmund Burke to Tony Blair*. New Haven, CT: Yale University Press, 2006.

Manlove, Colin. 2003. *From Alice to Harry Potter: Children's Fantasy in England*. Christchurch, New Zealand: Cybereditions, 2003.

Mare, Margaret, and Alicia C. Percival. *Victorian Best-Seller: The World of Charlotte M. Yonge*. London: George G. Harrap, 1948.

Masefield, John. *Martin Hyde: The Duke's Messenger*. Boston: Little, Brown, 1927.

McGinley, Phyllis. "Foreword." In Frances Hodgson Burnett, *A Little Princess*, 5–6. New York: J. B. Lippincott, 1963.

Mill, John Stuart. *Autobiography*, edited by Jack Stillinger. Boston: Houghton Mifflin, 1969.

Milne, A. A. *The End of a Chapter*. In *By Way of Introduction*. London: Methuen, 1929.

———. *It's Too Late Now: The Autobiography of a Writer*. London: Methuen, 1939.

Milne, Christopher Robin. *The Enchanted Places*. Harmondsworth, UK: Penguin, 1974.

Moore, Doris Langley. *E. Nesbit: A Biography*. New York: Chilton Books, 1966.

Moore, Thomas. *Care of the Soul: A Guide for Cultivating Depth and Sacredness in Everyday Life*. New York: HarperCollins, 1992.

Moss, Anita. "E. Nesbit's *The Story of the Treasure Seekers*: The Idiom of Childhood." In *Touchstones: Reflections on the Best in Children's Literature*, edited by Perry Nodelman, 1:188–97. West Lafayette, IN: ChLA, 1985.

Musgrave, P. W. *From Brown to Bunter: The Life and Death of the School Story*. London: Routledge, 1985.

Nuding, Gertrude Prescott. "Britishness and Portraiture." In *Myths of the English*, edited by Roy Porter, 216–36. Cambridge: Polity Press, 1992.

Olsen, Bjornar. "The End of History? Archaeology and the Politics of Identity in a Globalized World." In *Destruction and Conservation of Cultural Property*, edited by Robert Layton, Peter G. Stone, and Julian Thomas, 42–54. New York: Routledge, 2001.

Ong, Walter J. *Orality and Literacy: The Technologizing of the Word*. New York: Methuen, 1982.

Orwell, George. "Boys' Weeklies and Frank Richards's Reply." In *An Age Like This 1920–1940: The Collected Essays, Journalism and Letters of George Orwell*, edited by Sonia Orwell and Ian Angus, 460–85. New York: Harcourt, Brace & World, 1968.

Osbourne, Lloyd. *An Intimate Portrait of R.L.S.* New York: Charles Scribner's Sons, 1924.

Parrinder, Patrick. *Nation and Novel: The English Novel from Its Origins to the Present Day*. Oxford: Oxford University Press, 2006.

Pears, Iain. "The Hero Gentleman and the Hero: Wellington and Napoleon in the Nineteenth Century." In *Myths of the English*, edited by Roy Porter, 216–36. Cambridge: Polity Press, 1992.

Philip, Neil. "*The Wind in the Willows*: The Vitality of a Classic." In *Children and Their Books: A Celebration of the Work of Iona and Peter Opie*, edited by Gillian Avery and Julia Briggs, 299–316. Oxford: Clarendon Press, 1989.

Pickering, George. *Creative Malady: Illness in the Lives and Minds of Charles Darwin, Florence Nightingale, Mary Baker Eddy, Sigmund Freud, Marcel Proust, Elizabeth Barrett Browning*. Oxford: Oxford University Press, 1974.

Plumb, J. H. *The Death of the Past*. London: Macmillan, 1969.

Poon, Angelia. *Enacting Englishness in the Victorian Period: Colonialism and the Politics of Performance*. Burlington, VT: Ashgate, 2008.

Porter, Roy. "Introduction." In *Myths of the English*, edited by Roy Porter, 1–11. Cambridge: Polity Press, 1992.

Priestley, J. B. *The Edwardians*. New York: Harper & Row, 1970.

———. "Little Englanders." In *Writing Englishness 1900–1950: An Introductory Sourcebook on National Identity*, edited by Judy Giles and Tim Middleton, 26–27. London: Routledge, 1995.

Quayle, Eric. *Ballantyne the Brave: A Victorian Writer and His Family*. London: Rupert Hart-Davis, 1967.

Quigly, Isabel. *The Heirs of Tom Brown: The English School Story*. London: Chatto & Windus, 1982.

Quindlen, Anna. *Imagined London: A Tour of the World's Greatest Fictional City*. Washington, DC: National Geographic, 2004.

Ransome, Arthur. *The Autobiography of Arthur Ransome*, edited by Rupert Hart-Davis. London: Jonathan Cape, 1976.

Reynolds, Kimberley, and Nicola Humble. *Victorian Heroines: Representations of Femininity in Nineteenth-Century Literature and Art*. Hemel Hempstead, UK: Harvester Wheatsheaf, 1993.

Richards, Jeffrey. *Happiest Days: The Public Schools in English Fiction*. Manchester: Manchester University Press, 1988.

Roberts, Helene E. "Marriage, Redundancy or Sin: The Painter's View of Women in the First Twenty-Five Years of Victoria's Reign." In *Suffer and Be Still: Women in the Victorian Age*, edited by Martha Vicinus, 45–76. Bloomington: Indiana University Press, 1972.

Robson, Catherine. *Men in Wonderland: The Lost Girlhood of the Victorian Gentleman*. Princeton, NJ: Princeton University Press, 2001.

Rose, Jonathan. *The Edwardian Temperament 1895–1919*. Athens: Ohio University Press, 1986.

Rosenthal, Michael. *The Character Factory: Baden-Powell and the Origins of the Boy Scout Movement*. New York: Pantheon Books, 1986.

Royde-Smith, Naomi. *The State of Mind of Mrs. Sherwood*. London: Macmillan, 1946.

Rudd, David. "From Froebel Teacher to English Disney: The Phenomenal Success of Enid Blyton." In *Popular Children's Literature in Britain*, edited by Julia Briggs, Dennis Butts, and M. O. Grenby, 251–69. Burlington, VT: Ashgate, 2008.

Sale, Roger. *Modern Heroism: Essays on D. H. Lawrence, William Empson, and J. R. R. Tolkien*. Los Angeles: University of California Press, 1973.

Sandbach-Dahlstrom, Catherine. *Be Good Sweet Maid: Charlotte Yonge's Domestic Fiction. A Study in Dogmatic Purpose and Fictional Form*. PhD diss., University of Stockholm. Stockholm: Almquist & Wiksell International, 1984.

Sanders, Andrew. *Charles Dickens*. Oxford: Oxford University Press, 2003.

Saper, Craig J. *Artificial Mythologies: A Guide to Cultural Intervention*. Minneapolis: University of Minnesota Press, 1997.

Sayer, George. *Jack: A Life of C. S. Lewis*. Wheaton, IL: Crossway Books, 1994.

Sentamu, John. "Archbishop's Speech on 'Englishness.'" Paper delivered at the Sunday Times Literary Festival, Oxford, April 4, 2009.

Sewell, Mary. *The Children of Summerbrook: Scenes of Village Life. Described in Simple Verse*. London: Jarrold & Son, 1859.

Seymour, Michael, Jocelyne Couture, and Kai Nielsen. "Introduction: Questioning the Ethnic/Civic Dichotomy." In *Rethinking Nationalism*, edited by Jocelyne Couture, Kai Nielsen, and Michael Seymour, 1–61. Calgary: University of Calgary Press, 1996.

Shapiro, Marc. *J. K. Rowling: The Wizard Behind Harry Potter*. New York: St. Martin's Griffin, 2000.

Shelley, Hugh. *Arthur Ransome*. New York: Henry Z. Walck, 1960.

Shippey, Tom. *J. R .R. Tolkien: Author of the Century*. New York: Houghton Mifflin, 2000.

Sibley, Brian. *Through the Shadowlands: The Love Story of C. S. Lewis and Joy Davidman*. Grand Rapids, MI: Revell, 1994.

Singh, Rashna B. *Goodly Is Our Heritage: Children's Literature, Empire, and the Certitude of Character*. Lanham, MD: Scarecrow Press, 2004.

Smiley, Jane. *Charles Dickens: A Penguin Life*. New York: Viking, 2002.

Smith, Dennis. "Englishness and the Liberal Inheritance after 1886." In *Englishness: Politics and Culture 1880–1920*, edited by Robert Colls and Philip Dodd, 254–82. London: Croom Helm, 1986.

Stevenson, Robert Louis. "A Humble Remonstrance." In *Henry James and Robert Louis Stevenson: A Record of Friendship and Criticism*, edited by Janet Adam Smith, 86–100. London: Rupert Hart-Davis, 1948.

Stone, Harry. "Fairy-Tale Form in *A Christmas Carol*." In *Charles Dickens*, edited by Clarice Swisher, 74–81. San Diego, CA: Greenhaven Press, 1998.

Stoney, Barbara. *Enid Blyton: The Biography*. London: Hodder & Stoughton, 1992.

Stott, Anne. *Hannah More: The First Victorian*. New York: Oxford University Press, 2003.

Streatfeild, Noel. *Magic and the Magician: E. Nesbit and Her Children's Books*. London: Ernest Benn, 1958.

Sturrock, June. *"Heaven and Home": Charlotte M. Yonge's Domestic Fiction and the Victorian Debate over Women*. Victoria, BC: University of Victoria, 1995.

Summerfield, Geoffrey. *Fantasy and Reason: Children's Literature in the Eighteenth Century*. London: Methuen, 1984.

Sutton, Mike. "England, Whose England? Class, Gender and National Identity in the 20th Century Folklore Revival." *Musical Traditions Internet Magazine*, June 2, 2000. http://www.mustrad.org.uk/articles/england.htm.

Talfourd, Thomas Noon. *The Letters of Charles Lamb with a Sketch of His Life*. New York: Harper & Brothers, 1837.

Taylor, Ann. *Original Poems for Infant Minds*. London: Darton, 1804–1805.

Taylor, Charles. *Sources of the Self: The Making of the Modern Identity*. Cambridge, MA: Harvard University Press, 1989.

Taylor, Ina. *The Art of Kate Greenaway*. Gretna, LA: Pelican, 1991.

Thwaite, Ann. *A. A. Milne: His Life*. London: Faber & Faber, 1990.

———. *Waiting for the Party: The Life of Frances Hodgson Burnett 1849–1924*. London: Faber & Faber, 1974.

Tolkien, J. R. R. *The Letters of J. R. R. Tolkien*, edited by Humphrey Carpenter. Boston: Houghton Mifflin, 1981.

———. "On Fairy-Stories." In *Tree and Leaf*. Boston: Houghton Mifflin, 1965.

Tompkins, J. M. S. *The Art of Rudyard Kipling*. London: Methuen, 1959.

Trease, Geoffrey. "The Revolution in Children's Literature." In *The Thorny Paradise: Writers on Writing for Children*, edited by Edward Blishen, 13–24. Harmondsworth, UK: Kestrel Books, 1975.

Tucker, Nicholas. *The Child and the Book: A Psychological and Literary Exploration*. Cambridge: Cambridge University Press, 1981.

Turner, E. S. *Boys Will Be Boys: The Story of Sweeney Todd, Deadwood Dick, Sexton Blake, Billy Bunter, Dick Barton, et al.* London: Michael Joseph, 1975.

West, Magda Frances. "'There Is No Devil,' Asserts Mrs. Frances Hodgson Burnett." In *The Secret Garden: Authoritative Text, Backgrounds and Contexts, Burnett in the Press, Criticism,* edited by Gretchen Holbrook Gerzina, 250–51. New York: W. W. Norton, 2006.

Whistler, Theresa. *Imagination of the Heart: The Life of Walter de la Mare.* London: Duckworth, 1993.

White, Michael. *Tolkien: A Biography.* New York: New American Library, 2001.

Wiener, Martin J. *English Culture and the Decline of the Industrial Spirit, 1850–1980.* Cambridge: Cambridge University Press, 1981.

Wullschläger, Jackie. *Inventing Wonderland: The Lives and Fantasies of Lewis Carroll, Edward Lear, J. M. Barrie, Kenneth Grahame, and A. A. Milne.* New York: Free Press, 1995.

Index

adolescence: as separate stage, 140; Stevenson and, 109
adults: Barrie and, 111; Grahame and, 99–100; Nesbit and, 103–104; Ransome and, 133; Victorian society and, 75. *See also* parent-child relationships
Adventure, 119
adventure stories, 52–66, 115; influence of, 3; in interwar period, 116–120; *Robinson Crusoe* and, 52–53; Tolkien and, 150; *Treasure Island* and, 107–110
aesthetic movement, 80, 90
affirmation, 139–158n45
agency, Burnett and, 143
Albert, prince-consort, 38, 96
Alice's Adventures in Wonderland, 4, 81, 84, 95–96
Allan Quatermain, 62
"All Things Bright and Beautiful", 20–21
Altick, Richard, 20
anachronisms, 9
Andersen, Hans Christian, 161
Animal Farm, 144–145
animals: Ballantyne and, 54–55; *Black Beauty* and, 9, 77–79
archetypes, 187
Arnold, Guy, 60
Arnold, Thomas, 44
Arthur, King, 7, 86, 179, 182, 187; as hero, 50; and public school code, 46
Aurora Leigh, 21
authority: Evangelicals and, 22. *See also* questioning
autobiographies, 166
autonomy, 139–158n45; Grahame and, 99; Nesbit and, 104; Potter and, 98; Rowling and, 169

Baden-Powell, Agnes, 121
Baden-Powell, Robert, 66–69, 121; life of, 66, 69
Baldwin, Stanley, 153
ballads, 87
Ballantyne, Robert, 53–56
Barczewski, Stephanie, 46, 86
Barrie, James, 82, 96, 111–112, 163–164; and Ballantyne, 53; and writing, 4, 130
Beautiful Child, 80, 127
beauty: aesthetic movement and, 80; Burnett and, 75, 76, 77, 80, 143; and picture books, 89
The Big Six, 132
biographies, 2, 50, 51, 58
birthrights, 188
Black Beauty, 9, 77–79
Blake, Sexton, 66, 116, 118
Blake, William, 24, 74, 91, 92
Blyton, Enid, 134–136, 184
Boer War, 65, 67
The Book of Dragons, 105
bookrights, 188
boy-man, 69, 97
boys. *See* men
Boy Scouts, 66–69
Boys of England: A Young Gentleman's Journal of Sport, Travel, Fun and Instruction, 64
Boys' Own Paper, 64
Brazil, Angela, 121–123, 135
Brent-Dyer, Elinor, 123
Bristow, Joseph, 65
Britishness, vi; term, 184–185, 189, vii. *See also* Englishness
Brooke, Rupert, 182
Browning, Elizabeth Barrett, 21
Bruce, Dorita Fairlie, 123
Bubbles, 80

About the Author

Rebecca Knuth has been a professor in the Library and Information Science Program at the University of Hawaii for sixteen years. She teaches classes in the history of books and libraries, intellectual freedom, public libraries services, children's literature, and young adult literature. Knuth uses an interdisciplinary approach and has written two books: *Libricide: The Regime-Sponsored Destruction of Books and Libraries in the Twentieth Century* (2003) and *Burning Books and Leveling Libraries: Extremist Violence and Cultural Destruction* (2006).